Comparative Early Childhood Education Services

CRITICAL CULTURAL STUDIES OF CHILDHOOD

Series Editors:
Marianne N. Bloch, Gaile Sloan Cannella, and Beth Blue Swadener

This series focuses on reframings of theory, research, policy, and pedagogies in childhood. A critical cultural study of childhood is one that offers a "prism" of possibilities for writing about power and its relationship to the cultural constructions of childhood, family, and education in broad societal, local, and global contexts. Books in the series open up new spaces for dialogue and reconceptualization based on critical theoretical and methodological framings, including critical pedagogy; advocacy and social justice perspectives; cultural, historical, and comparative studies of childhood; and post-structural, postcolonial, and/or feminist studies of childhood, family, and education. The intent of the series is to examine the relations between power, language, and what is taken as normal/abnormal, good, and natural, to understand the construction of the "other," difference and inclusions/exclusions that are embedded in current notions of childhood, family, educational reforms, policies, and the practices of schooling. *Critical Cultural Studies of Childhood* will open up dialogue about new possibilities for action and research.

Single-authored as well as edited volumes focusing on critical studies of childhood from a variety of disciplinary and theoretical perspectives are included in the series. A particular focus is in a reimagining and critical reflection on policy and practice in early childhood, primary, and elementary education. The series intends to open up new spaces for reconceptualizing theories and traditions of research, policies, cultural reasonings, and practices at all of these levels, in the United States, as well as comparatively.

COMPARATIVE EARLY CHILDHOOD EDUCATION SERVICES

International Perspectives

Edited by

Judith Duncan and Sarah Te One

COMPARATIVE EARLY CHILDHOOD EDUCATION SERVICES
Copyright © Judith Duncan and Sarah Te One, 2012.

First published in 2012 by
PALGRAVE MACMILLAN®
in the United States—a division of St. Martin's Press LLC,
175 Fifth Avenue, New York, NY 10010.

Where this book is distributed in the UK, Europe and the rest of the world,
this is by Palgrave Macmillan, a division of Macmillan Publishers Limited,
registered in England, company number 785998, of Houndmills,
Basingstoke, Hampshire RG21 6XS.

Palgrave Macmillan is the global academic imprint of the above companies
and has companies and representatives throughout the world.

Palgrave® and Macmillan® are registered trademarks in the United States,
the United Kingdom, Europe and other countries.

ISBN: 978–0–230–11976–5

Library of Congress Cataloging-in-Publication Data

    Comparative early childhood education services : international
perspectives / edited by Judith Duncan, Sarah Te One.
        p. cm.—(Critical cultural studies of childhood)
      ISBN 978–0–230–11976–5 (hardback)
       1. Early childhood education—Cross-cultural studies.
    I. Duncan, Judith, 1963– II. Te One, Sarah, 1954–

LB1139.23.C65 2012
372.21—dc23   2011044509

A catalogue record of the book is available from the British Library.

Design by Newgen Imaging Systems (P) Ltd., Chennai, India.

First edition: March 2012

10 9 8 7 6 5 4 3 2 1

Printed in the United States of America.

Contents

Figures and Table

Figures

Table

Series Editors' Foreword

Marianne N. Bloch, Gaile Sloan Cannella,
and Beth Blue Swadener

For over 20 years, early childhood educators and researchers around the globe have worked toward a reconceptualization of dominant knowledges and practices in fields that focus mainly on those who have been labeled "child." Grounded in social justice movements of the 1960s and influenced by the emergence of disciplines such as cultural and gender studies, as well as critical reconceptualizations of qualitative research, groups of scholars in education have practiced deconstruction, critique, and reconceptualization. Curriculum theorists in education have served as the initiators for notions of reconceptualizing as they have used critical histories and indigenous and traditionally marginalized knowledges to address systemic oppression and social injustice in education. Further, this work has delineated historical forms of education and both major and minor sites of educational practice that would move toward social justice. These conceptual locations include (but are not limited to) the critical work of educators such as Friere and Horton, as well as actual physical sites of critical education practice. Examples of community-based physical sites include the Highlander School in Tennessee, freedom schools throughout the southern part of the United States, integrated services community-based schools, and various community sites around the globe in which conceptualizations of pedagogy privilege learner knowledges and decision making while acknowledging that everything is political. A critical educational praxis has even been labeled "pedagogy of revolution." Postmodern critical perspectives, including feminist post-structuralism, postcolonial critique, and endarkened feminisms have been, and continue to be, brought to the center of deconstruction, reconceptualization, and rethought practice.

Early childhood scholars and educators have served as major voices in these practices of reconceptualization related to constructions of "childhood" generally, as well as the rethinking of notions of education and care and, to some extent, conceptualizations of family and social services. Scholarship has included critiques of "Western" assumptions concerning the child, as well as problematizations of authoritative structures such as discourses of "best practice," "quality," and "accountability" that have been/are used to construct power for some and for judgment and disqualification of "others." Early educators have pointed to the multidisciplinary nature of the field as it engages with critical psychology, sociocultural challenges to truth implied by notions of theory (whether Piagetian or Vygotskian), or feminist and critical examinations of medicine. Classroom practices have been reconceptualized as ranging from concern with equity, to the acknowledgement of sexuality for both teachers and children, to the implementation of a collectivist, culturally based curriculum. Early childhood schools, classrooms, and centers have been recognized as locations of minor politics, similar to freedom schools.

However, perhaps contemporarily the greatest challenge to reconceptualization is the neoliberal condition of late capitalism. This condition would market and privatize all constructions of child, family, community, education, and services, placing everyone and everything within the capitalist lens. Further, neoliberalism even creates and takes advantage of disaster to construct new forms of privatization and market products, as demonstrated in the construction of school sites for private education and care in various disaster locations. For these reasons, and to create lines of flight that do not lead back to capitalist objectifications of children and their families/communities, scholars and educators in early childhood education, care, and social services believe that the reconceptualization should be expanded. Disciplinary boundaries should be further challenged to create new sites of minor politics; all education/care/service practices should be recognized as political, and new, multiple forms of critical activism in partnership with communities, families, and those who are younger should be conceptualized.

The authors in this book generate just such reconceptualized practices as they rethink forms of integrated education and social services; partner with families and *whānau* (extended family); remind us of the diverse locations that can be conceptualized as childhood centers, such as prisons; and explore ways to construct large-scale qualitative studies that acknowledge funds of knowledge and community strengths. Reading these chapters can facilitate broadening of thought and possibility. We, as series editors, challenge the reader to engage with the text to construct previously unthought reconceptualizations and practices that can lead to increased social justice and possibilities.

FOREWORD

Peter Moss

This book is an important contribution to an important task: to reconceptualize the early childhood center. In today's dominant discourse, produced from an amalgam of neoliberalism and regulatory modernity, these institutions are understood as factories where human technologies are applied to young children and sometimes their parents (or, more precisely, their mothers) to produce a narrow range of predetermined outcomes; but also, increasingly, as private businesses, competing with other factory-businesses to sell to consumer-parents in a competitive market. Such thinking has extended furthest among English-speaking countries, from which the chapters in this book come, and has indeed gone furthest in my own, England. In 2010, more than three-quarters of places in nurseries providing full day care were supplied by the for-profit sector (Blackburn, 2010). A recent report from the English government states as its first aim for early childhood education and care "to foster a sector which in all its parts is: Entrepreneurial...actively markets itself to all parents...with healthy business models" (Department for Education/Department for Health, 2011, p. 33). But this mix of instrumental rationality, technical practice, and economic calculation is spreading much further afield, seeping into the early childhood services of nearly every country.

Space and purpose preclude a critique of the dominant early childhood discourse; that can be found elsewhere (cf. Moss, 2009). I want instead to add my voice to those in the book that insist there are other ways of thinking about early childhood centers. I would go further and say that if we are to have any chance of regaining a democratic politics of early childhood education—"education" being understood in its broadest sense—then we must resist the dictatorship of no alternative pursued by the dominant discourse, and proclaim and welcome a domain of plural perspectives and multiple alternatives. My contribution is to offer just one.

We must also rediscover the importance and pleasure of political questions, "not mere technical issues to be solved by experts…[but questions that] always involve decisions which require us to make a choice between conflicting alternatives" (Mouffe, 2007, n.p.). Political questions constitute and define a politics of education. Some of these questions are ontological. What is our understanding, or image, of the child, the parent, the educator, the early childhood center? How do we understand education? Some are epistemological. What is knowledge? How do we learn? Some concern other conflicting alternatives. What are the purposes of education? What should be its fundamental values? What should be its ethics?

This book engages with several of these questions, in particular the image of the child, the parent, the educator—and, in particular, the early childhood center, which is also the focus of this foreword. It does so in a way that combines strong theoretical and philosophical perspectives with empirical research. The answers offered in this book to the critical question—What is your image of the early childhood center?—are rich and hopeful, taking us away from the privatized, narrow, and technocratic understandings of the dominant discourse with its concern to govern child and parent by insistent conformity to norm. My own answer to the question, which has much in common with the authors in this book, has been the early childhood center as a public responsibility and a public institution; as a public space or forum where citizens of all ages meet; and as a collaborative laboratory or workshop, acting for the common good.

A recent paper for the Organisation for Economic Co-operation and Development (OECD) comments that "many preschool programs serve dual purposes—increasing the employment of mothers [*sic*] and enhancing child development" (Barnett, 2010, p. 3). But my image of the preschool, like that of the authors in this collection, goes far beyond single or dual purpose—childcare, education, development, or even education and care or care and development. This is the thinking behind the factory, a place for the large-scale and strongly managed production of a limited number of prespecified products.

The early childhood center, as I understand it, as a forum or a collective laboratory or workshop, is capable of many, many purposes and can produce many, many projects of common interest and benefit. Here are just a few that can be found today—not all in every preschool center, but some in most and many in a few:

- reproducing and co-constructing knowledges, values, and identities;
- co-constructing cultures of childhood and education;
- practicing and renewing participatory democracy and active citizenship;
- practicing and deepening relational ethics;
- providing family support;
- strengthening social cohesion and community solidarity;
- supporting the social inclusion of children and families;
- resisting dominant discourses and other forms of oppression;
- constructing new discourses and working for social change;
- sustaining diversity of cultures and languages;
- developing the economy and increasing employment;
- experimenting with new pedagogical and social projects;
- promoting gender and other equalities.

While most readers will recognize such projects, we have too few documented examples of this diversity. There is an urgent need for the more extensive and systematic documentation of the potentiality of early childhood centers, another reason for welcoming this book (for another example, England's Sheffield Children's Centre, see Broadhead, Meleady, & Delgado, 2008; Delgado, 2009).

This thinking about the potentiality of the early childhood center has much in common with my thinking about young children's learning. Both involve the productiveness of assemblages of people, objects, and desires, and the interconnections that occur within these assemblages from encounters with difference, a productiveness expressed as movement, transformation—or, to use the concept of Deleuze and Guattari—as lines of flight creating something new, whether new thought, new experimentation, or new projects.

From time to time though, there are moments where something new and different may happen, something that increases all participants' capacity to act and create interesting connections and features in between teachers and children as well as between the form and content of the practice. These are the moments of the lines of flight...When something new and different is coming about, when the lines of flight are created and activated in the practices, it is never taking place as a rationally planned and implemented change by specific individuals. Rather, there are from time-to-time magic moments where something entirely new and different seems to be coming about. This is recognized only by the tremendous intensity and, very often, the physical expression of goose bumps that take possession of participants (Olsson, 2009, p. 62).

Here Olsson, in her book in the series *Contesting Early Childhood*, is writing about pedagogical work in one particular Swedish preschool. But something new and different may happen—lines of flight—in the other encounters or assemblages possible in an early childhood center that understands itself to be a public space, a forum, and a collective workshop; lines of flights involving connections not only between children and teachers, but also with other staff, parents, and the center's local community.

This creativity happens not by imposing predetermined means and ends. On the contrary, it happens by enabling the unexpected to escape all attempts to tame, predict, supervise, control, and evaluate against preset goals. The challenge here is to turn away from trying to know what a preschool—or a child—is, to resist transmitted representations, to let go of expert assurances of guaranteed returns; and to turn instead toward the center—and child—as a potentiality, a not-yet, a becoming, a multiplicity, a case of and...and...and. If *quality* and *outcome* are important concepts for understanding the rationality of the dominant discourse, then surprise and wonder are similarly important in an alternative discourse.

So rather than a closed system intended to ensure the implementation of prescribed technologies to attain prescribed outcomes in a known world, I desire an openended early childhood education in a center that occupies and contributes to an unfinished world, a place of infinite possibilities. This image of the early childhood center connects to two important concepts that embody potentiality: *immaterial production* and *democratic experimentalism*. Hardt and Negri (2005) define the former as "the production of ideas, images, knowledges, communication, cooperation and affective relations...social life itself" (p. 146); such production, they argue, calls for continuous cooperation, being achieved "not by individuals but collectively in collaboration" (p. 187), for "its foundation is the common" (p. 147). Roberto Unger (2005), speaking of the latter concept, argues that

[t]he provision of public services must be an innovative collective practice, moving forward the qualitative provision of the services

themselves. That can no longer happen in our current understanding of efficiency and production by the mechanical transmission of innovation from the top. It can only happen through the organization of a collective experimental practice from below....Democracy is not just one more terrain for the institutional innovation that I advocate. It is the most important terrain. (pp. 179, 182)

The early childhood center can be understood as a collective workshop for the collaborative production of immaterial products and the conduct of democratic experimentation, varied in nature—social, cultural, political, ethical, affective—and often highly original. Furthermore, it can be a place where the benefits of such production and experimentation, which are not just narrowly economic, accrue to the common good. This is a long way from the early childhood center of the dominant discourse as a tightly managed factory for producing predetermined goods and as a business providing products to consumers and profit to entrepreneurs.

The rationale for early childhood education and the early childhood center, from this perspective, is not an investment decision based on an economic calculation that a given amount of *taxpayers' money* will produce a predicted return, a predefined and fixed relationship between inputs and outputs expressed in terms of a contractual relationship, with *payment by results* as its extreme manifestation. Rather it is a *political* decision based on a public recognition of the potential importance of early childhood centers for a cohesive and solidaristic society; on public hope in their productive potential for creating new learning and new projects; and on public faith in the capacity of human beings for intelligent judgment and action if proper conditions are furnished.

Those *proper conditions* are many and varied. For now, though, I want to focus on one political condition: democracy as a fundamental value inscribed in how decisions are made, in how relations are conducted, in how educational practices and projects are conducted, and in how evaluation is undertaken. This is democracy as a set of formal procedures for governance and decision making, from preschool through commune to national government. But it is also democracy understood in another and more pervasive sense: as a way of thinking, as a way of being and acting, as a way of relating and living together. This is democracy as "values and practices [that] shape not just the formal sphere of politics but the informal sphere of everyday life" (Skidmore & Bound, 2008). This is democracy, in the words of John Dewey, as "a mode of associated living embedded in the culture and social relationships of everyday life" and as "a way of life controlled by a working faith in the possibilities of human nature...[and] faith in the capacity of human beings for intelligent judgment and action if proper conditions are furnished" (Dewey, 1939). This is democracy, as Hannah Arendt sees it, as a form of subjectivity expressed as a quality of human interaction (Biesta, 2007).

Democracy, understood in this way, can be seen not only as a political principle but as a relational ethic that can and should pervade all aspects of everyday life. It is "a way of being, of thinking of oneself in relation to others and the world...a fundamental educational value and form of educational activity" (Rinaldi, 2006, p. 156). When democracy is adopted as a fundamental value and practiced throughout the life of the early childhood center, when adults and children alike *do democracy* in the everyday, the center becomes a site for democratic practice and for constructing democratic subjectivity through participation in that practice. The practice flows through all parts of the center: in the way that its work is conducted; in the way children and adults relate in everyday life; in the way decisions, from smaller to larger, are made; in the way the potential of the center is realized; and in the way that potential is evaluated. As such, it can contribute to the renewal of democracy in modern societies, through widening and deepening its reach. The preschool can then be part of a coalition to oppose what Morin calls "the regression of democracy," where "all problems, having become technical, elude the grasp of citizens to the profit of experts" (Morin, 1999, p. 70). It becomes an example of how, for Negri and Hardt (2005, p. 355) "the institutions of democracy today must coincide with the communicative and collaborative networks that constantly produce and reproduce social life."

The democratic school practicing democratic education is not, of course, a new idea; democracy is one of five recurring themes that Darling and Norbenbo (2003) argue characterize approaches to schooling in the tradition of progressive education. There are numerous examples past and present of attempts to develop the democratic school. More recently, the democratic early childhood center has also come into the picture. The Swedish preschool curriculum defines democracy as "the foundation of the preschool," adding that "all pre-school activity is to be carried out in accordance with fundamental democratic values." The centers in Reggio Emilia, the municipal schools for young children, provide one well-documented examples of democracy in action, defining participation as a key value in their work (Rinaldi, 2005; Vecchi, 2010)—though this expression of democracy should be seen as typical of a wider "municipal school revolution" that saw many towns and cities in northern Italy develop early childhood education from the 1960s onward with a strong democratic ethos (see Lazzari, 2011, for the work of Bruno Ciari as head of education in the city of Bologna between 1966 and 1970). A recent project in nurseries in a German town—*Living democracy in day care centre*—concludes "that the basis for an everyday democratic culture can indeed already be formed in the day nursery" (Priebe, cited in George, 2009, p. 14).

Democracy, as value and practice, finds no place in a neoliberal-inscribed dominant discourse: they are quite incommensurable. Democracy rejects the investment logic, the instrumental rationality, the deference to experts. It values collective choice exercised in democratic processes, over individual choice exercised by consumers. It values democratic accountability over managerial accountability. It values the political and ethical over the technical. And it values collaboration over competition as the way to create not only the kind of preschool and pedagogical work envisaged in this book, but also for the production of creative responses to the grave dangers we face as a species. Shah and Goss argue that

> our society faces challenges where we need to act collaboratively more than ever. We need to deepen democracy through more deliberative and participative democratic mechanisms that spread democracy into the "everyday" of our lives. And we need to foster a stronger public realm and associative democracy with organisations that bring people together to live and learn together. (Shah & Goss, 2007, p. 26)

I want to end by making three disparate observations, triggered by reading the following chapters. First, a democratic early childhood education that is at ease with and values diversity and multiple perspectives and is also a public responsibility has to work on developing a nuanced view of outcomes. If we understand early childhood centers as a public responsibility and as public institutions, worthy of public commitment and funding, then citizens, through democratic government, should place certain requirements or expectations on them. But while there should be some predetermined outcomes, there should also be an appetite for other outcomes, outcomes that are not predetermined, outcomes that are new, outcomes that trouble our assumptions and disturb our complaisance, outcomes that are a cause of wonder and surprise. This way we may escape from the atrophy of only seeing what we are looking for and the danger of governing people by norms.

Second, while there is much reference in this book, and in many others on early childhood services, to *parents*, what is usually meant is *mothers*. While the use of the generic rather than the gendered term is understandable and, in some ways, commendable, seeking to avoid an assumption that young children are solely or primarily women's responsibility, it can nevertheless serve to render the crucial issue of gender invisible. We must remember, too, that those working in these services are overwhelmingly women, early childhood being one of the most gendered fields of paid work in all societies—and proving stubbornly resistant to change. It seems to me that one of the possibilities of the early childhood center could be as a place where the politics of gender and care are explicitly addressed, though this I readily concede, is more easily said than done. However, if we are to stand any chance of creating societies that are more equal and that attach due value to care as an essential ethic and practice, then it is a nettle we must grasp: men as well as women must be included in early childhood education.

Third, I am increasingly persuaded that early childhood education needs to engage with all other forms of education, not in a subservient way (*preparation* or *readying* for school), but on the basis of what OECD's *Starting Strong* reports term a "strong and equal partnership (OECD, 2001, 2006). A starting point would be to enter into dialogue about the sort of political questions I have proposed above, to see the scope for shared answers. There is much in this book about the image of the early childhood center that might be relevant to a reconceptualized school, a school like the early childhood center based on democracy. We all, of course, are absorbed in our own field, fascinated by its complexities, problems, and possibilities, and we live in societies that seem ever more specialized and narrowly focused. But in the case of early childhood education, to continue with this introversion is particularly short-sighted and dangerous.

As this book illustrates, some of the most innovative and important work in any field of education is to be found in early childhood education—yet it is little known and understood elsewhere. Early childhood education needs a more assertive voice, reflecting a readiness and desire to engage with compulsory education and beyond, insisting on the important answers it is producing to those political questions that define all education, calling for a pedagogical meeting place where equals can dialogue, argue and create new, shared meanings. To fail to take this long view, to continue to look no further than itself, is dangerous; for early childhood education will find itself defenseless against being forced into the subservient position of handmaiden to a conservative and narrow compulsory education, a trend already clearly visible in many countries as early childhood education is reduced to one more means of boosting school attainment and national performance in international league tables.

The introduction to this book by Judith Duncan and Sarah Te One argues that "ECEC [Early Childhood Education and Care] services can, and should, play pivotal roles in building democratic communities, family resilience and family wellness; presenting possibilities for inclusion...and providing a range of integrated services." I would agree, but I would also suggest that we might broaden the statement to ECEC services and schools. In a dangerous world, driven by multiple crises and in the grip of an economic system that is unsustainable and inimical to human flourishing, we should be calling for nothing less.

References

Barnett, W. S. (2010). *Benefits and costs of quality preschool education: Evidence-based policy to improve returns.* Paris: OECD. Retrieved from http://www.oecd.org/officialdocuments/publicdisplaydocumentpdf/?cote=EDU/EDPC/ECEC/RD(2010)4&docLanguage=En

Biesta, G. (2007). Education and the democratic person: Towards a political understanding of democratic education, *Teachers College Record, 109* (3), 740–769.

Blackburn, P. (2010). *Children's Nurseries UK market report.* London: Laing & Buisson Ltd.

Broadhead, P., Meleady, C., & Delgado, M. A. (2008). *Children, families and communities: Creating and sustaining integrated services.* Maidenhead: Open University Press.

Darling, J., & Norbenbo, S. E. (2003). Progressivism. In N. Blake, P. Smeyers, R. Smith & P. Standish (Eds.). *The Blackwell guide to philosophy of education* (pp. 288–308). Oxford: Blackwell.

Delgado, M. A. (2009). *Community involvement in services for children, families and communities.* Saarbrücken: VDM.

Department for Education/Department for Health (England). (2011). *Supporting families in the foundation years.* Retrieved from http://media.education.gov.uk/assets/files/pdf/s/supporting%20families%20in%20the%20foundation%20years.pdf

Dewey, J. (1939, October). "Creative democracy—The task before us." Address given at a dinner in honor of John Dewey. New York. Retrieved from http://chipbruce.files.wordpress.com/2008/11/dewey_creative_dem.pdf

George, S. (2009). *Too young for respect? Realising respect for young children in their everyday environments.* Den Haag: Bernard van Leer Foundation.

Hardt, M., & Negri, A. (2005). *Multitude.* London: Penguin Books.

Lazzari, A. (2011). *Reconceptualising professional development in early childhood education: A study of teachers' professionalism carried out in Bologna Province.* Unpublished doctoral thesis, University of Bologna.

Moss, P. (2009). *There are alternatives! Markets and democratic experimentalism in early childhood education and care.* The Hague: Bernard van leer Foundation. Retrieved from http://www.bernardvanleer.org/publications_results?SearchableText=B-WOP-053

Morin, E. (1999). *Homeland earth: A manifesto for the new millennium.* Cresskill NJ: Hampton Press.

Mouffe, C. (2007). Artistic activism and agonistic spaces. *Art and Research,* *1*(2), 1–5.

OECD. (2001). *Starting Strong I.* Paris: Organisation for Economic Co-operation and Development.

OECD. (2006). *Starting Strong II.* Paris: Organisation for Economic Co-operation and Development.

Olsson, L.M. (2009). *Movement and experimentation in young children's learning: Deleuze and Guattari in early childhood education.* London: Routledge.

Rinaldi, C. (2006). *In dialogue with Reggio Emilia: Listening, researching and learning.* London: Routledge.

Shah, H., & Goss, S. (Eds). (2007). *Democracy and the public realm.* London: Compass & Lawrence & Wishart.

Skidmore, P., & Bound, K. (2008). *The everyday democracy index.* London: Demos.

Unger, R. M. (2005). The future of the Left: James Crabtree interviews Roberto Unger, *Renewal, 13* (2/3), 173–84.

Vecchi, V. (2010). *Art and creativity in Reggio Emilia: Exploring the role and potential of Ateliers in early childhood education.* London: Routledge.

Acknowledgments

Ehara taku toa, he taki tahi, he toa taki tini

My success should not be bestowed onto me alone, as it was not individual success but success of a collective

We would like to acknowledge the children, families, *whānau* (extended family), teachers, and colleagues from the five countries included in this volume, who have joined us in the research endeavors that are reported here. It is the experiences of these community members that have enabled the writers in this book to explore the notions of community, family, *whānau*, child development, resilience, and cultural inclusion. We wish to acknowledge their stories, time, and expertise that they have shared with us, all of which have made this book possible.

Each author, in their chapter, has also acknowledged other contributors, including funding sources for the research and individuals who have supported and guided them. We wish to acknowledge these individuals and organizations also. Without the support of government and nongovernmental funding to sustain research in early childhood education, our increasing understanding of the field and our ability to develop new and innovative ways of support child development, family resilience, and community wellness would not be possible.

On a personal note we would like to thank and acknowledge Maggie Burgess, Dunedin, New Zealand, who has assisted us with the editing and production of this book.

CONTRIBUTING AUTHORS

Judith Duncan
Judith Duncan is an Associate Professor in Education, School of Māori, Social and Cultural Studies in Education, at the University of Canterbury College of Education, Christchurch, New Zealand. Prior to this position Judith was employed at the Children's Issues Centre, University of Otago, where for nine years she researched and taught in the area of early childhood education and children's participation. Judith is an established researcher with over 15 years of research experience, predominantly using qualitative research methods in a range of education settings. Her research and teaching interests include early childhood education, children's voices, gender and education, and education policy and practice. Since her doctoral studies, which examined teachers' perspectives of education reforms in the kindergarten sector, she has been involved in a range of projects that examine early childhood, from multiple and interdisciplinary perspectives, placing central to each research project the perspectives of children and their families.

Hillel Goelman
Hillel Goelman is a Professor at the University of British Columbia (UBC) Canada Department of Educational and Counseling Psychology, and Special Education <http://www.ecps.educ.ubc.ca> and an associate member of the Department of Pediatrics and the Department of Population and Public Health at UBC. He currently serves as chair of the Interdisciplinary Studies Graduate Program at the UBC. His research focuses on the short- and long-term effects of early childhood interventions on child development. He is currently director of *The Consortium of Health, Intervention, Learning and Development (CHILD) Project*, a collaborative, interdisciplinary research project. He is also director of a study on the development of child graduates of neonatal intensive care units and on maternal and child mental health. Almost everything he knows about early child development he learned from his sons, Zachary and Nada, and from his wife, Sheryl Sorokin, a child and family therapist.

Dawna Holiday

Dawna Holiday is a doctoral student in Curriculum Studies at Arizona State University, United States. Her research focuses on analyzing children's perspectives on stereotypical popular culture, Hollywood-fashioned Native Americans, and the dominant ideologies that exist in films. With the saturation of stereotypical figures depicted through the media, her dissertation research will include a comparative analysis of the perspectives of seven- to eight-year-old Native American and non–Native American children, living on and off the reservation. She recently worked with the qualitative component of the *First Things First* external evaluation project, focusing on families, community stakeholders, and children's narratives.

Rachel Holmes

Rachel Holmes is a Reader in Cultural Studies of Childhood in the Educational and Social Research Institute, Manchester Metropolitan University, United Kingdom (U.K.). Her research interests are among the interstices of applied educational research, social science research, and arts-based research within the field of childhood. She has interests in notions of childhood territories, such as ways childhood becomes imag(in)ed through fictional, documentary and ethnographic film; children's child(self)hood, identities and objects; and ways to (left)field childhood via opening up off-center research methodologies. Currently, she is involved in evaluating innovative work within a *Mother and Baby Unit* located in a prison, as well as developing a film and seminar series project, funded by the Economic and Social Research Council.

Jamie Patrice Joanou

Jamie Patrice Joanou is a doctoral candidate in Educational Leadership and Policy Studies at Arizona State University, U.S. Her research focuses on adolescents in context, particularly the effects of landscape and context on identity development and performance. Her dissertation examines the reciprocal relationship between outreach organizations, the urban landscape, children and adolescents working on the street, and the ways in which this relationship promotes the adoption of a street identity. She is also the evaluation coordinator for the qualitative portion of the *First Things First* External Evaluation, which is evaluating the efficacy of this voter-approved early childhood initiative.

Liz Jones

Liz Jones is a Professor of Early Childhood and Education at the Educational and Social Research Institute, Manchester Metropolitan

University, U.K. She has over 20 years' experience of teaching in both mainstream and special education. Her research interests lie within poststructuralist theory, feminist theory, and social constructions and deconstructions of *the child* and *childhood*. Currently, she is working with colleagues in partnership with Manchester Science Museum on an Economic and Social Research Council–funded case studentship. Additionally, she is involved in evaluating innovative work within a *Mother and Baby Unit* located in a prison and with the Fatherhood Institute's initiative where the aim is to encourage fathers, particularly the young and more vulnerable, to become proactive in the care of their children.

Debora Lee

Debora Lee is a lecturer and practicum coordinator (ECE) at the Faculty of Education, University of Auckland, New Zealand. Her research interests include the complexities of the early childhood practicum and GLBTT (*Gay, Lesbian, Bisexual, Transgendered, Transsexual*) experiences of education. In 2006, she engaged in a study exploring the experiences of gay mothers and their families in early childhood education settings. Her latest research project involves examining visibility and inclusion issues for GLBTT in tertiary education.

Maggie MacLure

Maggie MacLure is Professor of Education in the Educational and Social Research Institute, Manchester Metropolitan University, U.K. She started her career as a researcher on the influential *Bristol Language Development Project*, and later moved to the National Foundation for Educational Research, where she helped to develop the national framework for the assessment of *oracy*, for the Assessment of Performance Unit. She has continued to carry out research on language and discourse, and is also interested in the development of theory and methodology in applied social research. She is a member (from September 2006) of the Executive Council of the British Educational Research Association. Her book, *Discourse in Educational and Social Research*, won the 2004 Critics' Choice Award from the American Educational Studies Association.

Bruce Maden

For the last 19 years Bruce has provided leadership for the Te Aroha Noa Community Services, an integrated multidisciplinary community-developed agency situated in the heart of a lower socioeconomic and culturally diverse community, Palmerston North, New Zealand. Bruce has interests in community development, strengths-based work, and practice research. He deeply believes that communities should be involved in developing services and discovering solutions to community issues.

Robyn Munford

Robyn is Professor of Social Work and director of the Practice Research and Professional Development Hub, School of Health and Social Services, Massey University, New Zealand. She has qualifications in social work, disability studies, and sociology and is the co-leader of a project researching young people's pathways to resilience and a longitudinal project researching the transitions made by young people focusing on their work, education, and life projects. Both projects are funded by the government agency, *Ministry of Science and Technology (MSI)*. Robyn has extensive experience in disability and family research, including research on family well-being, using participatory and action research methodologies, and has published internationally on this research. She has recently completed an action research project that explored social and community practice in community-based settings and strategies for building inclusive communities to support families and children. Robyn has published widely on social and community work theory and practice including strengths-based practice; disability studies; community development, bicultural practice, and indigenous approaches; research methods and research ethics; children and young people; and family well-being.

Peter Moss

Peter Moss is a historian by background and has wide-ranging research interests including services for children, the workforce in these services, and including services for children, their workforce and democratic practice in these services; gender issues in work with children; and the relationship between employment and care, with a special interest in leave policy. He is also interested in social pedagogy and radical education. He has a good understanding of early childhood policies in most EU member states, including early childhood education and care and parental leave. His work with Gunilla Dahlberg on postmodern thinking in ECEC, and ethics in ECEC are leading texts that are used internationally.

Jayne Pivik

Jayne Pivik is a community psychologist with a background in developmental psychology and environmental influences on health. Her research interests are in identifying how communities can positively influence child/youth health, development and well-being; services and interventions promoting child and youth development; human-environmental interactions; methods for engaging children and youth in services that impact them; and equitable access for individuals with disabilities and the elderly. She is founder and CEO of Apriori Research <http://www.aprioriresearch.com> and an honorary associate of the Human Early Learning Partnership, UBC, Canada.

Frances Press

Frances Press is senior lecturer in early childhood education at Charles Sturt University, Australia, with a strong interest in the way in which governments' construction and enactment of early childhood education and care policy supports or works against the creation of a strong, robust, and child-responsive early childhood sector. She has been co-director and primary contributor to Australian and international reviews of early childhood policy, including the *OECD's Thematic Review of Early Childhood Education and Care: Australian Background Report* (2000). Frances's recent research has examined Australian integrated child and family services (with Jennifer and Sandie). She is a chief investigator on a number of research projects concerning early childhood education, including collaborative practice across professional disciplines (with Jennifer and Sandie) and two Australian Research Council (ARC) grants. Frances has particular research interests in early childhood programs for infants and toddlers; the construction and enactment of quality in early childhood education and care settings; and the creation of sustainable integrated services for children and families.

Jackie Sanders

Jackie is an Associate Professor in the School of Health and Social Services, Massey University, New Zealand. Jackie has qualifications in Sociology and Children's Studies and is co-leader of an international, longitudinal study of young people's pathways and transitions funded by the Ministry of Science and Innovation (MSI). She has undertaken youth, family, and child well-being research and has published extensively in these areas.

Jennifer Sumsion

Jennifer Sumsion is Foundation Professor of Early Childhood Education at Charles Sturt University, Bathurst, Australia. Her current research focuses on workforce capacity building and *quality* in early childhood education, and early childhood curriculum and policy. Her research has been supported by a range of external funding bodies, including the ARC. She currently holds two ARC grants. Jennifer has recently completed (with colleagues Frances Press and Sandie Wong) a national research project focussing on Australian integrated child and family services funded by the Professional Support Coordination Alliance. With Frances and Sandie, she is about to commence a research project investigating collaborative practice in integrated child and family services for the Victorian Department of Education and Early Childhood Development. Jennifer has published an edited book and more than 65 journal articles and book chapters.

Beth Blue Swadener

Beth Blue Swadener is Professor of Childhood Studies and Educational Policy at Arizona State University, U.S. Her research focuses on internationally comparative social policy, child and family issues in sub-Saharan Africa, and children's rights and voices. She has published eight books, including *Reconceptualizing the Early Childhood Curricula; Children and Families "At Promise"; Does the Village Still Raise the Child?; Decolonizing Research in Cross-Cultural Context;* and *Power and Voice in Research with Children* and numerous articles and book chapters. Beth is currently co-directing a statewide external evaluation project of *First Things First*, a health and early education initiative for children birth to age five and their families in Arizona, utilizing a mixed-method longitudinal design.

Sarah Te One

Sarah Te One is a lecturer at the Victoria University of Wellington, New Zealand. Sarah's interests are in children's rights and advocacy for young children and early childhood education policy, including curriculum and assessment issues. She is also interested in parent support and development in early childhood education and communities. Recent research experiences include two Centres of Innovation, a Ministry of Education project on involving children in research, and a *Teaching and Learning Research Initiative* (TLRI) *project* (with Judith Duncan). Sarah has over 25 years' experience in the early childhood sector.

Maureen Thomas

Maureen Thomas is a Bachelor of Education (Hons) graduate who has taught in primary schools in the UK and New Zealand. After having three children of her own, she followed her interest in children's development in early childhood and attained a Graduate Diploma in ECE. Maureen is now a team leader at the Whanganui Central Baptist Kindergartens.

Sandie M. Wong

Sandie M. Wong is a postdoctoral research fellow within the Research Institute for Professional Practice, Learning and Education at Charles Sturt University, Australia. Her research focuses on the role early childhood education and care services play in supporting families, especially those from marginalized groups, both today and historically. Sandie has extensive experience in early childhood program delivery and evaluation. She contributed to the *OECD Thematic Review of Early Childhood Education and Care Policy: Australian Background Report* (authored by Dr. Frances Press and Professor Alan Hayes). She recently completed (with colleagues Jennifer Sumsion and Frances Press) a national research project focusing on Australian integrated child and family services funded by the Professional Support Coordination Alliance. With Jennifer and Frances, she is about to commence a research project investigating collaborative practice in integrated child and family services for the Victorian Department of Education and Early Childhood Development. Sandie's work has been published in a book chapter, several peer reviewed and professional journals, and numerous evaluation reports.

CHAPTER 1

Early Childhood Education Services: The *Heart* and *Hearth* of Communities; International Perspectives

Judith Duncan and Sarah Te One

INTRODUCTION

This international collection reconceptualizes the positions and roles of early childhood education within communities, challenging the traditional practices of *involving families* or *partnerships with parents* in early childhood services. The chapters in this volume argue that a shift in the perspectives of teachers, management, and service providers within early childhood services toward incorporating new ways of working with, alongside, and in collaboration with family, *whānau* (extended family), and the wider community is both timely and global. So often the involvement of children's *whānau* is directed and dictated by the teachers' agendas for supporting the educational programs or activities; for example, parents are often called on to support children's learning assessments, mow lawns, repair equipment, or organize fund-raising events. While there has been a shift to supporting more authentic relationships between teaching staff and families in many early childhood settings across the globe, the authors in this volume argue for a shift in positioning early childhood services both as the *heart of the community* and as the *heart and hearth of the community*, rather than as just an added option to a program. They argue that Early Childhood Education and Care (ECEC) services can, and should, play pivotal roles in building democratic communities, family resilience, and family wellness; in presenting possibilities for inclusion, while challenging heteronormativity, racism, and language barriers; and in providing a range of integrated services that ensure that children and their family and *whānau* can access the education, health, and social services they need for positive outcomes for their children. These ideas are the *heart* of this book.

CONTEXT

ECEC centers are pivotal places for communities and the families within these same communities. This has become particularly obvious for communities (in suburbs) where neoliberal politics in many countries have closed small local schools. Where facilities such as health and postal/communication services are no longer present in suburban or rural areas, the ECEC center has become the only meeting place for parents. Historically ECEC centers, represented in the countries in this book, have been community-based. This has encouraged both the inclusion of families and the sustained presence of the center in the community, with often the same staff in the center over many years. Teachers who know the children, families, *whānau,* and community through the early years of parenting and family development are a key resource within the community and play a role in the social cohesion of that community.

PARENTAL PARTICIPATION

How parents, families, and *whānau* participate in their child's ECEC setting has changed and developed over the last 20 years. The discourses range from working with parents, parent helping (in centers), parent support (for fundraising and working bees), parent partnership (for management and interactions in the center), to the more recent parent collaborations (working together for children's learning outcomes). While all of these discourses have positioned parents in active involvement with the staff and children of an ECEC service, they have not often involved authentic or reciprocal relationships with parents, families, and *whānau* where the outcome of the interaction may be of benefit for the family themselves. Most commonly, centers and services have been the recipient of the activity of the parents, and while this has benefited the learning opportunities for children, it has not been of equal benefit for families, or for the community the service resides within.

Internationally, there is recent research that has highlighted gains that parents (usually mothers) experience through participating in early childhood education (Duncan, Bowden, & Smith, 2004; Duncan, Bowden, & Smith, 2005, 2006a, 2006b; Hayden & Macdonald, 2000; Podmore, & Te One, 2008; Powell, et al., 2006; Smith et al., 2000; Wylie, 1994). This research has set the scene for reconceptualizing the role, perceptions, discourses, and activities that surround early childhood. ECEC services can and do help families develop supportive relationships and networks and in doing so influence the amount and quality of social capital available to families in times of crisis. Whether or not a family is resilient may depend not only on the family having access to strategies that will enable them to cope, recover, and protect themselves, but also on their ability to appraise the needs of a situation or crisis, match appropriate strategies with particular problems, and implement strategies effectively. Families should have access to personal, family, and community developmental programs and support services of high quality. ECEC centers can help families gain access to these forms of informal and formal support, and in doing so assist families to build social capital and resilience. To do this, however, ECEC staff, management, and teachers will need to reconceptualize both their role in the *community* and their *relationships with families.*

Community

Building, supporting, and growing communities is often the subject of debate among social services and educational agencies, but is less often heard in the market place or political sectors. Where a community does come to the attention of media, or political gazes, is when the *community* is needed to support a function that any particular service or government no longer wishes to take responsibility for; for example, support for the elderly or mental health disabilities where care has been *returned* to the community from government-supported agencies or institutions. ECEC has, traditionally, already been offering care in their communities—both formally for children and families and *whānau,* and informally for the wider community.

Research Evidence that ECEC Contributes to Community Building

Research has established that good quality early childhood education can contribute to ameliorating the effects of poverty and risk for children (Barnett, 1998; Smith et al., 2000). However, it cannot solve the problem of poverty, but it can help families and *whānau* cope with the stresses and challenges of modern-day life. Early childhood education should not, however, be considered the only context for intervention with families and *whānau* in need. It can and should be considered as a valuable part of the solution to the problems facing modern families and *whānau* that requires a multiperspectival and multisector approach.

Hayden and MacDonald (2000) argue that early childhood centers are well situated to adopt this new role, one that moves beyond a child-centered program focus. They argue that it is time to transcend the traditional discourses that view early childhood centers as support for working parents, as compensatory programs for children with additional needs (disadvantaged children), or as programs for developing school readiness. By changing attitudes and policies, early childhood services can be reformulated to assume the critical task of developing and facilitating social relationships, networks, and interagency collaborations—and play a central role in building communities and civil society. Hayden and MacDonald argue that early childhood centers should be seen as offering a service to the community and that a new discourse be developed that incorporates a community-oriented approach to service delivery. This discourse would recognize that many early childhood centers and services help build community connectedness by being a vehicle whereby links, relationships, and opportunities for networking develop—both on a micro, personal level between families and early childhood centers, and on a community level between agencies and organizations, early childhood centers, and families.

The research that has addressed parent participation in early childhood programs has begun to demonstrate the positive impact it has on family members, in addition to the child who is attending. Wylie (1994), in a review of early childhood policy and programs, found that parents involved in early childhood programs experienced enhanced relationships with their children, alleviation of maternal stress, upgrading of education or training credentials, and improved employment status. Wylie, Thompson, and Kerslake Henricks (1996) reported that parents in the Aotearoa New Zealand *Competent Children at 5* study identified the benefits from being involved in their child's early childhood service as support, friendship, and company. For those parents, who were the main caregivers of their children, gaining a better understanding of their children and the early childhood program and improving their own skills were identified as benefits.

The trend internationally in early childhood education is to provide a comprehensive approach that focuses not only on children, but also on their families (OECD, 2001; Powell, 1997). A *family systems perspective* (St. Pierre & Layzer, 1998) suggests that programs that focus only on children will not produce the best results. Programs that are delivered to whole families are more likely to be effective in breaking the cycle of poverty. *Head Start Family Services* and programs such as the *New Chance* and the *Comprehensive Child Development Program* in the United States are initiatives that have focused on the whole family and their multiple needs for services. In an OECD report (2001) reviewing ECEC provisions in 12 countries, the reviewers identified key programs that linked early childhood centers, parents, and communities through meaningful and supportive mechanisms. The authors of the report argued that ECEC programs can strengthen and build the social cohesion between families, communities, and government and nongovernmental sectors. They identified how multi-agency initiatives, incorporating early childhood provisions, more adequately meet the needs of today's parents and, when located in areas of high need, promote equal educational opportunities without stigmatizing individual children (OECD, 2001, p. 84). They offer several international examples of these forms of provision, including England's

> *Early Excellence Centres,* government supported models of exemplary practice, [who] offer a range of integrated services, including early years education for 3-4 year olds, full-day care for children birth to 3 years, drop-in facilities, outreach, family support, health care, adult education and practitioner training. (OECD, 2001, p. 84)

Wigfall (2002) describes the *one-stop-shop* approach taken by the Coram Community Campus, an innovative model of service provision in inner London, where a range of services for young children and their families include care, education, health, parent support, and other services (e.g., a child psychologist and social worker) on one site. This approach was developed in order to overcome the problem of compartmentalization and fragmentation in traditional children's services and is based on research that focuses on the importance of early preventive work with parents in supporting resilience.

The Pen Green Centre, in Corby, United Kingdom, is also internationally cited as a multidisciplinary/multifunctional model, where working collaboratively with children and their families has made a significant impact on the wider community. Its *one-stop shop* for families with young children in the community has provided quality services for the wider community since 1983 (Whalley & the Penn Green Centre Team, 2007).

The Contents of the Book

This book brings together research and researchers from five countries—Aotearoa New Zealand, Australia, Canada, the United States, and the United Kingdom. The examples included in this book are not exhaustive, nor do they purport to represent all the communities that early childhood services are situated within, or groups they work alongside, but together the authors theoretically interrogate different contexts and discourses across a range of settings, population groups, and historical times. The authors in this collection draw on a range of theoretical positions to highlight the emerging research and understandings in this field within their own contexts, linking to the broader themes of this book and providing provocations to traditional ways of viewing and thinking about ECEC.

The first three chapters are based on results from two New Zealand and one Australian research project, which have each concentrated on one multidisciplinary ECEC setting, to demonstrate innovative ways of supporting quality education and wider family and community involvement and outcomes associated with these services.

In chapter 2, Duncan, Te One, and Thomas begin the contributions with a discussion at the heart of this collection—how teachers can reframe their work with parents, families, and *whānau* to improve both children's learning outcomes, but also family and community resilience and well-being. The authors report on working with teachers, management, and a *whānau* support worker within four ECEC centers in Aotearoa New Zealand, using sociocultural theories as the foundation for their shared research. They discuss a research tool, which worked both as a data-gathering tool, but more importantly as a professional development and reflection tool for the teachers in their inclusion of parents in the ECEC centre environment.

In chapter 3, Sumsion, Press, and Wong develop insights into the tensions that can arise from integrated services in ECEC, the ways in which services negotiate these tensions, and implications for how children, families, and practitioners experience integrated services. They call on data drawn from their commissioned study of Australian integrated services that investigated elements perceived to contribute to successful integration. Using examples from two such Australian services (Ngala and Gowrie SA) they contend that integrated services are sites of intersecting discourses. As authors they bring their three distinct voices to the discussion, reporting on the data through three different theoretical lenses to highlight the potential difficulties, dilemmas, and opportunities operating in integrated services—conceptualizations from communitarianism (Sumsion), Habermas (Press), and Cultural Historical Activity Theory (CHAT) (Wong). Together they highlight the complexity and visionary possibilities of integration for ECEC services.

In chapter 4, Munford, Sanders, and Maden discuss the experiences of one Aotearoa New Zealand community-based agency, *Te Aroha Noa*, which has developed effective strategies for enhancing family and community well-being. It provides an ECEC service and a range of other services developed with innovative approaches for nurturing the strengths of families. *Te Aroha Noa* has also contributed to building the capacity of the community within which it is situated. The authors present the agency's experiences in developing their approach to practice that spans early childhood, family and community work, and adult education. This chapter explores the key concepts that are central to this practice and provides examples from the early childhood center, which is located on the main site of the agency, and the parenting support and education programs provided to families that are delivered on site and in-home. The authors take a strengths-based approach to working with families and capacity building in the community. They use the metaphor of the *Spinifex*, a perennial grass that thrives in difficult environments and is well-adapted to coastal environments and the problems posed by unstable sand dunes, to represent the resilience of families and children and define the agency's presence in this community.

The following six chapters incorporate research results from a range of ECEC settings, either as multiple research sites, or drawing on participants who have been spread across multiple ECEC settings, positioning the role of ECEC in challenging discrimination, disadvantage, and racism and promoting inclusion, resilience, and well-being.

In chapter 5, Duncan continues to explore ECEC centers as places for building family resilience. Drawing on Foucault's notions of discourse, Duncan synthesizes the results from four Aotearoa New Zealand research studies, jointly undertaken with colleagues over a seven-year period. She argues that as ECEC centers are safe places, based within and around community life, they are the best places for supporting families and *whānau*, in comparison to targeted services, which create barriers for those most at risk. Together, the studies demonstrate that everyday teaching practices can make a significant difference for families and can reconceptualize ECEC settings as places for the community, as well as for children.

In chapter 6, Joanou, Holiday, and Swadener draw their chapter from a longitudinal, mixed-method evaluation of a statewide initiative for children birth-to-five and their families in Arizona, U.S. The authors situate family and community engagement in a state-wide perspective and draw from one aspect of the evaluation—a qualitative study of diverse families, early childhood providers, and children—in an attempt to foreground their voices and perspectives. These voices provide a very powerful chapter that demonstrates the complexity of children's and families' lives and the skill needed by ECEC providers to ensure that all children and their families are included, safe, and can access the education and support that the ECEC services could be providing. The problems identified in current delivery of programs are highlighted, but the authors draw on a *funds of knowledge* perspective that attempts to honor and understand the life experiences, aspirations, and perspectives of diverse families as well as the views of community members whose lives are spent trying to address the needs of families in Arizona.

In stark contrast to chapter 6, Lee's research in chapter 7 examining the experiences of lesbian mothers in Aotearoa New Zealand ECEC centers showcases teachers who actively worked to combat heternormativity and include *other* parenting styles into the everyday of the ECEC center. Lee builds her discussion around Kant's notion of *hospitality* as a responsibility to a common humanity. She argues that hospitality can be viewed as necessary for a civil society, and, in fact, as a moral imperative. Positioning the ECEC teachers within this theoretical construct of *hospitality*, Lee identifies the tensions and constraints of the mothers and the authentic and responsive relationships that were shared within the center—that was not always possible outside of the center. This small-scale qualitative study demonstrates that when inclusion works well for children and their families and *whānau*, family life is enhanced.

Building on Lee's examples, in chapter 8, Te One shares the success of a parenting program—*Supporting Parents alongside their Children's Education* (SPACE)—within an established ECEC service at Te Marua/Mangaroa Playcentre, an Aotearoa New Zealand Playcentre. This chapter reports on how the SPACE program created a sense of community for first-time mothers. The author shares findings from a three-year research study that demonstrated enhanced collaborative relationships between community agencies and first-time parents by "nurturing a culture of care" in the program. The combination of experienced facilitators, guest speakers, and the *whānau*-friendly environment of the playcentre encouraged supportive networks across the different settings these new parents participated in. Te One draws on sociocultural and ecological theories to interpret the findings and demonstrate that the SPACE program nurtured parent and child well-being and, at the same time, community wellness.

In chapter 9, Jones, Holmes, and MacLure discuss first-time mothers as well, but the context is very different from that of chapter 8. In their chapter, they examine the ways in which a prison-based Mother and Baby Unit (MBU) strives to develop different ways of working with diverse family cultures. The chapter draws on data that were collected while undertaking an evaluation of the MBU and introduces examples of data that, when read within a Foucauldian framework, foreground some of the tensions between the philosophy and practices of the MBU and the locations of *prison, prisoner, mother,* and *child.* Jones, Holmes, and MacLure encourage the reader to reconsider taken-for-granted teaching and parenting practices, where in the context of the MBU, everyday interactions occur in an extraordinary context and pose as examples for reconsideration. The authors explore the tensions provided by these readings and open a debate and dialogue to make space for renewed discussions that relate to both early childhood education, as well as what might constitute the resilient family.

The final research chapter, chapter 10, presenting a different context from the previous chapters, is based on an ambitious Canadian multidisciplinary longitudinal study. Goelman and Pivik describe the CHILD (Consortium for Health, Intervention, Learning and Development) Project, a five-year, collaborative interdisciplinary program of research in early child development. The CHILD Project was a collaboration of university researchers and community professionals that examined early child development through ten linked studies in four thematic clusters: the early identification of at-risk infants, toddlers and preschoolers; the implementation and effectiveness of early childhood program interventions; the impacts of governmental social policy on children and families; and the health and development of indigenous families. By using the metaphor of collaborative play, the authors identify how the project enabled interactions between university researchers and practitioners to articulate and share their meanings of *children* and *childhood,* inviting them to engage in the process of extending and co-constructing new meanings through collaborative discourse, problem finding, and problem solving. Similarly, the collaboration of community professionals and university researchers allowed for an ongoing exploration of how the worlds of professional practice and academic research construct meaning and knowledge of the conditions, policies, and programs that best support children and their families.

In the final chapter, chapter 11, "Reconceptualizing Early Education: Crossing Borders to Build Community," we, the editors, Duncan and Te One, identify the common themes and contextualize these within the overarching purpose of the book: to reconceptualize the space and place of early childhood services in communities by presenting new possibilities and potentialities for mutually beneficial collaborations between teachers, parents, *whānau,* and communities. In the first instance, political, economic, and cultural drivers of education policy cannot be ignored. Education is political, and therefore, shifting the lens from the individual child or family to the wider macro- and exosystem underpins a central challenge this book poses to readers. How can early childhood services enhance the well-being of children, families, *whānau,* and communities?

The fundamental value of a *strength-based approach* shines throughout the chapters. *Belonging and connectedness* to a community is critical to well-being in the broadest sense: the well-being of the child, of the parents, of teachers, and of services themselves. Rather than using a child-centered lens to assess well-being, the authors in this book illustrate how organizational and community lenses offer multiple perspectives that in turn create numerous possibilities for strengthening communities. Without exception each chapter presents research-based evidence of multiple *collaborations* and *networks* within, among, and between the diverse community contexts. A final theme to emerge from the data illustrates how *resilience* and *identity* within communities are enhanced when strengths as opposed to deficits are promoted.

In this volume, we bring together international thinking about how early childhood services can and do shift the balance of power situated within such services by crossing traditional boundaries into different spaces (homes, neighborhoods, and communities) where children, families, and *whānau* spend time. Our hope is that this book will encourage readers to reconceptualize their own existing frames of reference, beyond the center or service, and move out-the-door and into communities.

REFERENCES

Barnett, W. S. (1998). Long-term cognitive and academic affects of early childhood education and poverty. *Preventive Medicine: An International Journal Devoted to Practice and Theory, 27*(2), 204–207.

Duncan, J., Bowden, C., & Smith, A. B. (2004, November). *A gossip or a good yak? Reconceptualising parent support in early childhood centre based programmes.* Paper presented at the NZARE Annual Conference, Wellington, NZ.

Duncan, J., Bowden, C., & Smith, A. B. (2005). *Early childhood centres and family resilience.* Report prepared for the Ministry of Social Development, Wellington, NZ.

Duncan, J., Bowden, C., & Smith, A. B. (2006a). A gossip or a good yack? Reconceptualizing parent support in New Zealand early childhood centre based programmes. *International Journal of Early Years Education, 14*(1), 1–13.

Duncan, J., Bowden, C., & Smith, A. B. (2006b). Aotearoa New Zealand early childhood centres and family resilience: Reconceptualising relationships. *International Journal of Equity and Innovation in Early Childhood, 4*(2), 79–90.

Freeman, C., Quigg, R., Vass, E., & Broad, M. (2007). *The changing geographies of children's lives: A study of how children in Dunedin use their environment.* Dunedin, NZ: Department of Geography, University of Otago.

Hayden, J., & Macdonald, J. J. (2000). Health promotion: A new leadership role for early childhood professionals. *Australian Journal of Early Childhood, 25*(1), 32–39.

OECD. (2001). *Starting strong: Early childhood education and care.* Paris: OECD.

Podmore, V. N., & Te One, S. (2008). *Nurturing a culture of care for infants and first-time parents: The SPACE programme at Te Marua/Mangaroa Playcentre early childhood centre of innovation (Round 2).* Final research report for the Ministry of Education. Wellington, NZ: Ministry of Education.

Powell, D. (1997). Parent support programmes: Opportunities and challenges. *Childrenz Issues, 1*(2), 9–11.

Powell, K., Cullen, J., Adams, P., Duncan, J., & Marshall, K. (2006). *The effect of adult playcentre participation on the creation of social capital in local communities.* Report prepared for the New Zealand Playcentre Federation, Wellington, NZ.

Smith, A. B., Grima, G., Gaffney, M., & Powell, K. (2000). *Early childhood education: Literature review report to Ministry of Education.* Children's Issues Centre, Dunedin, NZ.

St. Pierre, R. G., & Layzer, J. I. (1998). Improving the life chances of children in poverty: Assumptions and what we have learned. *Social Policy Report (Society for Research in Child Development), 7*(4), 1–28.

Whalley, M., & the Penn Green Centre Team. (2007). *Involving parents in their children's learning* (2nd ed.). London: Paul Chapman Publishing.

Wigfall, V. (2002). "One-stop shopping": Meeting diverse family needs in the inner city? *European Early Childhood Education Research Journal, 10*(1), 111–121.

Wylie, C. (1994). *What research on early childhood education/care outcomes can and can't tell policy makers.* Wellington, NZ: New Zealand Council for Educational Research.

Wylie, C., Thompson, J., & Kerslake Hendricks, A. (1996). *Competent children at 5: Families and early education.* Wellington, NZ: New Zealand Council for Educational Research.

Mapping Parents' Movements and Interaction: Reconceptualizing Parent Support

Judith Duncan, Sarah Te One, and Maureen Thomas

INTRODUCTION

Early Childhood Education and Care (ECEC) centers are often considered solely as child spaces, child places, and child-focused environments. As discussed in chapter 1, we argue that ECEC services are uniquely positioned to provide quality ECEC and to support parents, *whānau* (extended family), and families. Internationally, ECEC services have been trialing innovative and inclusive programs that position the child and their families and *whānau* as important partners in supporting the learning and growth of children and the resilience of the family and *whānau* (Dalli, 1997; Hayden, 2002; Hayden & Macdonald, 2000; Munford, Sanders, Maden, & Maden, 2007; Shulruf, 2005; Whalley, 1999, 2006). These models and initiatives have included parents and family members as integral to the ECEC setting, and the benefits of such initiatives are beginning to be recognized by governments, as well as by communities themselves (see also chapters 4, 5, 6, and chapter 11 in this volume for further discussions of these themes).

This chapter emerges out of a *New Zealand Teaching and Learning Research Initiative*– funded project,[1] examining how adult participation in an early childhood education context can support positive child-learning outcomes and general community wellness. The research is a two-year project involving five centers (four ECEC centers in New Zealand, and a parenting resource center attached to the education complex) begun in 2010. The research team is made up of two academic researchers (Duncan and Te One) and all of the teaching, management and support staff at the five centers. Our research question for the project is:

> How does active adult participation in early childhood education enhance positive outcomes for children and their *whānau?*

Over the two years of the project we have been using a mosaic of research methods (Clark, 2010) to capture the perspectives of staff, parents, and children, and to record and document reconceptualized pedagogical practices that include active adult participation. While many early childhood centers promote parent-partnerships or working with parents, we propose a substantial rethinking of the discursive positions offered to both teachers and parents by these traditional ways of viewing adults within early childhood education. Working with the *Central Baptist Kindergarten* (CBK), where parent support has been their focus for some time, has enabled us to test a range of approaches to parent support, parent involvement, and adult participation that we propose can turn the *extraordinary* into the *everyday practices* of early childhood education in every setting.

Background

The four ECEC centers in this project have had a background of explicitly working with families, *whānau,* and community within and alongside their ECEC services for many years. Over 2006–2009, the ECEC centers in Whanganui, known as the CBK, received funding from the *New Zealand Ministry of Education/Ministry of Social Development's Centre-Based Parent Support and Development (PSD) Pilot Project (2006–2009)*[2] to support the work of their parent resource center. This center, known as *303* (after the street address), is where social support provision was established for both center families and *whānau,* and other families and *whānau* from the wider Whanganui community.

The CBK ECEC centers are known locally and nationally in Aotearoa New Zealand for having a focus on supporting parents, for example: creating a welcoming and trusting environment for parents at the kindergartens; employment of staff empathic to parents' needs; the provision of parent groups, playgroups, and parenting classes; holding parent events/conferences; visiting parents at homes, and providing meals when there was a need (e.g., a new baby). The addition of the parenting support center was an extension to this existing work with families, *whānau*, and community. Significantly, a key difference between *303* (the parenting support center) and other parenting provisions in Whanganui has been the nature of the *wrap-around support,* which included both the ECEC component and the ability of the team to respond to a wide range of issues or concerns; for example, health, violence, budgeting, nutrition, parenting, and so on. The CBK has entwined a range of other professionals and programs, around *303* and the ECEC centers, to ensure this broad base, wrap-around approach to parenting in the preschool years. These programs include: *Home Intervention for Parents of Preschool Youngsters* (HIPPY),[3] *Strategies with Kids/Information for Parents* (SKIP),[4] and *Supporting Parents alongside Children's Education* (SPACE)[5] to support parents with preschoolers within the home and community environments. These programs operate out of the CBK buildings, and the staff interact regularly between the programs and ECEC centers. Increasingly, parents from the ECEC centers are gaining employment as HIPPY coordinators, and teaching staff are sharing the facilitation of SPACE sessions, which increases the strength of, and links between, the ECEC centers with parents, *whānau,* and the wider community.

An equally important aspect of the wider parent support provided by CBK is the location of the centers and programs—right behind the main street of the town, and built alongside the Whanganui Central Baptist Church. The church buildings provide another avenue for parents to meet others (regular coffee mornings) and for the staff working in any of the ECEC services or programs to hold gatherings, private meetings, or groups. The physical location of the church alongside the CBK enables ongoing links to wider community and resources. In addition to the church's physical availability, its social services are characterized by openness to the community (not just its own congregation), which provides very real support for CBK and the parenting work, they engage with.

Figure 2.1 demonstrates the model and activities developed within CBK and its connections with both early childhood education and the wider well-being of *whānau* and the community. It is on this model that this research project took its activities and frame of reference.

This integrated or *wrap-around* model, implemented by CBK, as an effective model of parent support, is supported by other research

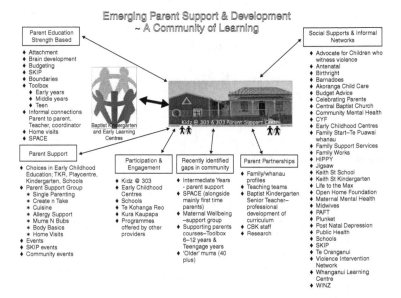

Figure 2.1 CBK model of supporting *whānau* in the Whanganui community

and reviews of such services. In their review of Canadian parenting programs, Corter and Arimura (2006) concluded:

> The dazzling variety of family support programs may support better parenting and better outcomes for children but the evidence is mixed and most popular approaches remain unevaluated. An important conclusion from the literature to date is that different approaches are required for different groups and different contexts. Integrated service approaches have the advantage of offering parents more choice. One size does not fit all. (p. 1)

RESEARCH APPROACH

Building on the ECEC centers' approaches to supporting and working with family and *whānau*, our research project was designed to investigate how encouraging adult participation makes a difference not only to family life, but to children's learning outcomes and the functioning of the wider community around the services.

Research examining early childhood education in Aotearoa New Zealand has demonstrated a gap in provisions in regard to parent participation and partnership and has called for more *action* and more *investigation*. Mitchell and Cubey (2003), in a review of professional development for enhancing children's learning in ECEC, concluded that a key to enhanced learning was the inclusion of children's families and *whānau*. They argued for strong links between ECE (Early Childhood Education) teachers and centers with families and *whānau* because this

- makes a key contribution to children's learning and wellbeing (p. vii);
- challenges teachers'/educators' beliefs and assumptions and acknowledges the knowledge and skills of families and children (p. vii);
- assists in creating coherence and continuity in children's lives (p. x);
- changes parents' perceptions of their roles with their children, and creates greater understanding of their children's interests and experiences (p. x);
- supports an approach to education where teachers, children and their *whānau* co-construct learning together (p. 8);
- provides opportunities of home and early childhood settings to reinforce one another (p. 79). (Mitchell & Cubey, 2003)

A study by a combined research team from Massey University and the Children's Issues Centre (2005) examining "the effect of adult playcentre participation on the creation of social capital in communities" found that parents identified increased confidence in their parenting, personal confidence, sense of involvement and belonging in the community, and in later employment opportunities (Powell, Cullen, Adams, Duncan, & Marshall, 2006, p. 1). This sense of belonging and the important role that ECEC plays in this for families and *whānau* was also reported in studies by Duncan, Smith and Bowden (2006) investigating early childhood centers' impact on family resilience, in studies by Duncan, Dalli et al. (2006) investigating under-three-year-olds' experiences of kindergarten, and in Duncan's (2009) report of parents' current experiences of kindergarten services (see chapter 5 of this volume). This role that ECEC plays in terms of support and education programs is also becoming more generally understood. In their research, Podmore et al. (2008) found that first-time mothers who participated in a playcentre parenting programme (SPACE) overcame the feelings of isolation that can often overwhelm first-timers (see chapter 8 of this volume). The researchers' findings "concluded that good parenting skills were beneficial in the long term" (Podmore et al., 2008, p. 4). Together, these Aotearoa New

Zealand studies argue that ECEC services can and do make a significant difference in families' lives, particularly when adults are actively involving themselves in this aspect of their young children's lives.

International research continues to demonstrate that ECEC plays a significant role in families' lives and that now is the right time to begin to address how and why ECEC can play a more explicit role in families' lives and in developing resilient and democratic communities.

While earlier research has set a foundation for inquiry, our research at the Whanganui CBK has set out to investigate and gather evidence on what difference active adult participation makes not only to children's learning but also for the benefit of the community. We have developed a range of methods and analyses with this challenge clearly in the focus of our investigations.

MAPPING MOVEMENTS AND INTERACTIONS

The spatial layout of buildings and urban places exerts a powerful influence on human behavior. The way that places connect is directly related to the way that people move, interact and transact. (http://www.spacesyntax.com/)

The method and tools discussed in this chapter were developed as one of the mosaic approaches (Clark, 2010) that we have used across the project. We began the research by focusing on relationship building between teachers and parents, teachers and teachers, and parents and parents. To be able to record, in some systematic way, the current effectiveness of the interactions in the centers between adults, we decided to record parent movements and interactions in the four ECEC centers and the parent support center. The intention was to be able to identify the amount of teacher-parent interaction and parent-to-parent interaction, plus the overall involvement by parents in the centers (how long did they stay? Who did they interact with? Did all parents know at least one other parent?). To this end we developed a tool, adapted from the method of *Spaghetti Mapping*[6] (Jacka & Keller, 2009), to help assess and monitor whether the interactions provided evidence for the development of relationships and networks that we know from research and experience *do* make a difference for families and *whānau* (Citizens Preschool and Nursery Centre of Innovation, 2008; Duncan, Bowden, et al., 2006; Duncan, Dalli et al., 2006; Podmore et al., 2008).

We began by thinking about what we knew about the daily interaction patterns between teachers and parents, and parents and parents. While anecdotally teachers were confident about the amount of interaction that occurred in the centers, together as a team (university researchers, teachers, and management) we decided to record these interactions, looking carefully at both the *quantity* of interactions (who with, and for long) and the *quality* of interactions (simple greetings, business of the center, or discussions based more on personal relationship).

To develop appropriate tools we moved outside of the traditional early childhood literature. We found interesting theoretical ideas around adult interactions within architecture and business theories (Hillier, 1996; Sailer & Penn, 2007) rather than within the expected ECEC literature. We found that the bulk of writing about environments in ECEC have primarily focused on the child-centered nature of environments and on how to support learning and development for children, and rarely discuss adults in the environment. Apart from the layout of environments and resources to maximize involvement or interactions with children or to minimize health and safety issues (storage facilities that do not involve back strain, for example), adults are seldom mentioned in ECEC texts and guides. Designing or structuring environments to include parents was noticeably absent in the education literature. One major exception to this is the work by Alison Clark and her colleagues using methods to gather children's understanding and use of space, which has extended into practitioner and parents' perspectives of design and space in early childhood centers for children (Clark, 2010).

A lack of consideration of the *adult in a space* has been commented on within research in other disciplines also. Several researchers have argued how space can be a "forgotten dimension" (Fischer, cited in Sailer & Penn, 2007). Using a theory called *space syntax*, researchers have shown how the way in which the parts (including the building) are put together plays a crucial role in the patterns of human movement and individual experience (Hillier, 1996; Sailer & Penn, 2007).

Peters (1993) argues that space can be the most effective tool in bringing about social change and enhancing learning (cited in Sailer & Penn, 2007, p. 2). Sailer and Penn (2007, p. 1) argue that "the relevance of space 'as a vector of social interactions'" is underacknowledged and that the spaces that people occupy and use have a significant influence on their social interactions.

Therefore, architectural theories provided us, as researchers, with a *window* of thinking that expanded our gaze from just recording interactions between parents and teachers to including a *mapping* of the interactions—space, place, and time, as well as who was talking to whom, and about what.

To begin, we concentrated on the physical layout of spaces and the uses that were made of them: that is, how *space* and *place* afforded or inhibited social interactions between adults. We then attempted to identify patterns of interactions within each of these spaces or places. This necessitated the use of a well-known observation method (event recordings) and the development of a new tool (mapping movements):

1. *Event recordings*: Using the usual method of counting interactions, at set intervals, we recorded numbers of interactions, who talked to whom and, where possible, about what. The teachers in the centers supported these event recordings with after-the-fact diary records of their interaction with parents, which enabled us to link the event recordings with the teachers' own records of the interactions.

2. *Mapping movements*: The mapping movements tool, which was new to us, was piloted first in one center, fine-tuned, and then carried out across all five centers (the four ECEC centers and *303*). They consisted of recording the parents' and teachers' movements and interaction points on the center room plans.[7]

How Our Mapping Tool Worked

It is this tool, our maps, that forms the rest of this chapter. We have found it to be not only an extremely useful tool for data collection, but also one that has prompted significant discussions, useful for teacher self-review of many different aspects of pedagogy and environment. Discussions with teachers outside of our research context have reinforced our belief that this tool has the potential to enable teachers to map a variety of aspects of their pedagogy in a reflexive and proactive way (Duncan, Te One, Eaton, & Dewe, 2011; Te One & Duncan, 2011).

We began by gathering floor maps of each center, including the outdoor environment (where possible). These maps were generally used for evacuation plans, so they were readily available. We enlarged them onto A3 sheets of paper: one version had clearly signaled markings and/or photos of the layout of the space—where the equipment, tables, and resources were positioned—and the second version was for the mapping exercise (see figure 2.2).

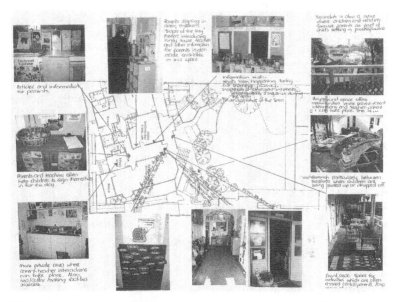

Figure 2.2 Positioning resources and equipment on the map at *Center One*

In this map the key locations were identified, and this enabled us to reflect on what the arrangement of furniture *afforded* for interactions; for example, the position of a couch may or may not encourage mothers to stay to breastfeed or parents to linger to share children's portfolios, and so on. The possibilities for adults to interact with other adults appeared to be directly related to particular areas of the center where tasks were required of the adult on arrival or departure; for example, signing in the child's attendance on a roll sheet, or hanging up the child's bag. Having a visual image of these was helpful in the analysis of the maps.

At two or three key times through the day an observer (a teacher from the center) would track the movements and interactions of the parents in each space. Research undertaken by Duncan, Bowden et al. (2006) had highlighted that there are key times that parents were more likely to be available to interact with teachers and each other in ECEC centers—for example, at drop-off and pick-up times from the centers—and this seemed to fit with the cycles of the four ECEC centers as well. The parent center (*303*) had different critical times for its context and so it followed a slightly different mapping schedule but used the tool in the same way.

Each mapping episode began by tracking each parent as they entered the center, then, using a variety of marks (e.g. ∗ or x). The mark would be entered to indicate when the parent stopped for an interaction with another parent or teacher. The tracking followed the parents' movements until they left. The colors of the mapping changed with different time periods over any one mapping exercise so that a sense of time and interactions could be seen at a glance on the maps. In this way we had very colorful maps for each 45–60 minute period of the day, with the colors changing every 10–15 minutes (see figures 2.3, 2.4, and 2.5). At the same time as the mapping exercise was taking place, one member of the research team would be observing the adult interactions, and the teachers involved in such interactions would record these in a journal later in the day. Generating multiple sources ensured robust and trustworthy data.

This map is of the start of the day—the *drop-off* time at the ECEC centers. In this map the cluster of parents around the doorway tracks the movement from hanging the child's bag in the hallway, entering the center, placing the child's lunch-box in the named shelf, and signing in on the daily roll. These three activities are all around the entranceway, which enables a parent to undertake the required tasks and then exit the center, which the majority of the parents did on this particular morning. The few parents that moved across to the other side of the room and exited the doorways on the opposite side of the center were entering the playground. This exit also contained access

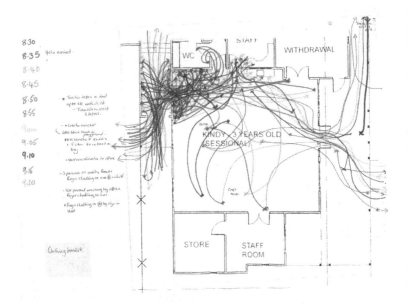

Figure 2.3   Mapping at the beginning of the day

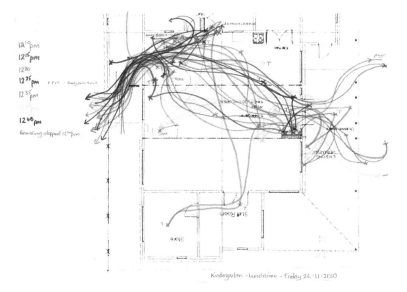

Figure 2.4 Mapping in the middle of the day at "change-over time" for several of the children (leaving and joining the group).

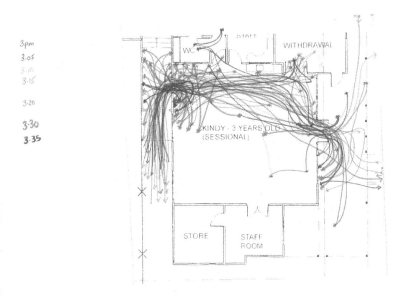

Figure 2.5 Mapping at the end of the day

to another center and an exit gate to the street (hence the different directions of the arrows on exit). As indicated (by the *, or x), the only parents who had interactions with other adults (teacher or another parent) were those that crossed the center, rather than those who only moved inside the door, to complete the beginning-of-the-day tasks, and left again.

A different pattern can be seen in the middle of the day. At this time of day, a smaller number of parents come and go from the center. These parents are either collecting a child, or are arriving with a child for the afternoon program. As tracked on this map, the movement around the center is wider, with parents seeking out their children to collect them, or finding the child's friend prior to the parent leaving. Both the wider sweep of the center and the fewer children arriving and leaving increased the number of adult-to-adult interactions, as demonstrated by the increased asterisks/crosses on the map in comparison to the morning arrival times.

The end-of-day pattern is similar to that of the morning. The parents collect the lunchboxes and bags and sign the child out around the doorway. The main difference is that more of the parents move around the center collecting the children from the playground or from different areas of the center, and so the number of potential and real interactions increased—there were more opportunities for parents to talk with other parents, and for teachers to engage with parents. However, the map also captures that there is still a significant number of parents who manage to remain near the doorway, and therefore are not as likely to engage with another adult.

WHAT DID THESE MAPS TELL US?

Overall, the mapping presented the research team with a graphic representation of the way in which parents and other adults were interacting with the people, places, and things in the center environment. Looking at the above examples it became clear where the parents entered, lingered, and left the center. There were natural gathering places; for example, places for putting the child's bag and lunch box away, for signing in the register for the time that the child arrived and left, and then for settling children and/or talking with staff, or other parents. The accompanying notes from the researcher (taken at the time of mapping) gave further insight into the occurrences that significantly affected the patterns of flow during that sample time (e.g., the arrival of a family bringing their pet lamb into the playground; a family arriving with their newborn baby). These were important to note as they indicated that the mapping flow may differ from an *ordinary* day—if there can ever be such a thing in an ECEC center where the *extra-ordinary* is often the business of many days. Discussions with the teaching teams in each center also fleshed out these observations and added to the data's influence within pedagogical reflection.

What Did We Learn from This Data?

We re-presented each map, to the individual teaching teams, for their reflection and discussion, using reflective questions to engage their thinking, such as:

1. How does the center layout support and encourage (or inhibit) adult involvement with children, with teachers, with other adults?
2. Is the center *family-friendly*? (i.e. easy to use? ...or not?)
3. How welcoming is the center?
4. Are there spaces for discussion? Spaces for privacy?
5. What (in the center environment) affects the flow patterns?
6. Do we (as teachers) greet/ acknowledge/ interact with every adult who enters the center? If not, why not?

Not only was this data-gathering method useful for providing rich insights into the research, the data formed a useful tool for self-review: reflection, discussion, and critique about parent participation and parent involvement through mapping both *how* the adults used the *spaces* in the *places* and the *quantity* and *quality* of interactions that occurred each day between parents and teachers, then parents and parents.

This discussion between teaching colleagues, centered on the mapping evidence, served to highlight for teachers what is important for center philosophy and culture. If the aim is to support and facilitate active parent participation within the center community, then looking closely at how the environment is set up and the effect which this has on the observed flow patterns of adults using the center space is a powerful tool. Considering what helps (affords) and what hinders (constrains) interactions and adult participation can begin to reshape pedagogical and professional practices. What became clear to us, as researchers and teachers, was that the need to be seen within an environment was a pivotal affordance for interactions. If a teacher could physically *see* the parent in the environment, and vice versa, then an interaction was more likely to occur. Similarly, if parents could *see* each other, either in passing, or more generally in the center environment, then they were more likely to engage in an interaction together. As Sailer and Penn (2007, p. 10) argue:

> Interaction patterns depend very much **on seeing and being seen.** Often the need and motivation for informal and unplanned encounter arises only in the very moment of seeing someone. The more some-one sees—and is seen—the larger are the possibilities for interaction. [Emphasis added]

WHAT CHANGES HAVE RESULTED FROM OUR REVIEW OF THE DATA? ONE CENTER'S EXPERIENCE

First and foremost, the teaching team's sharing of the data and the resultant discussion, reflection, and self-review led to a reexamination of the dynamic between the physical layout of the center and center systems and procedures around arrivals and departures. As the lead ECEC teacher described:

> Our awareness was raised of the adult movements across the centre lay-out and this led to further reflection and discussion about the way in which we had set up our center environment. The mapping data (and also the reported observations of the researcher who was recording the mapping data) raised our awareness of what was happening at that time with teacher positioning in the environment.

The maps, in the particular center included in this chapter, demonstrated that the teachers were positioned (while engaged in working with the children) with their backs toward the main entrance door. This was an unintended consequence of the layout of the center, where the position of the tables enabled teachers to scan the room for children, but placed them with their backs to the door. This highlighted several issues for the teachers regarding the ease with which teachers could effectively scan the center area, supervision of the other children in the room, ability to notice other adults entering the space and to make a connection with them, and availability for interactions with adults.

After the discussion with the teaching team, using the mapping data as the reflective tool, changes were made to the center environment. The teachers changed their position within the room at the key times, moved the *sign-in* sheet to the other side of the room from the main entrance door (to draw parents into the center, rather than by the entrance door), and a more-welcoming area was created by the main entry door. In addition, the sofa was moved and turned to face the parents as they entered the center, a carpet mat was placed in front of the sofa, and the children's Profile Books (assessment folders for the children and parents) rack was repositioned alongside the sofa. As the lead teacher reflected on these changes:

> We recognised that our ability and our opportunities to connect are limited if parents and other adults are not drawn further in...and can see a comfortable place to linger.

Re-review after the Changes

Following these physical environmental changes, further data were collected at a later date (using the same mapping method of data collecting) as a comparison. The team noticed less *peak-time* congestion around the main entry door. Conversations and interactions appeared to be more spread out across other parts of the center area. Interactions were still largely focused around where teachers were, and so the positioning of teachers within the environment was recognized as continuing to be hugely important for parents as well as the children. The immediacy of the change in patterns and interactions from the slight movement of the furniture and the increased understanding of the role of *place* and *space* by the teachers together afforded this new level and style of parent participation and interactions.

Conclusion

Parent interaction with other adults in the environment is a powerful *affordance* for parent participation in ECEC and in their children's learning. International and national research has demonstrated that parent interaction and participation increases the learning outcomes of children and increases skills of parents (Gray, 2001; Mitchell & Cubey, 2003; Powell et al., 2006; Wylie, 1998, 2001; Wylie & Thompson, 2003; Wylie, Thompson, & Kerslake Hendricks, 1996; Wylie, Thompson, & Lythe, 2001), as well as contributing to family resilience (Duncan, Bowden et al., 2006).

This chapter describes one research tool for assessing and evaluating parent interactions in an ECEC setting. The tool enabled us to gather information about the regular movements of parents in the centers, and also provided us with a reflective tool to engage in pedagogical discussions around parent participation in children's learning and the teachers' roles in supporting community wellness.

This mapping exercise highlighted the importance of teacher positioning within the environment. Where the teacher was placed in an ECEC center environment was an affordance or a constraint to *seeing and being seen*—important precursors to parental interactions and involvement with others. While reflective practice in pedagogical discussions usually centers on teaching and learning for children, the discussions held by the teaching teams in the CBK around adult interactions, as a result of the mapping movements data, demonstrated the effectiveness of increasing this focus as an important aspect of teaching and learning in ECEC services.

Notes

1. The *Teaching and Learning Research Initiative* is managed by the New Zealand Council for Educational Research and is funded by the Ministry of Education to support partnership projects and new knowledge around teaching and learning.

2. New Zealand Ministry of Education/Ministry of Social Development's *Centre-Based Parent Support and Development* (PSD) Pilot Project (2006–2009): "The Early Childhood Education (ECE) centre-based Parent Support and Development (PSD) programme trialled by the Ministry of Education was intended to provide early interventions that targeted vulnerable parents through a universal service. A total of 18 pilot ECE sites were selected and funded to provide PSD for a three-year period starting from 2006. Pilot sites were selected, in part, on the basis of the high concentration of vulnerable families living in the surrounding area. The sites offered a wide range of activities including educational, social support and outreach activities" (quoted from http://www.educationcounts .govt.nz/publications/ece/74648).

3. HIPPY (Home Intervention for Parents of Preschool Youngsters) is a home-based program that supports parents in becoming actively involved in their four- and five-year-old children's learning. Parents and children work together for 15 minutes a day with storybooks, puzzles, and learning games that help children become successful learners at school. The HIPPY program builds on the bond between parents and children. HIPPY believes parents play a critical role in their children's education. HIPPY offers support that builds upon parental strengths so that parents can provide their children with necessary skills and confidence to begin school with a positive attitude toward learning. The work children and parents do together in their own home with the HIPPY materials is

complemented by what they can gain from attending their local early childhood education. For further information see http://www .familyservices.govt.nz/working-with-us/programmes-services /early-intervention/home-interaction-programme-for-parents -and-youngsters.html.

4. Strategies with Kids/Information for Parents (SKIP) provides support, information, and parenting strategies for parents and caregivers of 0–5-year-olds. SKIP's vision is for all children in New Zealand to be raised in a positive way by parents and caregivers who feel confident about managing children's behavior as part of a loving, nurturing relationship. SKIP works with national and local organizations to support all New Zealand parents. For more information see http://www.skip.org.nz.

5. The SPACE program is mainly for first-time parents with newborn babies. Sessions run weekly at a playcenter or suitable community venue for three to four terms, extending through the first year of the child's life. SPACE provides a quality curriculum in order that the parent may maximize on this valuable time with their child. For more information see http://www.space.org.nz.

6. Spaghetti mapping is known in the business and health sectors for streamlining work-flow. See: http://www.ehow.com/how_4803373 _spaghetti-diagram-lean-process.html.

7. We fondly called our maps "spaghetti junctions" (after the look of the final product). This name led us to the field of the Spaghetti Diagram or Standard Work Chart, which are used in streamlining work-place environments (see http://www.systems2win.com/solutions /layout.htm or http://www.ehow.com/how_4803373_spaghetti -diagram-lean-process.html). We have used a similar technique, but for very different purposes and outcomes from the ones suggested.

References

Citizens Preschool and Nursery Centre of Innovation. (2008). *Collaborations: Teachers and a Family Whānau Support Worker in an early childhood setting*. Final report for Centre of Innovation Research (2005–2007). Retrieved from http://www.educate.ece.govt.nz/Programmes/Centres OfInnovation.aspx

Clark, A. (2010). *Transforming children's spaces: Children's and adults' participation in designing learning environments*. Milton Park, Oxon: Routledge.

Corter, C., & Arimura, T. (2006). *Community vitality: Literature review on parent support*. Report prepared for Invest in Kids, Toronto, Canada.

Dalli, C. (1997). Early childhood centres as parent support: A personal perspective. *Childrenz Issues, 1*(2), 21–24.

Duncan, J. (2009). Aotearoa New Zealand kindergarten parents reflecting on kindergarten: 2006–2007. *The Open Education Journal, 2,* 1–10.

Duncan, J., Bowden, C., & Smith, A. B. (2006). *Early childhood centres and family resilience*: Ministry of Social Development. Retrieved from http://www.msd.govt.nz/about-msd-and-our-work/publications-resources/evaluation/early-childhood-centres-and-family-resilience/index.html

Duncan, J., Dalli, C., Becker, R., Butcher, M., Foster, K., Hayes, K., & Walker, W. (2006). *Under three-year-olds in kindergartens: Children's experiences and teachers' practices*. Wellington, NZ: Teaching and Learning Research Initiative.

Duncan, J., Te One, S., Eaton, S., & Dewe, R. (2011, July). Who are the teachers? Who are the learners? Challenging the spaces in-between. Workshop presentation at the annual conference of *Te Tari Puna Ora o Aotearoa*, Rotoura, NZ.

Gray, A. (2001). *Family support programmes: A literature review*. (Prepared for the Ministry of Education). Wellington, NZ: Ministry of Education.

Hayden, J. (2002). Revisiting the early childhood-health dyad: Implicatons for policy and practice of health promotion in early childhood settings. *Delta, 54*(1&2), 57–70.

Hayden, J., & Macdonald, J. J. (2000). Health promotion: A new leadership role for early childhood professionals. *Australian Journal of Early Childhood, 25*(1), 32–39.

Hillier, B. (1996). *Space is the machine: A configurational theory of architecture*. Cambridge, UK: Cambridge University Press.

Jacka, J. M., & Keller, P. J. (2009). *Business process mapping: Improving customer satisfaction* (2nd ed.). New Jersey: John Wiley and Sons.

Mitchell, L., & Cubey, P. (2003). *Characteristics of professional development linked to enhanced pedagogy and children's learning in early childhood settings*. Wellington: Ministry of Education.

Munford, R., Sanders, J., Maden, B., & Maden, E. (2007). Blending whānau/family development, parent support and early childhood education programmes. *Social Policy Journal of New Zealand, 32*(November), 72–87.

Podmore, V. N., Te One, S., with Dawson, L., Dingemanse, T., Higham, J., Jones, J., Matthews, K., & Pattinson, S. (2008). *Nurturing a culture of care for infants and first-time parents: The SPACE programme (Supporting Parents alongside Children's Education) at Te Marua/Mangaroa Playcentre as an early childhood Centre of Innovation (COI)*. Retrieved from http://www.educationcounts.govt.nz/publications/ece/22551/22579

Powell, K., Cullen, J., Adams, P., Duncan, J., & Marshall, K. (2006). *The effect of adult playcentre participation on the creation of social capital in local communities*. Report prepared for the New Zealand Playcentre Federation, Wellington, New Zealand.

Te One, S., & Duncan, J. (2011, September). *Getting to know each other: Adults in early education services*. Presentation at the University of Victoria Spring Early Childhood Research Seminar. Wellington, New Zealand.

Sailer, K., & Penn, A. (2007, May). The performance of space—Exploring social and spatial phenomena of interaction patterns in an organisation.

Paper presented at the *Architecture and Phenomenology Conference*, Haifa.

Shulruf, B. (2005). Parent support and education programme: A systematic review. *New Zealand Research in Early Childhood Education, 8*, 81–102.

Whalley, M. (1999, August). Parents' involvement in their children's learning. Keynote address at the *Seventh Early Childhood Convention*, Nelson, NZ.

Whalley, M. (2006). Leadership in integrated centres and services for children and families—A community development approach. *Childrenz Issues, 10*(2), 8–13.

Wylie, C. (1998, December). *The Competent children project—The contribution of early childhood education, school, and home to children's progress between 5 and 8.* Paper presented at the Annual Conference of New Zealand Association for Research in Education, Dunedin, NZ.

Wylie, C. (2001, October). *Why quality matters in early childhood education: The research evidence.* Paper presented at the Early Childhood Education for a Democratic Society, Wellington, NZ.

Wylie, C., & Thompson, J. (2003). The long-term contribution of early childhood education to children's performance—Evidence from New Zealand. *International Journal of Early Years Education, 11*(1), 69–78.

Wylie, C., Thompson, J., & Kerslake Hendricks, A. (1996). *Competent children at 5. Families and early education.* Wellington, NZ: New Zealand Council for Educational Research.

Wylie, C., Thompson, J., & Lythe, C. (2001). *Competent children at 10: Families, early education and schools.* Wellington, NZ: New Zealand Council for Educational Research.

CHAPTER 3

Theorizing Integrated Service Provision in Australia: Policies, Philosophies, Practices

Jennifer Sumsion, Frances Press, and Sandie M. Wong

INTRODUCTION

In Australia, as in many other countries, there is strong government interest in the potential of integrated services, in which professionals from a range of disciplines—including Early Childhood Education and Care (ECEC)—work together to enable families, especially those dealing with multiple challenges, to have seamless access to a variety of services. This interest reflects a growing recognition of the interrelatedness of complex social and health problems experienced by many families and has been widely welcomed in Australia, not only for its potential to provide more effective support for families, but also for opening up new possibilities for partnerships between government, families, services, and practitioners (Nichols & Jurvansuu, 2008; Press, Sumsion, & Wong, 2010). This chapter builds on our interest in exploring the nature and scope of those possibilities.

Like Nichols and Jurvansuu (2008, p. 119), we have an ongoing research interest in the multiple policy framings of integrated services and "the complex interactions between policy, services, practitioners and families" and indeed, the wider community. We are especially interested in integrated services as sites of intersection of multiple discourses about early childhood education. Particularly salient are two broad categories of discourses and policy framings: those that frame society primarily in economic terms as comprising interconnected acts of investment, production, exchange, and consumption (Taylor, 1997), including investment in and the production of human capital; and those that emphasize dialogue, relationships, and trust in working toward the common good. Rather than positioning these discourses as binary oppositions, however, we concur with Moss (2009) that it is more productive to consider the conditions under which services might flourish within and across these respective discourses. We consider it important to develop insights into the tensions that can arise from these discourses, the ways in which services negotiate these tensions, and implications for how children, families, and practitioners experience integrated services.

In this chapter, we explore these ideas further with reference to a commissioned study we undertook of Australian integrated services that investigated elements perceived to contribute to successful integration (Press et al., 2010). It involved, among other components, case studies of ten services across several Australian states and the development of a definition of integration commensurate with Australian government policy. Following considerable consultation, the definition arrived at was that, in Australia,

> integrated services provide access to multiple services to children and families in a cohesive and holistic way. They recognise the impact of family and community contexts on children's development and learning and focus on improving outcomes for children, families and communities. Through respectful, collaborative relationships, they actively seek to maximize the impact of different disciplinary expertise in a shared intent to respond to family and community contexts. (Press et al., 2010, p. 53)

This definition encompassed human investment discourses (development, outcomes) seemingly prioritized by government and dialogic, participatory democratic possibilities of integrated services.

The parameters of the commissioned study, along with funding and time constraints, precluded opportunities to explore extensively and explicitly with participants whether, and how, they worked within and across these discourses. Nevertheless, data gathered through interviews, focus groups, and observations illustrated the capacity of organizations to steer their way through various policy contexts while maintaining internal philosophical fidelity. To highlight this capacity, in this chapter we present profiles of two of the case-study services: Ngala and Gowrie South Australia (SA). Drawing on a variety of theoretical tools, we then critically reflect on the work of these services and identify issues that we believe warrant further investigation.

ORGANIZATIONAL PROFILES

We focus on Ngala and Gowrie SA because their case studies were particularly rich. Their long-standing commitment to integration pre-dates current policy interest in integrated provision and their journeys toward integration have been characterized by in-depth thinking and a preparedness to introduce new structures that support integration at all levels within their organizations. Ngala's profile foregrounds community, while Gowrie's profile describes in some detail a pivotal early-intervention parenting program.

NGALA

Established in 1890 in Perth, Western Australia (WA), Ngala is a not-for-profit organization providing integrated services for families and children. Ngala takes its name from an Aboriginal word from the *Bibbulmun* dialect meaning *we two*, mother and child. Originally known as the House of Mercy and later as a *mothercraft home*, for many years Ngala provided short-term care for children from birth to three years, as well as an adoption service and a center for training mother-craft and child health nurses. The organization has continued to evolve in response to social, cultural, and economic changes, expectations, and priorities. On its website, for example, it commends the Western Australian government's apology to mothers whose babies were adopted, a widespread practice in Australia from the 1940s to 1980s, and expresses regret for the trauma caused to the mothers and their children.

The organization now provides three types of services:

- universal services open to all families (e.g., telephone helpline, website resources, long day-care centers offering full-day education and care for children aged from birth to five years);
- targeted services for particular cultural, geographically based, or other specific groups (e.g., indigenous parent groups; playgroups in remote regions; programs to support children following family separation); and
- intensive services offering specialized, interdisciplinary support for individual families (e.g., a prison parenting program; an *overnight stay* program for families with young children that provides 24-hour support). (Ngala, 2007–2008)

Underpinning and unifying all its services are strong philosophical commitments to children's rights and interests; to ecological perspectives (following Bronfenbrenner, 1979) that view children and families within the context of their communities; and to fostering inclusivity, collaboration, and community building.

Each year, Ngala assists more than 25,000 families across the geographically vast and sparsely populated state of WA. In any one year, it has direct contact with more than half of the families in the state with newborn babies (Ngala, 2007–2008). Ngala's leaders note with quiet pride that most families that approach the organization do so through word-of-mouth recommendations or the widely advertised Ngala Helpline, and attribute the high level of self- referral by families to the high community regard in which the organization is held (Ngala, 2008).

Ngala's focus on community has multiple strands. It continually seeks to strengthen its relationships with local communities, for example, by offering "assistance, support, and ideas" (Ngala, 2008, p. 38). It also strives to foster partnerships within communities, on the premise that communities are strengthened when people in the community work together to develop locally relevant strategies to achieve locally identified common goals and address locally identified problems. Where feasible, it endeavors to include families and children in aspects of organizational decision-making processes as a way of encouraging them to feel part of the Ngala community.

Fostering a sense of community among Ngala staff, with their diverse disciplinary backgrounds and professional expertise (e.g., early childhood education, health, counseling), is another key strand of Ngala's community building. Transparency and open communication are considered essential. For example, from an internal website, all staff can access minutes from meetings of various groups within the organization, including executive decision-making meetings. Reflecting Ngala's commitment to interdisciplinarity, its board members, at the time of the study reported in this chapter, included a business development/property specialist, a pediatrician, an accountant, a lawyer, a marketing specialist, a clinical researcher, and an early childhood education academic. While their role accountabilities suggest a hierarchical structure, in practice organizational leaders and key staff have worked collaboratively to establish common program policies and practices that characterize the interdisciplinary *One Ngala* ethos and approach.

The notion of *One Ngala* facilitates community building within the organization as well as externally. A defining feature is the strong commitment to a *common language* and to an overarching framework to guide interdisciplinary professional practice throughout the organization, including at senior management level. The practice framework is known as the *C-Frame* because of its emphasis on the themes of *connect, collaborate,* and *change*. Grounded in relationship building and emphasizing the development of mutual trust, the framework encompasses four nonsequential and overlapping phases:

- creating collaborative relationships;
- developing a commitment to change;
- contextual analysis; and
- negotiating change and intervention.

Across all four phases, practitioners are expected to engage in sustained reflective practice or action learning and, importantly, are provided with time to do so. An organizational expectation is that professional decision making and practice will be informed by evidence, including evidence generated by reflective inquiry.

The practice framework also emphasizes respect: for all staff, for all families and children accessing Ngala services, and for communities. Valuing diversity and embracing a commitment to "learning from our experiences with each other" are seen as integral to "the Ngala way" (Ngala, 2007–2008, p. 3). In brief, the practice framework and its underpinning principles, according to service documentation,

> provides a process and tools for practitioners to connect on the one hand with families and work collaboratively with them towards positive change, and on the other hand to connect with colleagues and work collaboratively towards positive change and an increase in skills in the workplace. (Ngala, 2007–2008, p. 34)

The intent, and in many respects the effect, is a blend of clarity, consistency, and flexibility that is respectful of, and able to accommodate, difference, with expectations of a willingness to negotiate differences and a commitment to trying to arrive at some common understandings. The aim is to ensure that families and children experience Ngala as accessible, responsive, trustworthy, and *seamless* in the support it provides.

Gowrie SA

Gowrie SA is located in South Australia, and is situated in two Adelaide suburbs, Thebarton, a mixed residential/industrial area, and Underdale, a new housing estate adjacent to a higher education precinct. Originally known as the Lady Gowrie Child Centre, the service was first funded in 1940 by the Australian government as a demonstration preschool. It is one of six Lady Gowrie Child Centres, one in the capital city of each state, all established in the 1940s with the objective of testing and demonstrating "methods for care and instruction of the young child" and to study problems associated with "physical growth, nutrition and development" (Gowrie SA, n.d., n.p.). It is a nonprofit organization managed by a board with a mix of academic, parent, and community representation.

The Lady Gowrie Child Centres have, throughout their history, provided care and education services to children and families as well as resources for the early childhood field. Over time, Gowrie SA has evolved into an integrated, multidisciplinary service offering a range of universal and targeted programs for children and families, as well as advice, training, and support to the early childhood sector. It provides

- early childhood education and care (sessional and full-day programs);
- early intervention and parenting support programs; and
- professional development, support, and resources to the South Australian early childhood field through the Gowrie Training Centre and a specialist Resource Centre.

Included in its suite of services are playgroups; a multisite early intervention parenting program—*Through the Looking Glass (TtLG)*—which has components of an intensive mothers' group and sessions for fathers; and a children's mental health initiative (Kidsmatter Early Childhood, n.d.). It also fosters practitioner research focusing on *leaderful* teams and improving outcomes for children.

Two developments in particular exemplify the journey and practice of integration. The first is the creation of fully integrated ECEC programs, from an initial base of separate childcare and preschool (kindergarten) services. The second development, the *TtLG* project, is a targeted intervention for families where mother-child attachment is threatened through risk factors such as anxiety, depression, and social isolation. The latter program provides intense multidisciplinary support to families across a number of early childhood sites. The integration of the preschool and childcare programs involved carefully challenging deeply entrenched community and staff perceptions and ways of working. The *TtLG* project involves health, education, and welfare in a collaborative early intervention and is available in five

ECEC sites. *TtLG* provides intensive psychosocial support, therapeutic intervention, and early childhood education for families with the aim of developing and supporting secure attachment relationships between mother and child (Aylward & O'Neil, 2009). The Gowrie SA ECEC services in Thebarton and Underdale both offer *TtLG*. The intervention involves

- the provision of up to two days ECEC per week;
- the implementation of a Primary Care Giving (PCG) model of ECEC. The PCG model provides a secure base for each child (a *special person*) and for each parent a primary contact;
- intensive individual work with a clinician (with a social work or psychology background). Family work and counseling is delivered at the ECEC center or through home visiting; and
- an 18-session weekly small-group project for two hours each week, conducted for the mothers while the child/children are in care. Each group comprises a maximum of seven mothers, the small group size contributing to a safe, secure environment for parents to share and explore their parenting experiences.

During the development stage of the project, a reference group with representation from ECEC, health, and welfare offered expert advice to inform its overall structure and direction. A staff member from the ECEC program was supported to undertake a master's degree in Infant Mental Health. She now works with staff to enhance their capacity to work with vulnerable families. The ECEC site provides a nonstigmatized site for ongoing support, and there has been a strong commitment to ensuring that parents feel welcomed into a nonjudgmental environment. The majority of *TtLG* families continue their child's enrolment after the formal intervention is complete. An evaluation of the project found that the vast majority of mothers reported a lasting positive impact from the intervention (Aylward & O'Neill, 2009). Importantly, staff engagement with the PCG model for *TtLG* has established a strong primary care–giving culture.

Although the integration of ECEC services and the *TtLG* project are distinct programs, they are also interrelated. The *TtLG* project is built on the strong foundations of the integrated ECEC programs. Staff and management across the entire service system have been engaged in strengthening interdisciplinary collaborations. Embedding profound and sustainable change in both the structure and practices of the organization has taken time, and one of the factors contributing to Gowrie's success in integration has been to tackle one issue at a time. Time has enabled staff and families to deeply engage with questions of philosophy (for instance, many months were spent examining the image of the child informing practice within the center), to learn, to try new things, and to discuss and challenge practices. The resulting cross-disciplinary approach has benefited children and families and enriched the knowledge base and work of staff.

Inspired and decisive leadership, coupled with the creation and implementation of a shared leadership model, have been important drivers of change. The implementation of a flatter leadership structure has afforded staff the opportunity to gain a broad organizational perspective and enabled emergent leaders to address challenging situations with the support of other members of staff. Such approaches have been important in nurturing *leaderful* teams.

There has been a deliberate focus on shifting disciplinary boundaries, accompanied by a preparedness to challenge deeply entrenched perspectives and practices. Professional dialogue and reflection is embedded in the organization's operations and in its philosophy, which states that Gowrie SA is "open to questioning what we do and why we do it" and that there is a shared "responsibility to keep connections alive by listening to and communicating with each other and being open to feedback" (Gowrie SA, 2008, p. 2). Staff meetings focus on professional learning arising from events at work; staff appraisals, and professional development support, personal and professional growth congruent with the organization's commitment to integration; staff placements are carefully organized to provide mentoring and the opportunity to learn from different disciplines; and professional learning encompasses training, mentoring, and theory, and supports staff in initiating and trialing new approaches to their work. For example, early childhood educators from the children's programs are placed with the training center to provide professional development to the field. In turn, one of the trainers from the training center works in a children's program one day a week. Early childhood educators are provided with nonteaching time to work with the *TtLG* clinician and health workers. Early childhood educators have been trained in, and now provide, parenting programs. Educators are also provided with opportunities to lead funded projects.

To sum up, both Ngala and Gowrie SA have spent some years working toward integration. Their service delivery has been altered considerably so that families, particularly those facing multiple challenges, are seamlessly supported. The development of strong, respectful partnerships between professionals from diverse disciplinary backgrounds and of partnerships with families has been a key achievement. These transformations have required time, commitment, and hard work.

CRITICAL REFLECTIONS

In the remainder of this chapter, we critically reflect on Ngala's and Gowrie SA's philosophies and approaches in order to deepen our understandings of possibilities for challenging, dismantling, or inadvertently reinforcing structural inequities and dominant power relations. By drawing attention to potential difficulties, dilemmas, and opportunities, we highlight the complexity and visionary possibilities of integration.

Earlier in the chapter, we contended that integrated services are sites of intersecting discourses. At this point, we return to the theme of intersections, and specifically to the generative spaces created when theories intersect. The employment of different theoretical lenses with the intent of finding points of intersection, as well as disjunctures, reflects how we try to work as members of an early childhood research community. Our research community is characterized by a commitment to valuing and *harnessing* the diversity of disciplinary backgrounds, theoretical perspectives, and methodological expertise of our team. In this way, we find that we are able to arrive at fuller and richer questions and explanations than would be possible otherwise.

In the following sections, we use an array of theoretical resources, drawing variously on conceptualizations from communitarianism (Jennifer), Habermas (Frances), and Cultural Historical Activity Theory (CHAT) (Sandie). Collectively, these resources assist in articulating some of the *macro* and *micro* levels of social realities (De Landa, 2006) that are integral to the work of organizations such as Ngala and Gowrie SA. From communitarianism, for example, we take tools for thinking about relations between the organization and communities. From Habermas, we identify the centrality of robust communicative spaces for organizational and individual transformation. From CHAT, we generate specific questions that may be helpful in guiding and grounding practitioners' reflection on practice and promoting action.

ON COMMUNITY (JENNIFER)

"Community" must surely be one of the most evocative, seductive, and pervasive terms in contemporary ECEC policy and practice

(Millei & Sumsion, 2011). Indeed, assertions that commitment to and connectedness with community is a distinguishing feature of the ECEC sector seem commonplace. Yet what is meant by community and implications of the emphasis on community rarely seem to be questioned despite *reconceptualist* challenges to many traditional views and assumptions about ECEC. The seeming disinclination to interrogate community in ECEC research, policy, and practice is doubly surprising given that it has been the focus of critical examinations in the broader sociological literature (e.g., Bauman, 2001; Delanty, 2010; Little, 2002). Using the case studies of Ngala and Gowrie SA as a provocation, I want to begin to tease out some of the complexities of community in ECEC.

Bauman (2001, p. 1) provides a useful starting point. He notes that "words have meanings: some words, however, also have a feel. The word community is one of them. It feels good: whatever the word community may mean, it is good "to have a community," "to be in a community." Yet it is precisely because this word has so many evocative and enticing connotations that critical theorists warn of "the dangers of employing naturalistic notions" of community (Hughes, 1996, p. 92).

Community and associated notions—connectedness, social and civic participation, building partnerships, having a voice—feature prominently in the Australian government's *Social Inclusion Agenda* (Australian Government, n.d.). Initially, the agenda had a strong focus on economic participation with Julia Gillard, then shadow minister for Social Inclusion and shadow minister for Employment and Industrial Relations, describing social inclusion as "in essence...investing in...[the disadvantaged] and their communities to bring them into the mainstream market economy" (Gillard, 2007, n.p.). The Social Inclusion Board, an influential advisory body established by the Rudd-Gillard government, took a far more comprehensive and values-based view. As a board member explained:

> What it means is that this is really about "us" not about some kind of imaginary "them." It's about all of us recognising that we have so much in common and that some of us, indeed many of us, some quite visible, some invisible are being left out or pushed out more to the point. It's the job and the responsibility of all of us to make sure that no one gets left out; that no one misses out on the opportunities that we understand as a nation are fundamental to what it is to be part of Australian society...[e.g.] some place you can feel safe and secure, a place you can call home, a sense of belonging, a sense of not being left

out, the opportunity to work, the opportunity to learn, the opportunity to get decent healthcare. (Falzon, 2009, n.p.)

The board was successful in moderating government views. While the "economic imperative" (Gillard, 2007, n.p.) remains clearly visible, it is now embedded in a noticeably more holistic, progressive discourse of social inclusion (Long, 2010). At the time of writing, the government's vision of a socially inclusive society

> is one in which all Australians feel valued and have the opportunity to participate fully in the life of our society. Achieving this vision means that all Australians will have the resources, opportunities and capability to learn, work, engage in the community and have a voice. (Australian Government, n.d.)

For Silver (2010, p. 208), the "distinctive refrain" in the government's social inclusion discourse of "making people 'feel valued' and respecting their dignity" has a notably communitarian flavor.

"Communitarianism," a term from social and political philosophy, generally refers to perspectives that view community as integral to individuals' sense of identity and as a "fundamental building block" of society (Little, 2002, p. 19). There are many variants of communitarian thought, and within each variant, community is conceptualized differently (Delanty, 2010; Hughes, 1996; Little, 2002). All share an emphasis, however, on an individual's responsibilities to the community rather than on individual rights and freedoms (Hughes, 1996). Traces of communitarianism are evident in Ngala's and Gowrie SA's requirement that all staff embrace a specific framework for professional practice: the *C-Frame* at Ngala, and *TtLG* at Gowrie SA. The rationale for this requirement is couched primarily in terms of strengthening community (including supporting individuals within those communities) within the organization itself, and in the communities served and fostered by the organization. To tease out some of the potential tensions and dilemmas of their strong community focus, I turn to three variants of communitarianism: moral authoritarianism, radical pluralism, and governmental communitarianism.

Moral Authoritarianism and Exclusion

Hughes (1996) suggests that moral authoritarian views of community are best summed up by the call "to restore civic virtues, for people to live up to their responsibilities and not merely focus on their entitlements, and to shore up the moral foundations of society" (Etzioni, 1995, p. ix). In Australia, moral authoritarianism can surface in response to almost any aspect of social, educational, indigenous, or immigration policy relevant to community. It is often visible, for example, in the media, in individuals' responses to media reports, in accusations aimed at government, and in government rebuttals. Moral authoritarianism can be a license for parochialism and bigotry (Little, 2002). I am interested in how organizations such as Ngala and Gowrie SA respond to such views and whether they respond differently according to who expresses them. Do they see a place for individuals, families, or groups with moralistic or authoritarian views within the Ngala/Gowrie SA community and in the communities they seek to serve and foster, or does holding such views constitute grounds for exclusion? Is moral authoritarianism more acceptable if it stems from the cultural values of an already-marginalized group that these organizations would normally place a high priority on supporting? If Ngala, Gowrie SA, or similar organizations deem exclusion necessary, how do they go about excluding without inadvertently succumbing, themselves, to moral judgementalism?

Radical Pluralism and Difference

In contrast to moral authoritarianism, radical pluralism explicitly values and seeks to accommodate difference (Little, 2002). Organizations that take a radical pluralist stance are likely to see community as an arena where individuals and groups actively contest ideas, values, and commitments. They recognize, therefore, that "at times there may be negotiation and compromise that is acceptable to all, in other debates the incommensurability of values may lead to...winning or losing the debate on specific issues" (Little, 2002, p. 81). They also recognize that conflicts cannot always be resolved through rational debate (Mouffe, 2005). Rather, radical pluralists call for the co-existence of different views and for the building of structures that allow dialogue across differences (Little, 2002). Solidarity, they argue, comes from joint acceptance of those structures and the importance of dialogue. Pluralist perspectives invoke questions about how much debate, and of what kinds, organizations such as Ngala and Gowrie SA consider desirable/allowable in their work with children, families, and communities. What structures are in place to support debate? (How) do they account for power relations (Hughes, 1996)? To what extent do they enable respect to be maintained in instances where different views reflect fundamentally different values (Sennett, 2003)?

Governmental Communitarianism and Control/Agency

Governmental communitarianism differs from moral authoritarianism and radical pluralism in its emphasis on "quasi-governmental" discourses of social management and the practices of "community experts"—such as Ngala and Gowrie SA—in regulating communities on behalf of the state (Delanty, 2010, p. 67; Rose, 1999). Governmental communitarianism can divert attention from the need for the state to take responsibility for devising "large-scale solutions to social problems" to local, not-for-profit, philanthropic, and/or volunteer endeavors (Delanty, 2010, p. 69; Rose, 1999, 2000). Through organizations such as Ngala and Gowrie SA, therefore, governments can steer at a distance the development of a responsible, skilled, stable, and self-disciplined citizenry and a globally competitive workforce. Hence, the work of these organizations can constitute technologies of subtle social surveillance, control, and risk management. Yet by fostering the development of skills and capacities, paradoxically a governmental focus on depoliticized human and social development can also become a force for (politicized) community agency (Delanty, 2010; Hughes, 1996). I am curious about how Ngala and Gowrie SA perceive and position themselves. Do they experience tensions between government priorities and their own? Do they consider themselves compliant to government or a force for democratic experimentalism, a term used by Moss (2009), influenced by Brazilian social theorist Roberto Unger, to refer to creative and dynamic ways of fostering relationships, dialogue, and democratic participation? Alternatively, do Ngala and Gowrie SA frame their focus on community in less dichotomized, more nuanced ways?

Using the lens of communitarianism, I have endeavored to highlight some of the tensions in visions and aspirations of community for organizations such as Ngala and Gowrie SA (Bauman, 2001). In Little's (2002, p. 28) words, "We need to think what communities actually are and what purposes we expect them to serve." This kind of thinking appears to underpin the work of Ngala and Gowrie SA.

ON CHANGE (FRANCES)

In order to understand the processes through which Ngala and Gowrie SA have achieved profound shifts in philosophy and practice,

I draw on Habermas to theorize organizational change. Ngala and Gowrie SA have relatively long histories in the context of Australian early childhood–oriented programs (Ngala, 121 years, and Gowrie SA, 61 years). From their inceptions, each has focused on working with children and families facing difficult circumstances. Over time, how this focus is addressed has changed in ways that reflect various social and political contexts, as well as their internal journeys of learning.

Longevity may well have an impact on the way each organization is perceived by, and is positioned within, its community. Certainly, it leaves an internal legacy of perspectives and embedded practice against which change must assert itself if new ways of working are to be more than transitory. Habermas's concepts of praxis, communicative action, and the public sphere are used here to understand how both organizations have made fundamental shifts in the nature of their work and their positioning and engagement of children and families.

Praxis encompasses both instrumental action (technical control and efficient use of technical knowledge) and communicative interaction (mutual understanding, recognized norms, and reciprocity) (Held, 1980, p. 257). When we seek to reach "an understanding about something in the world" we are engaged in communicative action (Habermas, 1990, p. 100). For Habermas, robust communication in the public sphere is at the heart of democracy, and a network or social space "for communicating information and points of view" is the public sphere. A requirement of the communication that Habermas exhorts as central to democracy and democratic solidarity is "citizens who respect each other as free and equal members of their political community" (Habermas, 2008, p. 3). Central to Habermas's philosophy is recognition of our interdependence and our intersubjectivity. We learn about ourselves through our interactions with others. Part of what defines our humanness is that we learn from one another (Habermas, 2008).

The case studies highlight each organization's emphasis on notions of community, the development of agreed-upon approaches to practice (supported by professional development), and the facilitation of communication. The preceding section problematized the use of the term "community" and highlighted the potentially coercive power of communitarianism. Community is amorphous. Membership may be bounded spatially or temporally, and there may be implicit or explicit rules of inclusion and exclusion. What might this mean for organizations that see themselves as being both embedded in community and as creators of community? Arguably, for Ngala and Gowrie SA, the decision to develop and deliver services in a more coherent manner has been driven by concerns about exclusion and inclusion, a consciousness that some families are left at the margins and that long-established norms have narrowed the boundaries of community.

The achievement of substantial and sustained change, therefore, has necessitated the abandonment of many existing norms and a preparedness to develop new forms of praxis. The search for new "organizational forms that produce solidarities" (Habermas, 2007, p. 399) has been guided by strategic action, that is, by action oriented to the achievement of a particular end (for instance, more effective engagement of potentially marginalized families) and coordinated by communicative interaction. Established and emerging practices and understandings are collectively scrutinized and subject to the test of the "generalisability of interests" (Habermas, 2007, p. 394) in order to develop a fuller understanding of their impact. The resulting strategically oriented decisions are "interlocked in a framework of norms and intersubjectively recognised rules of procedure" (Held, 1980, p. 257). That is, new norms are developed and embedded.

However, the altering of entrenched perceptions and ways of working is rarely easily achieved. Three types of knowledge generation identified by Habermas—instrumental knowledge (linked to causation), practical knowledge (linked to communication and understanding), and emancipatory knowledge (criticism, self-reflection, and utopian visions) (Coulhoun, Gerteis, Moody, Pfaff, & Virk, 2007)—contribute to understanding organizational transformation. The Gowrie SA experience highlighted that training in itself (instrumental knowledge) was not sufficient to transform staff practices. Although skills could be refined and developed through training and mentoring, real change came through the incorporation of theory (practical knowledge), accompanied by reciprocal questioning and discussion (emancipatory knowledge).

Evident in both Ngala and Gowrie SA is the active creation of networks and spaces for ongoing communication, questioning, and discussion (internal public spheres). These exist across various levels of each organization and are integral components of the services they deliver (for instance, parents' groups). Such fora are illustrative of Habermas's concept of deliberative communication,

> in which different opinions and values can be brought face to face, with an endeavor to ensure that each individual takes a stand by listening, deliberating, seeking arguments, and evaluating, while at the

> same time there is a collective effort to find values and norms that everyone can agree upon. (Englund, 2006, pp. 504–505)

Although consensus is not always possible, or perhaps desirable, aiming for consensus is in itself an important democratic process entailing a quest for reciprocal understanding, shared knowledge, and the development of mutual trust (Held, 1980, p. 333). For Habermas, the very act of speech is oriented to the idea of understanding. Ngala's and Gowrie SA's networks of communication can be considered democratic and potentially emancipatory projects. Of equal importance to the communicative spaces opened for praxis is the provision of public spheres for communities. Implicated in the notion of community is the dependence that we, as human beings, have upon one another. Our knowledge of ourselves is intersubjective. The creation of parents' groups, for instance, not only helps break down the isolation that some families may be experiencing, but can be individually and collectively transformational. Many of the families with whom Gowrie SA and Ngala work are potentially disenfranchised from the mainstream public sphere. Creating spaces for voice has the potential to validate individual personal experience and produce solidarities that can result in a public voice for those on the margins.

Additionally, in their journeys to integration, Ngala and Gowrie SA have redeveloped their philosophies in consultation with a range of stakeholders (staff, management, families, and representatives from other bodies). Both have actively sought to broaden their base of representation through their management, advisory structures, and networks. Both have attempted to become more transparent in their processes and decision making. Both have had to grapple with the consequences of differentials in status, between professionals from different disciplines and between professional versus family knowledge.

It would be simplistic to suggest that integration is ever fully achieved or that the routes taken are unproblematic. Community is a shifting horizon, and many communities exist. How integrated services invoke and respond to notions of community (including their internal communities as well as those of geography and population), who belongs, and who is excluded are important foci for consideration and debate.

Contemporary political rhetoric in Australia is conducive to a shift to integrated services provision. Although the political support of integrated services delivery is potentially beneficial to the work of Ngala and Gowrie SA, their journeys to integration preceded the potential interventions of government policy and arose from recognizing that previous approaches to working with families were failing a significant section of their communities. Here we see the interplay of government policy and the public sphere. Governments create policy in response to a perception of perceived problems or need. The creation of policies sympathetic to the work of integrated services has been influenced by a range of factors, including the advocacy and work of services that had already embarked on the journey. In creating this space for *voice,* organizations can be instrumental in bringing to the public sphere perspectives that may otherwise be hidden from view.

On Practice (Sandie)

In this section I take a practical turn and explore the micro level of integrated service delivery through the lens of Cultural Historical Activity Theory (CHAT) with the intent of highlighting the usefulness of this approach for supporting critical practitioner enquiry. Integrated services are complex, multidimensional systems of intersubjective human interactions, operating within larger sociocultural-political contexts. Like Edwards, Daniels, Gallagher, Leadbetter, and Warmington (2009), who use the approach to great effect to explore professional development in interagency work across services for school children and young people in the United Kingdom, I contend that CHAT offers a robust heuristic framework that can be used by practitioners in early childhood integrated services. CHAT is useful for analyzing the complexity of integrated services, for pulling them apart, and for exploring the relationships and contradictions within and between the constituent parts—*as a motive for transformation and development* [authors' emphasis] of the system (Daniels, Edwards, Engeström, Gallagher, & Ludvigsen, 2010; Engeström & Miettinen, 1999).

Through a CHAT lens, integrated service delivery is construed as a system of goal-directed actions (objects/goals and outcomes) performed by individuals or groups (subjects) and mediated by social and cultural materials and conditions (artifacts, rules, community of practice and division of labor) (Engeström & Miettinen, 1999). When these diverse elements are made visible and brought together under a theoretical gaze, contradictions and misalignments can be identified and challenged, generating a space for new ways of working. Using these elements as an organizing framework, I pose questions below that could be used by practitioners in integrated services to interrogate their own practices. As illustrative examples, I briefly address each question from the perspective of Ngala and/or Gowrie SA and suggest further probes for reflection.

Integrated services operate to achieve *outcomes*. But what outcomes, for whom, and are they well understood and agreed upon? Ngala and Gowrie SA, over their long history and through their commitment to reflective practice, have developed philosophies and practice statements that clearly articulate their desired outcomes for children, families, and communities. Do these outcomes reflect particular dominant discourses (e.g., investment and democratic participation) that produce certain types of citizens?

To achieve outcomes, individual or collective *subjects* engage in goal-directed activities. Each subject has their own history, knowledge and skills, desires and motives, and personal ethos and philosophy that they bring to the service. But is the work of the service considered from the perspectives of all subjects? Subjects in Ngala and Gowrie SA include both those employed in the service (professional and ancillary) and the families and children that use the service. Both services make attempts to include a range of voices (diverse professionals and families) in their decision-making processes. But are all voices, especially those of children, equally heard and listened to, or are some heard more than others? How are the perspectives of the most marginalized incorporated?

Subjects in integrated services perform actions, either consciously or unconsciously, to produce certain *objects or goals*. Are all the objects or goals clearly understood, or are some hidden and taken for granted? Ngala's tradition of providing time and resources for deep critical reflection on practice experiences is an example of how *hidden* practices may be teased out and made visible. It is often the unconscious or implicit behaviors, such as when a receptionist smiles and greets a family on their arrival, that have the most profound effect on families' experiences. How well are these behaviors understood and valued?

Mediating subjects' ability to achieve desired outcomes are *artifacts*—the tools at their disposal, such as curriculum materials and documents, space and time, that can have profound effects on the types of activity performed. Language, however, is perhaps the most important artifact. How is language used within the service? Both Ngala and Gowrie SA have worked extensively to develop common understandings about key terms such as *play* and *child* (Ngala's *C-Frame* and Gowrie's image of child). How are these understandings culturally and historically constructed?

Rules also mediate activity. They can be either formal, such as legislation and policies, or informal, such as cultural norms that may be historically and locally contingent; evidence from research might also be considered a type of *rule*. Which rules effectively guide the service practice and which constrict it? Both Ngala and Gowrie SA operate within practice and legislative guidelines and from a strong evidence base, but both services also challenge existing ways of working. How can this rule bending at a local level contribute to sustainable improvements in practices and procedures at policy levels?

A further factor impacting on the integrated service system is the *community of practice* in which it operates. Is the service working effectively *with* and *in* its community of practice? Ngala and Gowrie SA over time have forged strong links with their local and client communities to develop responsive services. But to what extent is community considered an integral part of the system? Community of practice also includes the professional community. How do the new and innovative ways of working in integrated services that challenge traditional professional boundaries impact on professional identities and sense of self?

A final aspect of the activity system considered by CHAT is *division of labor*—the ways that responsibility for the achievement of outcomes is shared. Is the work in the service equitably shared in ways that all parties are able to contribute their expertise and are fairly rewarded? Both Ngala and Gowrie SA seek to draw on and develop the expertise of their staff, for example, by developing flatter management structures. They have also made attempts to address inequality, for example, through pay structuring. As these new transdisciplinary ways of working are negotiated, and boundaries are continually blurred, how are issues of differential power and status addressed?

Using CHAT aids identification of diverse factors that impact upon an integrated services' ability to work effectively with communities. Identification of a system's constituent parts, however, is only the first step in a CHAT analysis. The next step is to explore the relationships between these parts and identify tensions, contradictions, and disruptions between them (Engeström & Miettinen, 1999). Questions that can be explored, for example, could include: How well aligned are the different elements of the system with the outcomes? How do rules governing the system impact on the ways work is divided? How are goals conceptualized differently by the diverse communities of practice? How are artifacts used by different individuals in the service?

Also important are the relationships between different activity systems, both within and across organizations. For example, in the case of Gowrie SA, how do activities such as the *TtLG* program work with the childcare services? And how do these services and programs work effectively to complement and contribute to the goals of external systems such as governments?

It is imperative that theorizing has some purpose and contributes to the social good. CHAT can contribute to this enterprise by alerting individuals within integrated services to the wide range of factors that can impact on these services. However, it is when the whole community comes together and enters into skeptical critical dialogue and exchange to confront contradictions between the constituent parts that old ways of working are challenged and change that responds appropriately to multiple perspectives becomes possible.

CONCLUSION

Ngala's and Gowrie SA's philosophies and practices provide a foundation for critical reflection enabling a deepened understanding of the ways integrated services might negotiate multiple discourses. Our particular interest in this chapter has been in the possibilities for integrated services to challenge dominant power relations and structural and social inequities through strengthening social relations and fostering dialogue and democratic participation. Utilizing an array of theoretical resources has added richness and depth to our insights into Ngala's and Gowrie SA's critical engagement with the opportunities and dangers arising from strong policy interest in integrated service provision. At a macro level, for example, communitarianism raises challenging questions about realities behind the rhetoric of community building. At a micro level, CHAT generates questions that individual practitioners might wish to ask themselves about their practices. Across both levels, Habermas provokes questions about how to establish communicative spaces that are sufficiently robust to enable organizational and individual transformation.

All three theoretical lenses highlight the importance of critical engagement (through critical dialogue, reflection, and action) with the policy environment, within the organization, and with the communities in which integrated services are embedded and serve. Indeed, for Ngala and Gowrie SA, critical engagement appears central to their capacities to negotiate government-driven agendas—without becoming enslaved to them—in ways that are consistent with their own philosophies and goals. Possibly those capacities have contributed to the longevity of both organizations and the high regard in which they are held.

This chapter has provided a welcome opportunity to highlight the impressive work of these organizations. It has also highlighted the capacity of theory to serve as a foil against complacency by opening up spaces in which to ask difficult questions, to articulate possibilities for change, and to engage critically with the challenges inherent in change.

ACKNOWLEDGMENTS

We are grateful to the Professional Support Coordinators' Alliance for funding the study from which this chapter is drawn. Sincere thanks to management and staff at Ngala and Gowrie SA and to our fellow researchers, Jan Duffie and Joy Goodfellow.

REFERENCES

Australian Government. (n.d.). *Social inclusion: Opportunity and capacity to learn. Overview.* Retrieved from http://www.socialinclusion.gov.au/Pages/Overview.aspx

Aylward, P., & O'Neil, M. (2009). *Through the looking glass: A community partnership in parenting. Invest to grow final evaluation report.* Adelaide: University of Adelaide and Gowrie SA.

Bauman, Z. (2001). *Community: Seeking safety in an insecure world.* Cambridge, UK: Polity.

Bronfenbrenner, U. (1979). *Basic concepts: The ecology of human development experiments by nature and design.* Cambridge, MA: Harvard University Press.

Coulhoun, C., Gerteis, J., Moody, J., Pfaff, S., & Virk I. (2007). Introduction to Part viii. In C. Coulhoun, J. Gerteis, J. Moody, S. Pfaff, & I. Virk (Eds.). *Contemporary sociological theory* (pp. 358–359). Malden, MA: Blackwell.

Daniels, H., Edwards, A., Engeström, Y., Gallagher, T., & Ludvigsen, S. R. (Eds.). (2010). *Activity theory in practice.* London: Routledge.

De Landa, M. (2006). *A new philosophy of society.* London: Continuum.

Delanty, G. (2010). *Community* (2nd ed.). Abingdon, Oxon: Routledge.

Edwards, A., Daniels, H., Gallagher, T., Leadbetter, J., & Warmington, P. (2009). *Improving inter-professional collaborations: Multi-agency working for children's wellbeing.* London: Routledge.

Engeström, Y., & Miettinen, R. (1999). Introduction. In Y. Engeström, R. Miettinen & R-L. Punamaki (Eds.). *Perspectives on activity theory* (pp. 1–16). Cambridge: Cambridge University Press.

Englund, T. (2006). Deliberative communication: A pragmatist proposal. *Journal of Curriculum Studies, 38*(5), 503–520.

Etzioni, A. (1995). *The spirit of community.* London: Fontana.

Falzon, J. (2009). *Transcript for Australian Social Inclusion Board interviews. Video 1: What does social inclusion mean to you?* Retrieved from http://www.socialinclusion.gov.au/Videos/asib/Documents/Transcript1.pdf

Gillard, J. (2007). *The economics of social inclusion.* Speech delivered to the Sydney Institute, July 12. Retrieved from http://www.thesydneyinstitute.com.au/podcast/the-economics-of-social-inclusion/

Gowrie S.A. (2008). *Lady Gowrie Child Centre Philosophy.* Lady Gowrie S.A.

Gowrie S.A. (n.d.). *History—Overview Lady Gowrie Child Centre.* Retrieved from: http://www.gowrie-adelaide.com.au/cms/?q=node/22

Habermas, J. (1990). *Moral consciousness and communicative action.* Cambridge: Polity Press.

Habermas, J. (2007). Civil society and the political public sphere. In C. Coulhoun, J. Gerteis, J. Moody, S. Pfaff, & I. Virk (Eds.). *Contemporary sociological theory* (pp. 388–408). Malden, MA: Blackwell.

Habermas, J. (2008). *Between naturalism and religion.* Cambridge, UK: Polity Press.

Held, D. (1980). *Introduction to critical theory.* London: Hutchinson.

Hughes, G. (1996). Communitarianism and law and order. *Critical Social Policy, 16*(49), 17–41.

Kidsmatter Early Childhood. (n.d.). Retrieved from http://www.kidsmatter.edu.au/ec/

Little, A. (2002). *The politics of community: Theory and practice.* Edinburgh: Edinburgh University Press.

Long, E. (2010). The Australian social inclusion agenda: A new approach to social policy? *The Australian Journal of Social Issues, 45*(2), 161–182.

Millei, Z., & Sumsion, J. (2011). The place of "community" in Belonging, Being and Becoming: An Early Years Learning Framework for Australia. *Contemporary Issues in Early Childhood, 12*(1), 71–85.

Moss, P. (2009). *Early childhood education and democratic experimentalism: Two models for early childhood education and care.* (Bernard van Leer Foundation Working Papers No.53). Retrieved from http://www.bernardvanleer.org/publication_store/publication_store_publications/there_are_alternatives_markets_and_democratic_experimentalism_in_early_childhood_education_and_care/file

Mouffe, C. (2005). *On the political.* Abingdon: Routledge.

Ngala. (2007–2008). *Annual Report.* Retrieved from http://www.ngala.com.au/files/files/152_Ngala_annual_report_07_08.pdf

Ngala. (2008). *Service delivery model.* Unpublished document.

Nichols, S., & Jurvansuu, S. (2008). Partnership in integrated early childhood services: An analysis of policy framings in education and human services. *Contemporary Issues in Early Childhood, 9*(2), 117–130.

Press, F., Sumsion, J., & Wong, S. (2010). *Integrated early years provision in Australia: A research project for the National Professional Support Coordinators' Alliance.* Bathurst: Charles Sturt University.

Rose, N. (1999). *Powers of freedom: Reframing political thought.* Cambridge: Cambridge University Press.

Rose, N. (2000). Community, citizenship, and the third way. *The American Behavioral Scientist, 43*(9), 1395–1411.

Sennett, R. (2003). *Respect: In a world of inequality.* London: W. W. Norton and Company.

Silver, H. (2010). Understanding social inclusion and its meaning for Australia. *Australian Journal of Social Issues, 45*(2), 183–211.

Taylor, C. (1997). Invoking civil society. In R. E. Gooding & P. Pettit (Eds.). *Contemporary political philosophy: An anthology* (pp. 66–77). Oxford, UK: Blackwell.

CHAPTER 4

Building Strengths in Families and Communities

Robyn Munford, Jackie Sanders, and Bruce Maden

INTRODUCTION

This chapter presents the experiences of one community-based agency, *Te Aroha Noa*, which has developed effective strategies for enhancing family and community well-being. The agency's name is derived from *te reo Māori* (the indigenous language of New Zealand) and embraces the idea of unconditional love and care. *Te Aroha Noa* provides early childhood services alongside a range of other services and has developed innovative approaches for nurturing the strengths of families. It has also contributed to building the capacity of the community within which it is situated. For over two decades, the agency has worked intentionally to understand the diverse needs of the families that come to *Te Aroha Noa* and has developed creative strategies for responding to these needs. Strengths-based and community-development perspectives inform the work and focus attention upon positive change strategies that enhance family and child well-being. This chapter presents the agency's experiences in developing an approach to practice that spans early childhood, family and community work, and adult education. It explores the key concepts that are central to this practice. The chapter draws on examples from the Early Childhood Education and Care (ECEC) center, which is located on the main site of the agency, and the parenting support and education programs provided to families that are delivered on-site and in-home.

Te Aroha Noa has provided services to people in Palmerston North (a provincial city of 80,000 people in the North Island of New Zealand) for over 20 years. It was established in the late 1980s when the Central Baptist Church made a decision to transfer its concern for people into action. It began with a counseling service located within the community so that the service was easily accessible to families. As time passed other services were added, including a play group that grew into a fully licensed ECEC center, parenting programs, adult education programs, an outreach social work and family support service, community development programs, and, more recently, programs for teenagers and for teen parents. Currently over 60 staff are employed across the agency's services and over 150 volunteers support the organization. The ECEC center has between 80 and 90 children on its roll; at any point in time over 200 families and individuals are receiving support from the agency. While many live in the immediate vicinity, those living in other parts of the city also utilize the agency's services.

The integrated service model has enabled families to address their immediate issues but also to seek out further opportunities for development and growth. The blending of individual and community development work and the focus on life-long learning creates the potential for change within families. This approach brings other, more general, benefits and has seen an increase in the confidence of local residents to engage with wider social and political institutions and with accessing other community resources and opportunities. Working with diversity is a key focus of practice. This includes understanding cultural frameworks and the range of life experiences of families (Munford & Sanders, 2008; Munford & Walsh-Tapiata, 2005). All of the agency's services, including the early childhood services and the parenting education and support programs, are based on a commitment to building collaborative partnerships with families and with the wider community. The location of these services within the neighborhood provides an anchor of support for families (Duncan, 2008) and engenders a sense of belonging where, in their interactions with families, staff in all of the agency's services demonstrate respect for the family's values and beliefs (May & Mitchell, 2009). The agency has been available and accessible to families and has been prepared to adapt its approaches to more effectively respond to the needs of families.

The remainder of the chapter outlines the key theoretical ideas that have informed practice at *Te Aroha Noa* and identifies a number of key concepts that are at the essence of this agency's work with families. The chapter concludes by considering reflective practice as a key strategy for sustaining the agency's commitment to developing responsive and effective services for families and children.

THEORETICAL PERSPECTIVES

Te Aroha Noa has engaged in research to identify the essence of their practice and to determine what interventions make a positive difference for those families attending their ECEC center, parenting programs, and other agency services. Several perspectives inform this work and enable agency staff to develop responses and interventions that work at different levels, ranging from the individual and family level to the systemic and community level (Handley et al., 2009, pp. 5–6). There is a dynamic interplay among theory, knowledge, and practice, where theory informs practice and where reflection on practice (Ruch, 2005) works to extend and advance knowledge about what works well and under what circumstances, and also reveals what strategies generate new possibilities for families and for the community.

Culture is a critical part of family and community life, and for this reason it is an important dimension of practice. Historically, practice discourses in Aotearoa New Zealand have been framed in terms of Western constructs, and it is only recently that indigenous knowledge has been recognized by mainstream practice and acknowledged as having a significant contribution to make to education and social and community work interventions (Munford & Sanders, 2008, 2011; Munford & Walsh-Tapiata, 2005). These recent developments locate cultural understanding at the center of practice and are connected to understanding how context shapes experience (Sanders & Munford, 2010). Of particular importance and central to achieving well-being is the connection with one's ancestry and generational links and a foregrounding of cultural meaning systems, including spirituality (Ruwhiu, 2009). This involves understanding connections to place and to people, including a person's position within their family and community (Munford & Sanders, 2011).

Structural theories have focused the agency's attention on how individual circumstances are connected to wider sociopolitical factors. Critical realism provides a useful explanatory framework for under-standing the relationship between structure and agency (Archer, 2002; Callaghan, 2008) and for exploring how families and commu-nities can work to change policies, structures and practices that under-mine their capacity to care well for their members (Handley et al., 2009; Munford & Sanders, 2005; Sanders & Munford, 2010). This explanatory framework enables an understanding about how material conditions and structures impact on family life and also assists agency staff in developing an understanding alongside families of how these circumstances can be overcome. These endeavors involve an exploration of the nature of complex systems and how these emerge from particular historical conditions (Callaghan, 2008).

Ideas derived from complexity theory have been of value in helping staff in all of the agency's services understand uncertainty and unpredictability, contradiction and tension (Handley et al., 2009, p. 9). They have developed an understanding of the nonproportional relation between cause and effect—the notion that small inputs can have large effects. In practice, this means being aware of how seemingly unrelated events can come together to provide a platform for positive change; learning how to hook into these opportunities and connect to emerging possibilities for change has been at the forefront of practice at *Te Aroha Noa*. Another concept from complexity theory is sensitivity to initial conditions. Durie and Wyatt (2007) assert that effective practice with families and communities requires an understanding of how complex conditions hold the possibilities of change. Staff at *Te Aroha Noa* understand that their "interventions can lead to the development of enabling conditions for transformational change" (Durie & Wyatt, 2007, p. 4), particularly in the ECEC center, where interventions and support provided in this setting hold great potential for change. Interventions with families are focused on identifying how "regeneration processes" (Durie & Wyatt, 2007, p. 5) emerge from the complexity of family and community life. Relationships are critical in complexity theory, and as noted throughout this chapter, well managed, careful relationships are key aspects of practice at *Te Aroha Noa*.

Educational theories such as the work of Freire (1985) and the focus on education and development inform engagement with families and with the community (Handley et al., 2009, p. 7). An approach to education that is based on emancipation and liberation is critical. This forms the foundation for building a learning community that reaches out to other resources and organizations and involves them in developing the vision for a strong and healthy community. The focus on education as liberation and as having the potential to open up new opportunities for families is closely connected to the agency's adoption of strengths-based practice that encourages all agency staff to identify the factors in clients' lives that contribute to growth and change. Strengths-based approaches underpin all aspects of the work at *Te Aroha Noa* and underline the centrality of clients in the change process (Handley et al., 2009, p. 7). For example, in the ECEC center, rather than beginning with a focus on what parents are not doing well, teachers support families to identify what is working well for them and their child, and they use the success here to strengthen other areas in the parent-child interaction. Drawing on constructionist perspectives, strengths-based approaches require professionals to understand the structures and experiences that shape clients' worlds. There is always more than one story to be told; families' worlds are complex and multilayered. They are not passive in these worlds but are active in making sense and meaning in their lives (Sanders & Munford, 2010 p. 32). Strengths perspectives urge us to think differently about family life and to understand that a focus on deficits and problems can mask the *multiple positions* families may occupy; it is these other positions or dimensions that hold the potential for change.

A focus on strengths does not ignore risks or issues but encourages professionals to find solutions by seeing and thinking beyond the challenges of family life (Munford & Sanders, 2005, 2008; Sanders & Munford, 2010). Families are active participants in the change process, and successful helping relationships are therefore based on actively engaging families in creating positive change for themselves and their children. The focus of all interventions with families is on what it is that enables families and communities to survive and grow. Relationships are central to successful change processes, and these are collaborative, transparent and respectful (Ruch, 2005). Underpinning strengths approaches is the belief that all families have a right to an ordinary life (Halvorsen, 2009) including having access to education and being able to participate in the activities of their neighborhood and wider community. Moreover, it is unhelpful to perceive those who face enduring challenges as suffering human beings living tragic and sad lives that need to be *fixed* before they can participate fully in their communities. Staff in all of the services at *Te Aroha Noa* understand the complexity of family life and aspire to being critically reflective in order to authentically engage with families. They understand that positive change for families will not arise from following a set of tightly prescribed rules or guidelines (Smith, 2011) but will rather emerge when the realities of family and community life are recognized as the driving force of change.

Strengths approaches have a strong affinity with ecological perspectives because they encourage us to think about the circles of relationships around individuals and families and to recognize the ways in which differing levels in the social ecology shape the approach to finding solutions. The agency has a strong focus on understanding the relationship between families and their social ecology and how, in the face of adversity, they have developed resilience and pathways for positive growth (Liebenberg & Ungar, 2009). Families build resilience by being able to successfully seek out resources, and an ecological approach to service delivery enables an understanding of how the different domains of a family's environment act to hinder or advance their ability to harness resources (Duncan, 2008). Central to such processes is being able to negotiate for resources that are culturally and socially meaningful and hold the possibilities for creating transformational change for families and their children (Dahlberg, Moss, & Pence, 2007).

THEORY INTO PRACTICE—THE DYNAMIC RELATIONSHIP BETWEEN THEORY AND PRACTICE

Defining key elements of intervention and change processes was a critical first step in the research on the development of the *Te Aroha Noa* practice model; this model has both individual- and community-level components. The research identified the key elements of practice and the agency embodied this in the metaphor of the *Spinifex* (Handley et al., 2009). The *Spinifex* is a perennial grass that thrives in difficult environments and is well adapted to coastal environments and the problems posed by unstable sand dunes. It is a tough plant that can cope with salt spray, drought, extreme temperatures, strong winds, and shifting sands. The plant puts out strong creeping runners across sand dunes and catches the sand as it blows up from the beach. The sand partially buries the plant but it continues to grow, stabilizing the dunes by holding the sand together. The strong creeping runners protect the plant from the wind and work beneath a turbulent surface to create stability in the environment. The seed heads of the plant tumble across the sand and inhabit new environments (Handley et al., 2009, p. 18).

The *Spinifex* metaphor represents the resilience of families and children and defines the agency's presence in this community. It works to provide stability and to also effect change. In this way, *Te Aroha Noa* is part of the journey that families take to achieve positive change; the staff across the agency's services clearly articulate their practice frameworks and the work they need to do at the micro and macro level to build capacity and to enhance participation in community life. Of significance is the commitment to life-long learning and education that includes ECEC education, parenting support, after-school homework programs, adult education, and individualized family support programs. Education has a central role in opening up new opportunities and pathways for positive change. We turn now to a discussion of some of the key ideas that inform the essence of practice at *Te Aroha Noa*.

UNDERSTANDING THE CONTEXT OF FAMILY AND COMMUNITY LIFE

Working to understand how context influences family and community life is a core element of practice at *Te Aroha Noa*. This includes understanding how political, social, economic, religious, and cultural factors influence family life and shape what it is possible for families to achieve. Taking a critical-realist position it is acknowledged that there will be constraining factors in people's environments but that equally there will also be opportunities for people to construct and define their situation positively and to create change for themselves (Houston, 2010). Professionals who fully understand the contexts of family life can assist families to connect with the meaning systems that will help them make sense of their worlds, such as cultural, religious, and spiritual beliefs. Examples include giving credence to the traditions families have around important activities, such as greeting and welcoming visitors, acknowledging ancestors, and the role that older members may play in supporting the family (Sanders & Munford, 2010, pp. 44–45). Regenerating connections with cultural meaning systems can assist the family to gain a sense of control over their experiences and situations and enable them to seek support from those who know and understand their history and contexts. For example, in the ECEC center, teachers and families are encouraged to use their own cultural processes in their work with children. Parents can become parent educators by participating in the activities of the ECEC center and can contribute their ideas for teaching and learning. They are supported to learn about child development and are encouraged to contribute ideas about how the activities reflect the experiences of children in their home context. For example, many of the children in the ECEC center are Māori (indigenous population of New Zealand), so *kuia* (elder such as grandmother) and *kaumatua* (elder such as grandfather), who are held in high regard by other *whānau* (extended family) members and are perceived as having much to offer succeeding generations, including caring for and teaching children and young people, are brought into the center to offer special programs. Through these activities the role of the extended family is reinforced as being a significant factor in the support of children's learning.

Understanding context also means that all agency staff challenge themselves to reflect on their own contexts and to understand how these may influence their work with families. They build an understanding of the nature of community life and explore whether the community is part of a network of support for the family or functions as an isolation and marginalization mechanism (Munford & Sanders, 2008). Of particular importance is aligning support to the lived realities of families. The agency has a key role in offering up new possibilities for vulnerable families and children (Sanders & Munford, 2010, pp. 45–46). Context-sensitive work intentionally focuses agency staff on understanding the ways in which wider factors (e.g., poverty and violence) in the environment influence the readiness capacity of families to embark on change.

The families that attend the ECEC center are invited to participate in other agency activities, such as becoming involved with community development processes that work to confront some of the wider community issues—for example, working to ensure that neighborhood resources reflect the needs of children and families, such as working with the local authority to upgrade the local park and play equipment so that it is safe and accessible. Families become involved in these initiatives, and over time they build a sense of agency by participating in activities that will transform their local environments. Involvement in community initiatives is important because it breaks down the sense that people come to *Te Aroha Noa* only when they have *problems*. These neighborhood initiatives provide opportunities for agency staff and families to work alongside each other on a common task, which challenges the *client-professional* demarcation. The close proximity of agency staff to the daily lives of families also guards against a social distancing and enables them to understand the complexities of everyday experiences (Smith, 2011). By joining with families to engage in neighborhood initiatives, agency staff come to know the daily struggles families face and demonstrate their commitment to the community and to the change processes that will enhance the well-being of families in this area. The trust and confidence that families build by being part of these processes enables them to work on some of their more challenging family issues, such as learning how to manage their children's difficult behavior and gain the confidence to confront those in their family who use violence to address their issues.

FOSTERING A SENSE OF BELONGING

The physical location of *Te Aroha Noa* within the neighborhood creates a sense of belonging for the families who, over time, come to view the agency as a key resource; they take pride in their participation in the agency and openly acknowledge the role the agency has had in creating positive change for their family (Handley et al., 2009). Gerald and McDonald (2010, p. 9) write of the important contribution community-based agencies make to their local neighborhoods; these agencies demonstrate a commitment to invest in the community and to support families within their own environments. As Gerald and McDonald (2010, p. 11) assert, agencies such as *Te Aroha Noa* are able to deliver deliberate and sustainable interventions that are family-oriented and strengths-based; they state that "one cannot underestimate the value of meeting the community and individual clients *within* their community, physically and psychologically." Community-based services can provide a sense of containment for families as they struggle with their daily challenges (Berry et al., 2006; Lightburn & Warren-Adamson, 2006). From a complexity theory perspective easy access to a place that is safe and supportive can be the right mix of initial conditions that creates the beginning of major change journeys for families and children. The integrated service model means that there are multiple pathways into the agency. There is no wrong door into the agency, and once families feel comfortable in the place they first make contact, such as the early childhood center, they can then begin to work on some of the more challenging issues they are facing. For example, they gain the confidence to work on their own development and on the issues that restrict their capacity to be available to parent well (Handley et al., 2009; Sanders & Munford, 2010).

Te Aroha Noa has fostered a learning community. Local people are supported and encouraged to grow in confidence and in their capacity to create a safe, supportive, and dynamic community (Handley et al., 2009, p. 6). Being located in the neighborhood and facilitating access to diverse service options means that there are many opportunities for forming respectful relationships (Ruch, 2005) and for creating foundations for new learning. *Te Aroha Noa* develops intentional and sustainable multileveled interventions and has become part of the everyday fabric of community life. The sense of belonging to the agency engenders a strong foundation for families. They see the agency as being able to welcome new people into a supportive environment that provides them with a safe place to work on challenging issues and to engage with others who are facing similar issues. Staff in all of the agency's services are highly inventive about finding routes to engagement and are always seeking moments for learning; within a culture of care they communicate to families a deep sense of respect for their traditions and values (Handley et al., 2009, p. 24). The ECEC center is central to this work, as the teachers encourage families to attend with their children, and this provides opportunities for parents to learn new skills and to meet with other parents to share stories in a nurturing, nonjudgmental environment (Handley et al., 2009). The ECEC center has had a key role in fostering a sense of belonging for families and in extending the support networks of families; for example, bringing families together to organize celebrations for their children such as birthdays and key life events such as moving from the ECEC center to primary school.

Strengthening Natural Support Networks and Sustainable Change Processes

Complexity theory reminds us that small steps play a significant role in major positive change (Sanders & Munford, 2010) and that good processes and respectful relationships can have ripple effects that stimulate ongoing change (Hudson, 2000, p. 221). Accordingly, networking and harnessing the opportunities and resources that already exist in families' worlds are important aspects of practice. The networking approach draws many people into the change process (such as extended family members and other agencies), and strengths-based conversations enable families to develop fresh perspectives on family life. This work enhances family and community capacity because it strengthens naturally occurring networks and support systems. Agency staff support families to identify the resources within the family system and to find the naturally occurring networks of support that can assist solution finding and capacity building; for example, connecting a young mother with the neighbor who is living away from her grandchildren and is keen to become involved in supporting a young family. The family remains at the center of helping processes and, as Gilligan (2004, pp. 101–102) asserts, professionals need to understand that they are not the exclusive source of help. In analyzing what creates change for clients within client/professional encounters Duncan, Miller, and Sparks (2004, p. 34) remind professionals to listen deeply to clients' stories; clients are experts on their lives and are the chief agents of change. This requires professionals to understand who is available to support the client through the change process and to identify who can assist to *get this back on track* when the client faces setbacks. It also alerts the client to what it is that may prevent them from taking ownership of the change process and being able to facilitate change.

Sustainable change takes time and requires that natural change processes are harnessed (Reeler, n.d.). In the ECEC center and the parenting programs the teachers actively create opportunities for hooking into the wider networks of support that are present in the local area. It is in these places that families are able to form new relationships and strengthen their networks. For many, their own networks are under pressure as they struggle to parent their children well with scarce resources. In the ECEC center and parenting program teachers bring parents together so that parents can develop mutual support networks (Bell, 2007) for their daily activities. For example, they have worked together to establish healthy eating options for their children and to find more appropriate methods for disciplining their children. What is significant here is that teachers support families to find information about parenting and child development and learn new skills. Families then use the relationships they have formed with others in agency programs to strengthen their learning and to change and grow. The circles of relationships created within the agency flow out into the community so that families are supported within their neighborhood when they adopt new ideas and practice new skills such as parenting strategies. Change needs to be supported and noticed by others in order to be sustained (Sanders & Munford, 2010). The use of naturally occurring networks is an intentional strategy for providing mutual support (Bell, 2007) and for achieving and sustaining change for the families who come to *Te Aroha Noa*.

Sharing and Respecting Diverse Knowledge

Valuing the expertise of all parties in a support relationship and intentionally recognizing and working with the rich knowledge all partners bring to the helping relationship are the cornerstones of strengths practice and of working collaboratively (Sanders & Munford, 2010). At *Te Aroha Noa* this orientation to practice is informed by a commitment to the Māori construct of *manaakitanga* (looking after people). This means that people are welcomed into the agency and that their diverse cultural backgrounds are acknowledged and respected. Families may come into the agency through different pathways—their children come to the ECEC center, families attend a mandated parenting program, couples are introduced to a counselor by a friend; whatever the pathway, they are welcomed in a respectful and careful way and they are honored for what they bring (Munford & Sanders, 2011). This approach, combined with a commitment to honestly facing tensions and contradictions and being open to diverse views, builds a strong foundation for establishing mutual learning processes.

Ako is a key concept in Māori pedagogy and gives prominence to the idea that learning, growth, and change are inherent human capacities and that all people are simultaneously teachers and learners (Handley et al., 2009, p. 21). This embraces the idea of mutuality and the ecological interdependence of living things (Reeler, n.d., p. 18), which creates connections and a solidarity between people who are all striving to learn how to adapt to and transform their environments. Unleashing the propensity for growth, through sharing knowledge and resources, is a primary focus of the work at *Te Aroha Noa*. The philosophy of *ako* provides a vehicle for families to enter into the agency as equals and to work with their own change but also to contribute to the wider changes within the agency and in the community. It brings humility into agency/family relationships as it recognizes that everyone has the capacity to impart knowledge and understanding and that in helping others to grow and change, staff themselves grow and develop (Handley et al., 2009, p. 21).

The agency draws in families to work collaboratively to develop new projects (individual, familial and community-wide). The collaborative approach engenders innovation, adaptation, and change as diverse ideas are brought to the table. An excellent example of this is encapsulated in the way the agency has worked to address the issue of family violence. The social workers and counselors working with families and with individuals on issues of violence noticed that while many had been able to change their approaches to one another and to the parenting of their children, the levels of violence in the community were not reducing. Using violence as a way to solve issues had an intractable presence in the community, and different approaches were required if this was to change in the long term (Handley et al., 2009). To address this issue *Te Aroha Noa* built upon relationships it had developed with other projects, such as parenting programs that worked collaboratively with families, and worked with local community leaders as *positive influencers*. These leaders worked with key community people to develop a vision of a *violence-free community* and to develop strategies for how this vision could be achieved.

What was significant in this project was the use of community leaders to cofacilitate the project and the commitment to using locally relevant knowledge and experience to build an engaged community (Mataira, 2002, p. 5). The processes that were adopted in this project were based on mutual respect and shared learning. Those involved in the project developed an understanding about the influence of historical experiences on current community issues, and their evolving connections generated new opportunities for change. The project was successful because trust was established through the support families had received in other domains, such as in their involvement with the ECEC center. Their positive experiences in these areas enabled them to face some of the more challenging long-term issues, such as confronting violence in their family and in the wider community.

Working with Complexity and Generating Possibilities for Change

Te Aroha Noa has grown out of its local environment and has adapted to the changing social, political, and economic landscape. It has worked with local social and cultural practices and, like the runners of the *Spinifex* plant, has provided stabilizing and growth-enhancing capacities. Staff in all of the agency's services understand that building resilience is a complex process; at times it will be the unexpected or unpredictable events that will enable a family to experience success and remain open to new possibilities and sources of support. At the heart of *Te Aroha Noa's* programs are respectful learning relationships that are established between the agency and families. They work to enable diverse voices to be heard so that different thinking can be generated; for example, using parents as cofacilitators in parenting programs so that those attending learn from real-life, local examples of family change. These approaches reflect thinking that has been established over generations to successfully adapt to challenging environments and issues and recognize that context and history are part of solution finding (Bessarab & Crawford, 2010). Those involved in *Te Aroha Noa's* programs recognize that traditional and indigenous approaches for generating healthy families and communities have often been ignored and discounted and there needs to be opportunities for regeneration and for putting these approaches at the center of solution finding. Drawing on the values, beliefs, customs, and cultural norms of local and indigenous helping practices (Gray, Coates, & Yellow Bird, 2008, p. 5) can generate new possibilities for creating healthy outcomes for families.

Te Aroha Noa works intentionally with both community and cultural leaders to foreground local knowledge and to nurture community processes to increase the strength of social networks. All agency staff are aware of the synergies that are created among people, events, and contexts and they are continually conscious of making *more* of situations and finding new possibilities for change and growth. They relate this to the metaphor of the *Spinifex,* where the seed heads of the plants travel long distances to find and transform environments (Handley et al., 2009, p. 21). The principle of *more* signifies how the agency seeks to influence places, people, and systems beyond the agency so that others become partners in effecting positive change processes with families and the wider community. The agency takes every opportunity for learning (Westley, Zimmerman, & Patton, 2006, p. 158) and supports people to discover new talents and capacities. This openness to learning creates synergies that generate individual and community resources (Handley et al., 2009, p. 22). For example, the ECEC center has a central role in the agency around which other services are arrayed (Munford, Sanders, & Maden, 2007). As a result of participating as parent educators in the ECEC center, parents have gained the confidence to become involved in their child's learning. They have been nurtured to develop their own agency and to dream about what might be possible for their children. Involvement in their child's preschool learning has enabled parents to become effective advocates for their child's life-long learning. Many have now been supported to make more deliberate decisions about what kind of education they would like for their child, including where they would like their child to go to primary school. These parents have established partnerships with early childhood teachers who assist them in this process and support them to meet with school teachers in order to facilitate a successful transition for their child from early childhood into primary school.

As well as using the strengths and possibility thinking orientation (Handley et al., 2009; Sanders & Munford, 2010) in their work alongside families, *Te Aroha Noa* uses this in their work with other agencies, including schools and other social service agencies. In understanding that change is often an unpredictable and emergent organic process agency staff have become attuned to noticing the opportunities for growth and development. One important example is inviting in other agencies to attend their community events and to welcome them into the agency through these events. As time passes possibilities emerge for developing stronger relationships, such as forming partnerships with child-protection agencies to work together to assist families to address their own issues and to learn new parenting strategies so that their children can be returned to them. *Te Aroha Noa* invites agencies to do their work with families on site; examples include sharing in the facilitation of family meetings and cofacilitating parenting programs. *Te Aroha Noa* provides a safe place for families to meet with agencies that may have been difficult to contact because of restricted appointment times, or because families may have felt alienated from organizational processes and protocols. As they build these relationships families learn to clearly articulate what they need from these agencies and how they wish to work with them. This practice happens with a diverse range of agencies, including education providers, schools, child- protection agencies, and health agencies. Over time, and as a result of their interactions with *Te Aroha Noa*, these agencies come to engage differently with the community; they begin to see the complexity of the issues in the community and they also become part of a process that other researchers have named co-evolving with the environment (Durie & Wyatt, 2007, p. 15). It is through this process that other agencies start to think differently about supporting families and children (Bessarab & Crawford, 2010). They come to see that they can connect with the issues in the community and form collaborative partnerships that enable them to become part of finding solutions to these issues.

Possibility thinking and working to find solutions in the complexity of family and community life is a practice orientation that informs all the agency's interactions; this requires openness and flexibility, a willingness to hold "professionalism lightly" (Handley et al., 2009), and active engagement with the solutions being offered by the community. Success involves positive change for individuals and families and it also opens up further opportunities for these families to engage in community life. Agency staff are attuned to the importance of relationship building (Ruch, 2005), as the seeds of change are found within these relationships. All agency staff at *Te Aroha Noa* know that major change has emerged from small beginnings; for example, the early childhood teachers have taken the time to understand family connections and have been able to bring others into the agency, such as grandparents, to contribute to the programs in the early childhood center. They have supported parents to learn about child development and gain the confidence to try out different parenting strategies, and parents have been encouraged to attend courses that will provide them with practical skills, such as obtaining their driver's license. While the initial connection with a family may be the provision of a direct service, such as at the ECEC center, teachers know that positive engagement in these services can lead to *more* and create the seeds for achieving transformational change for families (Handley et al., 2009).

BUILDING A REFLECTIVE AGENCY

The approaches adopted by agencies such as *Te Aroha Noa* require a commitment to ongoing critical reflection and to deep thinking about practice (Sanders & Munford, 2010, p. 171). This deep thinking occurs at an individual level as staff reflect upon their work with families: in supervision, in the integrated team meetings where staff work together to develop intervention plans, and in the ongoing research program the agency has developed over the past decade. *Te Aroha Noa* sees itself as a learning organization that is engaged in continual evaluation of its practice and of the processes it uses to engage with families, the community, and other agencies. Critical reflection creates an "open-mindedness" (Gardner, Fook, & White, 2006, p. 228) and embraces understanding of the individual in their social context (Fook & Gardner, 2007, p. 16). Critically reflective practice involves an integration of theory and practice (praxis) in the creation of knowledge (Sanders & Munford, 2010, pp. 172–173). It requires critical reflexivity on the part of the professional in order to understand their *use of self* and how they incorporate client knowledge and experience into practice wisdom. Critical reflection on practice reminds agency staff that families and children are not objects of intervention (Smith, 2011), but are partners in learning and in change processes. This reflexivity in practice assists staff to resist becoming subject to depersonalizing regulations and procedures that construct practice as an instrumental task that can further undermine the agency of families and their sense of control over their situation and experiences. They remain critical about their practice and work to form authentic and genuine relationships (Ruch, 2005) with families.

Critical reflection is a fundamental part of the essence of *Te Aroha Noa*. The commitment to action and reflection processes (Munford & Walsh-Tapiata, 2005, pp. 106-107) at all levels of the agency enables it to "remain flexible, innovative and prepared to change its approach as new challenges emerge" (Handley et al., 2009, p. 25). The combination of spontaneous and intentional development is part of a process of "crafting strategy" (Westley et al., 2006, p. 141) where the agency continually seeks new opportunities. This strategy identifies what is working well and puts in place processes for continuing and extending these activities. It also identifies areas for development; catalysts for change are identified that involve harnessing natural change processes and that also build upon community initiatives that are already present in the community or in the agency; for example, using the ECEC center as a site for facilitating parenting education classes so that learning can take place in a familiar and safe environment.

Research on practice has become an integral part of the agency; this research is based on collaborative and cooperative inquiry (Munford & Sanders, 2003) and is influenced by developmental and empowerment evaluation methods and appreciative inquiry (Fetterman & Wandersman, 2005; Reed, 2007) where the method for inquiry is openly negotiated and where all participants share responsibility for the outcome of the inquiry (Handley et al., 2009, p. 37). At *Te Aroha Noa* the *Spinifex* metaphor reminds those involved to look below the surface to find the factors that support families to survive and grow and to find stability. Sharing stories of family and community life, focused interviews, focus groups, and observation of practice encounters and key events have all been effective research techniques for discovering what has made a positive difference in the lives of families and in the wider community. Staff in all of the agency's services document change processes and keep records of what has created positive change for families across generations and within their extended family network. Understanding kin connections and connections with support networks is important information that can assist families to explore creative change options. The agency is interested in understanding the outcomes of service delivery and the contribution an integrated approach that combines education programs, therapeutic intervention, and community development can make in enhancing the well-being of families. Theoretical ideas such as those derived from ecological perspectives, critical realism, and complexity theory assist the understanding of the dynamic interplay between a range of factors, including the relationship between place and community processes and how these are related to outcomes (Durie & Wyatt, 2007).

What has emerged as one of the key findings in this ongoing research endeavor, and has been documented in the feedback loops that form part of the action and reflection cycle, is that success requires the creative management of relationships at many levels, both within the agency and in the wider community (Handley et al., 2009, p. 34). Change begins with the formation of collaborative partnerships that are generative and provide the foundation for a sensitized gradual accumulative development that moves beyond crisis-related and problem-saturated work to integrated strengths-based work.

Everyone is able to contribute their expertise to change; local wisdom combined with the practice knowledge and experience of agency staff creates a foundation for transformative change for the families coming to the agency and for the wider community.

CONCLUSION

This chapter has presented the experiences of one community-based agency that has engaged with ongoing critical reflection and research in order to identify the key elements of practice that can create positive change for families. This agency has created an integrated service model that includes early childhood and adult education, practical support, therapeutic interventions, and community development. In essence *Te Aroha Noa* takes a *whole family* and *whole community* approach to practice. By forming collaborative relationships with families, agency staff come to deeply understand the challenges they face and also the resources and expertise that are available within family and community networks, and interventions are more effective as a result. Staff understand the importance of seeking out the diverse knowledge frameworks that will contribute to successful outcomes for children and families. They have learned to work at multiple levels and understand that change is synergistic and that long-term and that sustained outcomes begin with small, gradual, proximal outcomes (Berry et al., 2006; Handley et al., 2009). *Te Aroha Noa* has been able to effect change at the micro level with individuals and families while working on a wider community level to address intractable issues such as family violence. Staff across the agency have brought new resources into the community by forming relationships with government and nongovernmental organizations and have educated those in key decision-making roles about the important role community-based services can have in supporting the well-being of families. *Te Aroha Noa* is focused on opening up opportunities for families; the agency's clear vision of supporting families to have big dreams for themselves and for their children guides their endeavors to seek out new possibilities for growth and development for families and for the wider community.

REFERENCES

Archer, M. (2002). Realism and the problem of agency. *Journal of Critical Realism,* 5(1), 11–20.

Bell, M. (2007). Community-based parenting programmes: An exploration of the interplay between environmental and organizational factors in a Webster Stratton project. *British Journal of Social Work, 37,* 55–72.

Berry, M., Brandon, M., Chaskin, R., Fernandez, E., Grietens, H., Lightburn, A., McNamara, P. M.... & Zeira, A. (2006). Identifying sensitive outcomes of interventions in community-based centres. *International Journal of Child and Family Welfare, 9*(1–2), 2–10.

Bessarab, D., & Crawford, F. (2010). Aboriginal practitioners speak out: Contextualising child protection interventions. *Australian Social Work, 63*(2), 179–193.

Callaghan, G. (2008). Evaluation and negotiated order. *Evaluation, 14*(4), 399–411.

Dahlberg, G., Moss, P., & Pence, A. (2007). *Beyond quality in early childhood education and care: Languages of evaluation.* London: Routledge.

Duncan, J. (2008, August). *Early childhood centres as places for family resilience and social capital.* Presentation to the Treasury Series on Social Mobility, Wellington, NZ. Retrieved from www.treasury.govt.nz/publications /media.../tgls-duncan-pres.pdf

Duncan, B., Miller, S., & Sparks, J. (2004). *The heroic client: A revolutionary way to improve effectiveness through client-directed, outcome-informed therapy.* San Francisco, CA: Jossey-Bass.

Durie, R., & Wyatt, K. (2007). New communities, new relations: The impact of community organization on health outcomes. *Social Science & Medicine, 65*(9), 1928–1941.

Fetterman, D., & Wandersman, A. (2005). *Empowerment evaluation principles in practice.* New York: The Guildford Press.

Fook, J., & Gardner, F. (2007). *Practising critical reflection: A resource handbook.* Berkshire: Open University Press.

Freire, P. (1985). *The politics of education, culture, power and liberation.* Basingstoke: Macmillan.

Gardner, F., Fook, J., & White, S. (2006). Critical reflection: Possibilities for developing effectiveness in conditions of uncertainty. In F. Gardner, J. Fook & S. White (Eds.). *Critical reflection in health and social care* (pp. 228–240). Berkshire: Open University Press.

Gerald, R., & McDonald, E. (2010). Building community *within* the community: Government-community partnerships in the District of Columbia's child welfare system. *Social Work Now, 45,* 8–14.

Gilligan, R. (2004). Promoting resilience in child and family social work: Issues for social work practice. *Social Work Education, 23,* 93–104.

Gray, M., Coates, J., & Yellow Bird, M. (2008). Introduction. In M. Gray, J. Coates & M. Yellow Bird (Eds.). *Indigenous social work around the world: Towards culturally relevant education and practice* (pp. 1–10). Aldershot, England: Ashgate.

Halvorsen, A. (2009). What counts in child protection and welfare? *Qualitative Social Work, 8*(1), 65–81.

Handley, K., Horn, S., Kaipuke, R., Maden, B., Maden, E.,...Sanders J. (2009). *The Spinifex effect—A theory of change.* Wellington, New Zealand: The Families Commission.

Houston, S. (2010). Prising open the black box: Critical realism, action research and social work. *Qualitative Social Work, 9*(1), 73–91.

Hudson, C. (2000). At the edge of chaos—A new paradigm for social work? *Journal of Social Work Education, 36,* 215–230.

Liebenberg, L., & Ungar, M. (2009). Introduction: The challenges in researching resilience. In L. Liebenberg & M. Ungar (Eds.). *Researching resilience* (pp. 3–25). Toronto: University of Toronto Press.

Lightburn, A., & Warren-Adamson, C. (2006). Evaluating family centres: The importance of sensitive outcomes in cross-national studies. *International Journal of Child and Family Welfare, 9*(1–2), 11–25.

Mataira, P. (2002). Treaty partnering: Establishment of a charter for Māori community based programmes. *Te Komako, Social Work Review, 14*(2), 5–7.

May, H., & Mitchell, L. (2009). *Strengthening community-based early childhood education in Aotearoa New Zealand: Report of the Quality Public Early Childhood Education Project.* Wellington, NZ: NZEI Te Riu Roa.

Munford, R., & Sanders, J. (with Andrew, A., Butler, P., & Ruwhiu, L.) (2003). Action research with families/whānau and communities. In R. Munford & J. Sanders (Eds.). *Making a difference in families: Research that creates change* (pp. 93–112). Sydney: Allen and Unwin.

Munford, R., & Sanders, J. (2005). Working with families: Strengths-based approaches. In M. Nash, R. Munford & K. O'Donoghue (Eds.). *Social work theories in action* (pp. 158–173). London: Jessica Kingsley Publishers.

Munford, R., & Sanders, J. (2008). Assessment of families. In W. Rowe & L. A. Rapp-Paglicci (Eds.). *Comprehensive handbook of social work and social welfare: Social work practice* (pp. 399–422). USA: Hoboken, NJ: W. John Wiley & Sons Inc.

Munford, R., & Sanders, J. (2011). Embracing the diversity of practice: Indigenous knowledge and mainstream social work practice. *Journal of Social Work Practice, 25*(1), 63–77.

Munford, R., Sanders, J., & Maden, B. (2007). Blending whānau/family development, parent support and early childhood education programmes. *Journal of Social Policy, 32,* 72–86.

Munford, R., & Walsh-Tapiata, W. (2005). Community development principles into practice. In M. Nash, R. Munford & K. O'Donoghue (Eds.). *Social work theories in action* (pp. 97–112). London: Jessica Kingsley Publishers.

Reed, J. (2007). *Appreciative inquiry: Research for change.* Thousand Oaks, CA: Sage Publications.

Reeler, D. (n.d.) *A theory of social change and implications for practice, planning, monitoring and evaluation.* Cape Town, South Africa: Community Development Resource Association.

Ruch, G. (2005). Relationship-based practice and reflective practice: Holistic approaches to contemporary child care social work. *Child & Family Social Work, 10*(2), 111–123.

Ruwhiu, L. (2009). Indigenous issues in Aotearoa New Zealand. In M. Connolly & L. Harms (Eds.). *Social work: Contexts and practice* (pp. 107–120). South Melbourne, Victoria: Oxford University Press.

Sanders, J., & Munford R. (2010). *Working with families: Strengths-based approaches.* Wellington, NZ: Dunmore Publishing.

Smith, M. (2011). Reading Bauman for social work. *Ethics & Social Welfare, 5*(1), 2–17.

Westley, F., Zimmerman, B., & Patton, M. Q. (2006). *Getting to maybe: How the world is changed.* Toronto, ON: Random House.

CHAPTER 5

Building Communities: Begins in the Early Years

Judith Duncan

INTRODUCTION

Aotearoa New Zealand has been seen as leading the world in its contribution to the growth, development, and learning outcomes for children in Early Childhood Education and Care (ECEC) services for children under the age of five years (in Aotearoa New Zealand children enter compulsory schooling at five). Internationally, educationalists and scholars have been impressed by the diversity of services (both the range and the philosophies); the early childhood education national curriculum, *Te Whāriki*; and the governmental support for early childhood services (in funding, teacher qualifications, and regulations). The focus for much of the development of ECEC in Aotearoa New Zealand has been on improving *access* for children and their families; improving *participation* of children in quality ECEC, especially for children who are ethnic minorities or are seen as at risk; and increasing the *quality* of ECEC. While these three factors are universally agreed by New Zealand governments, how these are supported and enacted differ with each government and their distinctive political philosophies. For example, in the strategic ten-year plan for 2002–2012 the government, of the time, focused on increasing qualifications of teachers (targeted for 100 percent for 2012), improving access and participation through heavily subsidizing parent fees (as a first step to universally affordable ECEC), and developing an active research program to build up understanding around best teaching and learning in ECEC (Ministry of Education, 2002). The priorities were reshuffled with a change of government in 2008 (midway through the ten-year strategic plan) where *access* and *participation* were reshaped as targeted assistance for those most at risk (including ethnic minorities and children with special needs), and increasing group sizes of children to accommodate increased participation. The government also began a process of rethinking teacher qualifications, lowering the target for 2012 to 50 percent qualified teachers with infants and toddlers, and 80 percent with other two-year-olds, and questioning the need for ECEC-specific qualifications by removing the requirement for compulsory-sector teachers to have to reeducate to work in ECEC settings (Ministry of Education, 2011).

Alongside this discourse of *targeting* those *in need* or *at risk*, families and *whānau* (extended family) requiring additional support have also come under the spotlight. Aotearoa New Zealand governments have acknowledged, for some time, that more support should surround families and *whānau* and have looked to models of parent support that are culturally appropriate, as well as financially manageable. However, once again, how parents, family and *whānau* are supported differs with each government's philosophy. *Targeting at risk* versus *universal provisions for all* are the constant discursive battles in Aotearoa New Zealand, and the programs, which are supported, fit with one or other of these discourses. This is where ECEC services are positioned to bridge competing discursive positions and provide sustainability in a contested funding and ideological context for communities, families, *whānau*, and children.

This chapter argues that ECEC settings are the ideal places for supporting parents in their early years of parenting, for family development, and the creation of community. This is not a new perspective. Internationally ECEC centers have been seen as places of social support for families (Whalley & The Pen Green Centre Team, 2007), forums for democratic practices (Dahlberg & Moss, 2005), key support for working parents, and growing the employment opportunities for women (Callister & Podmore, 1995; Gornick, Meyers, & Ross, 1997). In Aotearoa New Zealand the playcentre model of combining parenting and ECEC in a parent-supervised ECEC setting provided a model that benefits both parents and child (Densem, & Chapman, 2000); kindergartens regularly integrated parent participation and parent education programs into their pedagogy (Duncan, 2009); and *Ngā Kohanga Reo* (Māori immersion language ECEC centers) have focused on family and *whānau* cultural revival and survival, building resilient Māori *whānau* who are strong in their language and culture (Pohatu,

Stokes, & Austin, 2006; Tamati, Hond-Flavell, Korewha, & the whānau of Te Kōpae Piripon, 2008). What *is* new is the idea that ECEC services are also ideally positioned as hubs of the community, to foster and support social capital, resilience, health, overall well-being, and connections for families with preschoolers.

Drawing on several research studies undertaken by the author (in collaboration with colleagues), this chapter explores the role of building and maintaining networks and communities for healthy personal, family and *whānau* relationships (Duncan, 2006, 2009; Duncan & Bowden, 2004; Duncan, Bowden, & Smith, 2005, 2006a, 2006b, 2006c; Duncan, Dalli, et al., 2006). Research has overwhelmingly demonstrated that strong communities and networks support strong families and *whānau,* and strong families and *whānau* have fewer health, social, and mental and emotional issues (that is, they are more resilient) (Bianchi & Robinson, 1997; Chamberlin, 1996; Eldridge, 1994; Putnam, 2000).

DISCURSIVE CONSIDERATIONS

The discussions presented in this chapter draw on the notion of discourse as used by Foucault (1971). Foucault discusses discourse in terms of its role in shaping the social world through the production of meaning, knowledge, and power relations, which, in turn, shape our notions of reality, truth, and self (Foucault, 1971, 1977, 1980, 1991; Gordon, 1980). The relevance, or importance, of discourses is that they work to tell us what is possible to speak at any given moment, who can speak, and with what authority. Discourses then act as sets of rules and behaviors and these become the norm, or what is acceptable and expected. They, in turn, become our *taken-for-granted ways of working* (Foucault, 1970, 1971, 1980). For Foucault, discourses do not merely reflect what already exists, but they actually work to create this reality (Foucault, 1974, cited in Ball, 1990, p. 2). Individuals act on the basis of their ideas about how the world should be. Within discursive fields (i.e., the arenas, institutions, or organizations where discourses are occurring) complex negotiations and struggles among the various discourses occur over the meanings to be given *truth* status. These are then incorporated into outcomes, such as state policy (Yeatman, 1990) or early childhood provisions and pedagogies (Duncan, 2001).

The contested field of ECEC provisions and pedagogies provides an example of how our *taken-for-granted ways of working* are the product of discourses, which shape what is understood to be the role and purpose of an ECEC service, and what is not accepted as its role or purpose. The use of such concepts in this chapter is to demonstrate how the notions of both ECEC and community have taken on discursive positions within Aotearoa New Zealand, which have worked on different temporal occasions to position centers in positive and constructive ways, restrictive and limited ways, or a mixture of both depending on the context.

RETHINKING EARLY CHILDHOOD EDUCATION AS THAT WHICH BUILDS AND SUPPORTS COMMUNITY

Commentators on early childhood education often *take for granted* ECEC services' role in supporting women to attend work (babysitting function), and in the compensatory gains for children in attending (particularly for disadvantaged children). Research has established that good quality early childhood education can contribute to ameliorating the effects of poverty and risk for children (Barnett, 1998; Smith, Grima, Gaffney, & Powell, 2000). Critiques of early childhood education cite its perceived damaging effects, particularly on brain development and on social abilities for the very young children who attend for long hours, as well as the harmful effects on parent-child attachment (Atwool, 2002; Belsky et al., 2007). Both sides of the debates surrounding early childhood education focus on either benefits or harm to the child, most often presented in isolation from the child's own contexts: that is, the child separated from their family or from a range of community experiences. Presenting ECEC as *child focused* and *child centered* is rooted in the pedagogical shifts that have occurred internationally in an attempt to ensure positive learning environments for children (Fleer, 2002). This approach is not without its critics, however (see Cannella, 1997). Such discursive approaches to ECEC run the risk of positioning ECEC as a *place for a child without their family.* While many ECEC programs discuss notions such as *partnership with parents* or *collaborations with families,* the daily experience of children in ECEC is often separated from the daily realities of their community and *whānau,* or their parents and their working life (Brennan, 2007).

While Aotearoa New Zealand has not developed the same range or intensity of fully integrated multi-agency services as in other European countries, there is a strong philosophy that mainstream early childhood education programs have a major role in supporting families. The early childhood curriculum guidelines, *Te Whāriki* (Ministry of Education, 1996), has *belonging* as one of its five major focus areas:

> The families of all children should feel that they *belong* and are able to participate in the early childhood education program and in decision-making. (Ministry of Education, 1996, p. 54) [author's emphasis]

The goal of *belonging* aims to encourage the development of connecting links between early childhood centers and families. These connections can be expressed in a variety of different ways, dependent on the philosophies of the ECEC centre. Often these links can be restricted to one-way conversations and miss the rich opportunities that *connecting* can offer all parties—the child, the family, the *whānau*, the teachers, and the wider community.

A child's learning and development depends not only on the ECEC environment they experience, but also on their home and the wider social and cultural environments. The coming together of children and families in ECEC services provides opportunities for addressing health and social issues. Building strong links between ECEC services, antenatal programs, parents and *whānau*, parenting programs, schools, and health and social services can also improve a child's educational achievements. International research demonstrates that ECEC services can, and do, help families develop supportive relationships/networks and in doing so influence the amount and quality of social capital available to families in times of crisis. Families should have access to personal, family, and community developmental programs and support services of high quality. ECEC centers can help families gain access to these forms of informal and formal support, and in so doing, assist families to build social capital and resilience.

Connectedness with others through being part of a community has been identified as essential for building and maintaining personal and familial well-being and belonging. Many researchers and authors in the field of resilience and social capital argue that it is the nature of interaction that

> enables people to build communities, to commit themselves to each other, and to knit the social fabric. A sense of belonging and the concrete experience of social networks (and the relationships of trust and tolerance that can be involved) can, it is argued, bring great benefits to people. (Encyclopedia www.infed.org)

For example:

> Trust between individuals thus becomes trust between strangers and
> trust of a broad fabric of social institutions; ultimately, it becomes a
> shared set of values, virtues, and expectations within society as a whole.
> Without this interaction, on the other hand, trust decays; at a certain
> point, this decay begins to manifest itself in serious social problems. The
> concept of social capital contends that building or rebuilding commu-
> nity and trust requires face-to-face encounters. (Beem, 1999, p. 20)

This *trust* discourse is very apparent between families and the staff in
the ECEC centers in the research cited in this chapter.

Social capital is defined as existing in the social relations, networks, and norms (of trust and reciprocity) that exist among parents/
caregivers, between parents/caregivers and their children, and between
members of immediate and extended family/kin/*whānau,* and in
their relationship with the institutions of the community (Giorgas,
2000), that is, *connectedness.* ECEC centers are already positioned
within communities—either geographically, culturally, or socially—
and offer real potential to challenge the isolation of the child-centered
pedagogical approach and the isolation of nuclear families (which are
often physically or emotionally separated from extended families or
cultural groups). Challenging the traditional discourse of ECEC as a
place only for children, early childhood staff and employers can position themselves as the *heart of each community* and build their practices around discourses that support social capital, family resilience,
community cohesion, and society wellness.

An Aotearoa New Zealand Example

In recognition of research that demonstrates the value of commu-
nity to social, educational, and cultural well-being, the New Zealand
Ministry of Education, together with the Ministry of Social
Development, funded a pilot program entitled *ECE Centre Based
Parent Support and Development Project* (2006–2010) (PSD), an ini-
tiative to

> develop the role of ECE centers as a community hub, or venue, for
> the provision of parent support. It is a pilot project aimed at help-
> ing government to better understand what works in parent support
> programs in [New Zealand]. The project is aimed at families at risk
> of poor health, education and social outcomes and who have children
> aged birth–3. (Ministry of Education, 2006)

This initiative funded 18 centers to trial different methods and approaches to support families. These new initiatives systematically included early childhood centers as part of wider family and community support. They followed international moves toward such teaching practices (Whalley, 2006), and recommendations in Aotearoa New Zealand research for increases in such practices (Duncan et al., 2006a, 2006b, 2006c). Until recently, having a social worker or a support worker, to engage with families, has not been a part of early childhood centers in Aotearoa New Zealand. However, the *Social Worker in Schools* (*SWiS*) has been a successful part of the New Zealand primary and intermediate school sector for some time. The focus of the social worker is to work with the *whole family* at the school, and to network within the school and with community agencies. This model is one that ECEC is beginning to introduce into its centers, but it is still far from a universal model. Thus the ECEC PSD initiative enabled different models of family support to be introduced and evaluated. These sites have provided examples for the rest of the ECEC sector. An evaluation of the PSD pilots identified that

> interviews with parents provided strong evidence that positive outcomes were achieved for participating parents. Parents learnt about a wide range of things from specific topics relating to parenting (such as dealing with challenging behaviours, toilet training, seat belt safety, sleeping) to general life skills (such as financial literacy, dealing with domestic violence). Parents reported that participating in these activities made an important contribution to improving their overall quality of family life. In particular, parents reported increased confidence in their parenting abilities, reduced social isolation, enhanced sense of belonging to the community and increased access to other services which resulted in them participating more meaningfully in their community. Children benefited from the programme through parents improving their parenting style and, in some instances, through increased access to ECE (which gave them access to quality learning opportunities and the chance to form relationships with a wider group of peers). (Martin Jenkins & Associates Limited, 2010, p. 4)

Importantly, the evaluation concluded:

> Perhaps the most significant benefit was the growing sense of "community" and belongingness fostered amongst participants. In addition, the programme provided opportunities to learn and grow parents' skills not merely in their role as parents, but also in their roles as members of the wider community. (Martin Jenkins & Associates Limited, 2010, p. 6)

EXAMPLES OF EARLY CHILDHOOD
EDUCATION SERVICES AS SOCIAL SUPPORT FOR
CHILDREN AND FAMILIES—RESHAPING AOTEAROA
NEW ZEALAND ECEC

The New Zealand government's *Agenda for Children* (2000) policy document called for research to address understanding around the impact of community on children:

> We need information about: The effect of communities and their nature and level of well-being on children, the extent to which a particular neighborhood affects outcomes; and the characteristics of communities and neighborhoods that have the greatest effect on outcomes. (Freeman, Quigg, Vass, & Broad, 2007, p. 7)

Over the last decade, I have been engaged in several research projects, with colleagues in Aotearoa New Zealand, where we have examined a variety of ECEC centers that have been attempting to be places of wider support for families, and *whānau,* and position themselves as an important part of wider social support systems within local communities and national contexts.[1] From investigating these ideas with parents, teachers, managers of ECEC services, support practitioners from governmental, health, social welfare, and educational agencies, and from observing children in centers, we have identified some key findings, which when implemented into ECEC services, would enable centers to offer a wider range of social supports for *all* children and families. The following examples are from research projects discussing how ECEC can become a key social hub for parents, families, and *whānau* and the discursive constructions that have shaped these examples:

1. Ministry of Social Development–funded study: *Early childhood centers and family resilience* (Duncan & Bowden, 2004; Duncan et al., 2005, 2006a, 2006b, 2006c)

This study investigated how ECEC centers supported family resilience in their everyday practices. Resilience was defined as

> the ability of an individual and family to appraise the demands of different situations and to apply a set of skills and knowledge that enable the individual or family to "cope" with and "recover" from significant adversity or stress, in ways that are not only effective, but may result

in increased ability to "respond" to and "protect" their families from future adversity. (Duncan et al., 2006a, p. 3)

Three ECEC centers in low-decile areas participated in the study: one each in the regions of Gisborne, Wellington, and Dunedin, including one full-time ECEC center and two kindergartens. The study involved in-depth observation in the centers and interviews with key participants. A total of 29 families were interviewed: 10 families from Dunedin, 11 families from Wellington, and 8 families from Gisborne. Twelve ECEC staff and 13 representatives of advisory support and social agencies, nominated by staff of the ECEC center as providing vital support for their center and families, were also interviewed.

2. New Zealand Teaching Learning and Research Initiative–funded study: *Two year-olds at kindergarten—Children's experiences and teachers' practices.* (Duncan, Dalli, et al., 2006)

This project investigated the experiences of under-three-year-olds and teachers' practices in New Zealand kindergartens. Historically, kindergartens have provided an ECEC environment for three- to five-year-olds. As enrollments and waiting lists have dropped, kindergartens have opened their door to children under three years of age, taking them into an environment that was often structured for older children in a larger group setting. In this project we worked alongside kindergarten teachers to explore the impact of this change on two-year-olds' learning experiences, and on teachers' practices generally. Using investigative qualitative research methods, we conducted case studies of 18 two-year-old children in four kindergartens, two in Dunedin and two in Wellington, over a two-year period. The kindergarten teachers reflected on the narrative observations of the case-study children and their own teaching practices with the two-year-olds in their kindergartens. Parents of the case-study children were involved in reflective discussions of their child's narrative observations. The same case-study teachers met with other teachers in their geographical regions for five cluster group meetings over the two years, to explore the research questions and to support best practice with two-year-olds across their regions' kindergartens. In addition, we also conducted a national survey of associations about their policies and strategic planning related to under-three-year-olds in kindergarten.

3. New Zealand Ministry of Education—Centre of Innovation: *What counts as support for families? Citizens nursery and*

preschool in Dunedin. (Citizens Preschool and Nursery Centre of Innovation, 2008)

The staff from the *Citizens Preschool and Nursery Centre of Innovation* (now called *The Methodist Mission Early Learning Centre*) participated in a Ministry of Education three-year research project with Michael Gaffney and myself from the *Children's Issues Centre* at the University of Otago. The action research focused on the support given to families/*whānau* and the difference it makes for children's learning and development. Staff looked at what support works for families in the Nursery center (0–two-year-olds), using an investigation around their teaching practices, the introduction of a social worker into the teaching team, and the management practices of the centre.

4. University of Otago–funded study: *New Zealand kindergartens— Just another early childhood service or a distinctive part of New Zealand culture* (Duncan, 2009)?

The data reported here is from interviews from a larger national study looking at current kindergarten culture within the early childhood sector of this century. Sixty-one parents from across Aotearoa New Zealand were asked what they liked about kindergarten and what, if any, changes they would like to see in the kindergarten provision for their child and then for "kindergarten" as a national service.

Together these studies provide robust findings on the processes of social support for families through attendance at an early childhood center. While the centers represent community-based centers, and no private or corporate-owned centers are included in the studies reported here, the findings demonstrate discursive practices—new *taken for granted ways of working*—that all services and centers could position themselves within, irrespective of status of ownership (i.e., whether public, private, or corporate-led). Three discourses dominated the interview data from these four studies:

1. belonging and bonding;
2. networks and linking with others;
3. ECEC as the builder of community.

The resulting discursive practices involve a significant shift from perceiving ECEC as *only for children* or as *child centered* to prioritizing families, *whānau*, and community alongside work with children.

Discourse One: Belonging and Bonding

The discursive practices of belonging and bonding focused on the ECEC center's providing an environment where families could build *close* relationships/ties with staff and other families, on which families typically could rely on a day-to-day basis.

Almost all of the families, across the four studies, identified that their ECEC was somewhere they felt their child was safe, and where they felt a sense of belonging for themselves and their child. They, and several support agencies from the Duncan et al. (2006a) study, described their centers as warm, inviting, and friendly. For example:

> **Parent #11**: They are very welcoming. Like when you walk in the gate and you walk in the door, they greet every child by name and that child is made to feel quite special. And my kid, she gets quite embarrassed, but she loves it, absolutely loves it. The fact that someone would single her out and say "Hello [child's name]" you know, that makes her feel quite good, and makes us feel good. Like it makes you feel part of the [center] really. (Duncan et al., 2006a, p. 69)

Taking a genuine interest in the lives of family members was a strategy that was identified as helping families to feel welcome, supported, and safe about leaving their children at the early childhood center. For example, taking an interest in the activities of children that occur at home and attempting to link these with their experiences at the early childhood center was a daily practice by the early childhood staff. Similarly, the relationships that the staff had built up with the children were one of the main reasons that the parents felt good about the center and why other siblings were attending, or had attended, the center. These relationships took much pressure off parents, who saw the center as a place where they could relax about leaving their child, where they knew that the staff understood their child's unique needs, and where the environment was safe and designed for children. This was well expressed by this parent:

> **Parent #7**: But what really convinced me [to leave my child] was the teacher, [who] was a primary caregiver to [child], picked him up, and gave him a big kiss. And I thought "I just want someone who is going to love him. Someone who is going to teach him and care for him"...So it was that feeling it was the right place. He was happy and I was happy. (Duncan et al., 2006a, p. 69)

Across all the four studies parents and staff of the ECEC centers talked about the importance of trusting, caring, and stable relationships between early childhood staff and families. These relationships were the basis for building the sense of belonging.

Belonging was as important for other family members as it was for the children. A sense of belonging was needed for the bonding to occur for both the children and the family to, and with members of, the ECEC setting. As the ECEC staff identified, the child is part of a family, and to build a relationship with the child also means developing a relationship with the carers and the significant people in the life of that child. Actively promoting the family as part of the center community was an important philosophical goal of the all the ECEC centers in these studies.

DISCOURSE TWO: NETWORKS AND LINKING WITH OTHERS

Connecting with the community was repeatedly remarked on by the parents in all the four research studies—both rural and urban parents across Aotearoa New Zealand. A good relationship with what the kindergarten teachers described as the *wider community of the kindergarten* was seen by the teachers as important because of the opportunities it created for the ECEC center to connect with others beyond the child's immediate family or *whānau* (Duncan, 2009). In the Duncan, Dalli et al. (2006) study, when we asked the parents about the reasons that they had chosen the kindergarten for their child, being part of their local community and building up relationships was a key factor in several of the parents' reasons. All the parents discussed that they had chosen the kindergarten for their child for reasons of making social contacts for their children. They also talked about the importance of children making friends that they would go to school with and how good it was for the children to form relationships outside the family. Several families had chosen their particular kindergarten because of existing links with the community, for example, through church contacts, or from attending a shared playgroup (Duncan, Dalli, et al., 2006, p. 84).

Connecting with others and building links in the community was continually raised by the parents:

> **Urban Parent**: In a kindergarten situation you meet other parents and all of a sudden you start, you know, having play dates and stuff after [kindergarten] and you help out with each other's children if you can't pick them up. (Duncan, 2009, p. 6)

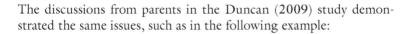

The discussions from parents in the Duncan (2009) study demonstrated the same issues, such as in the following example:

> **Urban Parent**: But it's more community, I think [kindergarten]'s more community.
>
> **Interviewer**: So you like the fact that there's community involvement?
>
> **Urban parent**: Definitely yeah. Well 'cause, you know, I moved up from [different geographical area] and like you get to meet everybody, aye. (Duncan, 2009, p. 6)

These features of the kindergarten, as places where parents can meet and connect together, cannot be underestimated. They play an important role both for individual families, as well as for communities, by building social capital (as has been found in other studies; see Powell, Cullen, Adams, Duncan, & Marshall, 2005).

Community and family isolation can place individuals in a heightened risk situation and decrease population health and educational achievement (Putnam, 2000). The ECEC centers in these studies played an important role in helping to combat the isolation of families in the community and by working toward building micro-communities (Scott, 2000). They also offered a safe, stable, protective environment for families who may live in high-risk situations and community environments. The very nature of ECEC centers just *being there* for families was a major theme recurring through all of the interviews with early childhood staff, support providers, and families:

> **Agency Provider #3**: There is a sense of being part of the community and meeting other people. You know, you get to meet other people who have got kids the same age to some extent or other and maybe also someone that you can talk to if you are feeling really stressed or freaked out about something in particular and you don't really know where else to turn. (Duncan et al., 2006c, p. 85)

In my research with kindergarten parents (Duncan, 2009), for the parents who had relocated to areas and had not known people, the link through the kindergarten proved to be a key for their families, both for general friendships but also for those times when family and family members are often depended on for support, such as in times of illness or at the birth of a new baby. For example:

> **Urban Parent**: We didn't know—we came here ... but I mean it's like we didn't even know anyone here really and—and we've met so many

friendly people, like all our friends now are from the [Kindergarten] so. When the baby was born—'cause I was—it really hit home because so many people came by and, you know, like dropped off, you know, a meal or whatever and the baby was in hospital for a few days and just to support us during that time was—it was amazing...it was great. (Duncan, 2009, p. 7)

Parents regularly used terms such as *networking, linking,* and *getting to know people* when talking about themselves and their kindergarten, and *making friends* when talking about their children:

Urban Parent: I think...like there's the sense of community not just—just being part of a family, which I think's important, but the fact that you're networking, you might just walk home with another group of kids, you know, the same direction or...you might meet up at the park and the kids—kids just feel like they—they know other people. And I mean my child care, because I don't have family here, are usually my [kindergarten] friends. (Duncan, 2009, p. 7)

Parents, in the kindergarten studies in particular, commented on the amount of parent involvement encouraged at their centers. Several of the parents saw huge gains and value in being involved in their kindergarten, not only for the benefit of contributing to keeping the kindergarten funded and supported, but in the enjoyment and pride that their children expressed in having their parent/s involved at their kindergarten.

Urban Parent: It's all about how community-based it is but also that opportunity to—even though it can be a—it's just that need for con-tribution, you know, physical—you know like whether it's grounds and I think it's kind of good for the kids to see you having that kind of input...and you know you're welcome. (Duncan, 2009, p. 7)

And:

Urban Parent: I like the fact that, you know, we have to do the things like take home the washing or go on those big trips or do fundraising, it kind of brings—you sort of have a greater sense of community...It's less a service and more of a community, that's how I feel about it. (Duncan, 2009, p. 7)

Across the studies we identified that the ECEC centers (whether they were kindergartens or childcare centers) have four main structural opportunities that increase participation by parents and so help to develop connections:

1. dropping-off and picking-up time;
2. participation in the program;
3. attending social events;
4. becoming a committee member.

Participating in the program appears to be an important variable in making contacts through the center. It appeared from the reporting of the participants across all the four studies that the level of involvement that parents had within the ECEC center greatly affected the amount and type of relationships they developed with other families. For example, those parents who reported that their level of involvement was restricted to dropping their children off, or who did not want a great deal of involvement with their ECEC center, tended not to report having made friendships or having developed relationships with other families through the ECEC center. This was in contrast with others who reported having some, to a considerable amount of, involvement in the center and having formed friendships and relationships with other parents within the ECEC center setting and those that extended beyond that setting.

Those who were unable to participate in the program during the day identified other times that offered them opportunities to connect with others. Walking to, dropping off, and picking up children from the ECEC center enabled several parents to form acquaintances and friendships with other parents/caregivers:

> **Parent #16**: I have made friends who I wouldn't have met under any other conditions except from the [center]. And because they live locally, it's very easy to have a true friendship. You start out just chatting and walking together...and go to their houses, and they come to my house, and it's the children that know each other. It's something that I always thought was important that you attend the facilities in your neighbourhood. That you don't live here and go to school across town. And it's for those very reasons; it creates, I don't know, a feeling of community, that you count, that you belong, that people notice you, that you notice them. (Duncan et al., 2006a, p. 74)

Center-organized social events and activities (e.g., fundraisers, working bees, cultural nights, shared meals) appeared to be a successful means of connecting families. These gatherings allowed parents/ caregivers to share information and knowledge, discuss issues, raise concerns, and seek help. In several cases providing a point of contact and center for parents with common interests to meet led to parents/caregivers forming relationships and becoming involved in other activities outside of the ECEC setting. This was identified as particularly helpful for parents who have difficulty making friendships and who feel they are isolated within their community:

> **Parent #11**: It's kind of like team building, you know, like you become a team, a culture in itself. Yeah, and you feel like you are part of that team and you all get together. I mean no-one really wants to come along to watch the kids ride their bikes round the cones, but the kids love it and you go along. Like, it's the same with the garage sale, you know, you end up, it's like camaraderie forms. Quite often, unfortunately it's only a small group, you know, you are not talking about 60 parents because you know that never happens but, you know, it spreads the net. I mean it's essential really, because you sort of, you come in here as an individual, you know and you leave as an individual. Whereas in situations like that you see that you are actually part of a team and it's sort of a bigger group of people and you are all working towards the same aim. You know educating your child, and hopefully your kid has a very nice time while they are here you know. Those things are really important I think. (Duncan et al., 2006, p. 74)

In the Citizens Nursery the teachers and social worker planned family events to ensure communication opportunities for the families. The teaching team held a *Celebration for Families* evening as a way to strengthen their relationships with the families enrolled at the center and to enable families to develop a stronger connection with the center as a community. These celebrations were held once a year and involved both the Nursery and Preschool of the ECEC complex. The aim was for families to develop their own connection with the environment where their children spent their days, and to feel that they were part of the family environment at Citizens. The evenings were rolling events from 3.30 to 6.30 p.m. so that parents could participate at the time that suited them. Entertainment and activities (bubble machine, story teller, face-painting, clay work) occurred during this time. Food and drinks were always available in both the Preschool and Nursery. The projector screen was set up in the Preschool so that parents could watch an ongoing screen show of photos of the children. Parents' and grandparents' comments demonstrated the success of these evenings:

- what a wonderful environment for my grandchild;.
- really enjoyed the screen show of the pictures and appreciated seeing the pictures of our children;

- it was great to see people come to this event;
- great food and it just kept coming;
- when is the next one? (Citizens Preschool and Nursery Centre of Innovation, 2008, p. 90)

The overwhelming responses from parents across the four studies discussed here acknowledge how the ECEC services offered the parents a way of joining the community and facilitated friendships that parents were able to form with others at their ECEC center.

DISCOURSE THREE: ECEC AS THE BUILDER OF COMMUNITY

All the participants identified the provision of an ECEC center in the community as a key form of family support. This cannot be overemphasized in its importance to families and their communities.

> **Parent #18**: Well, it's a connection thing really. Just, it makes me feel that, y'know I'm not an island…I think that anything that makes you feel part of your community, that makes even my sister's family feel part of the flow of what happens in [city], and that involves the kindergarten, the school, the [suburb] shops, the library. They're all as familiar to my niece as they are to my own children. (Duncan et al., 2006a, p. 51)

We note that if *no* other factor had been identified as important to support families, the mere presence and availability of the centers in their communities was a major factor in the families' lives across all of the four studies.

The parents identified that access to a quality early childhood service, in particular, provided parents and family members with much needed *time-out* from parenting demands. Time-out from parenting demands while their child was at a center enabled parents to undertake other tasks that were needed for family functioning, time-out from the stresses of parenting, and time to meet their own needs. This support impacts not only on the individual, but also on the way the individual interacted with others in the family; for example, allowing mothers to rest and then spend more quality time with the child. The support provided by the ECEC centers also enabled parents to recharge and look after their own well-being so that they could better provide for their family. It also allowed parents time to focus on the other family members who may have required special attention (e.g., those with special needs and illnesses).

Parent #18: When I was pregnant, it was...I could sleep every after-noon, knowing that [eldest child] was y'know occupied, busy, safe, having fun, and I wheel [son] home in the buggy. By the time we got home he was ready to be popped into bed, and then I could sleep—every afternoon for two hours. And that was a lifesaver actually, a life-saver. And to know it was going to happen every afternoon and...to rest...And it certainly it meant that the whole family benefited from the fact that I was, had enough energy to keep going for the rest of the day. (Duncan et al., 2006a, p. 51)

Having a space and place that was always there in the community, *for* the community, and to work *with* the community builds and cre-ates a community within and supports a community outside, and around, the ECEC service. Without a doubt, when put together, these four studies provide narratives to support ECEC as essential places for creating well-being among children, families, *whānau,* and communities.

Conclusion

The studies presented in this chapter collectively demonstrate a dis-cursive position for an early childhood center to be at the heart of any community. The ECEC centers are where the discursive practices (*taken-for-granted ways of working*) are centered around the *whānau,* their children, and the community. In the ECEC centers in the four studies explored in this chapter, early childhood staff focused on building networks, establishing family links, and enhancing micro-communities. Arguably, discursive positions for ECEC to be at the heart of any community have been demonstrated through these four studies:

- families felt comfortable approaching the ECEC centers and staff;
- the ECEC centers were able to reach out to families from an accessible, nonstigmatized setting (unlike social welfare ser-vices, or other settings that were identified as focusing on family deficits);
- the ECEC centers' support was *universal* and not *targeted at a risk group*—it was offered to all families, so those who needed it most could avoid feeling targeted and stigmatized;
- the ECEC centers' support goals were about supporting chil-dren and supporting families from a strengths-based model rather than from a deficit or abuse-prevention model.

Together, the research studies have identified that ECEC settings can, by everyday pedagogical practices, support extraordinary outcomes for children, families, and *whānau*. Changing the discourses surrounding ECEC from solely *child-centered* and building on the resultant new discursive practices where ECEC is a *community and family/whānau* service alongside an educational experience for the children, the connectedness and well-being of and for communities will be well supported.

It is time for ECEC staff, management, and settings to explore the key role they play in being the *heart of the community* and the positive impact they can have in supporting and building communities that will last long after the child, and the family, ceases to attend the ECEC setting.

Notes

I wish to acknowledge the funding and support from the following organizations and funding grants that made the research discussed in this chapter possible: New Zealand Ministry of Social Development, New Zealand Ministry of Education (Centres of Innovation), New Zealand Teaching and Learning Research Initiative Funding, University of Otago Research Grant, and a University of Otago Humanities Research Grant.

1. For full discussion of the studies used for these findings see: Citizens Preschool and Nursery Centre of Innovation (2008); Duncan, Bowden, & Smith (2006); and Duncan (2009).

References

Atwool, N. (2002). Attachment and the developing child. *Childrenz Issues, 6*(2), 21–43.

Ball, S. J. (1990). *Foucault and education: Disciplines and knowledge.* London: Routledge.

Barnett, W. S. (1998). Long-term effects on cognitive development and school success. In W. S. Barnett & S. S. Boocock (Eds.). *Early care and education for children in poverty: Promises, programs, and long-term results* (pp. 11–44). Albany, NY: State University of New York Press.

Beem, C. (1999). *The necessity of politics. Reclaiming American public life.* Chicago, IL: University of Chicago Press.

Belsky, J., Vandell, D. L., Burchinal, M., Clarke-Stewart, K. A., Mc Cartney, K., Owen, M. T., & the NICHD Early Child Care Research Network. (2007). Are there long-term effects of early child care? *Child Development, 78*(2), 681–701.

Bianchi, S., & Robinson, J. (1997). "What did you do today?" Children's use of time, family composition, and the acquisition of social capital. *Journal of Marriage and the Family, 59*(2), 332–344.

Brennan, M. (2007). Beyond child care—How else could we do this? Sociocultural reflections on the structural and cultural arrangements of contemporary Western child care. *Australian Journal of Early Childhood, 32*(1), 1–9.

Callister, P., & Podmore, V. N. (1995). *Striking a balance: Families, work and early childhood education.* Wellington, NZ: New Zealand Council for Educational Research.

Cannella, G. S. (1997). *Deconstructing early childhood education. Social justice and revolution.* New York: Peter Lang.

Chamberlin, R. W. (1996). "It takes a whole village": Working with community coalitions to promote positive parenting and strengthen families. *Pediatrics, 98*(4), 803–807.

Citizens Preschool and Nursery Centre of Innovation. (2008). *Collaborations: Teachers and a family whānau support worker in an early childhood setting. Final report for Centre of Innovation Research (2005–2007).* Retrieved from http://www.educate.ece.govt.nz/Programmes/CentresOfInnovation.aspx

Dahlberg, G., & Moss, P. (2005). *Ethics and politics in early childhood education.* London: Falmer Press.

Densem, A., & Chapman, B. (2000). *Learning together: The playcentre way* (Revised ed.). Auckland, NZ: New Zealand Playcentre Federation.

Duncan, J. (2001). *Restructuring lives: Kindergarten teachers and the education reforms 1984–1996.* A thesis submitted for the degree of Doctor of Philosophy, University of Otago, Dunedin, NZ.

Duncan, J. (2006). Collaborations between New Zealand early childhood centres and community resources. *Childrenz Issues, 10*(2), 14–19.

Duncan, J. (2009). Aotearoa New Zealand kindergarten parents reflecting on kindergarten: 2006–2007. *The Open Education Journal, 2,* 1–10.

Duncan, J., & Bowden, C. (2004). Promoting stress-resilient families, positive parenting practices and experiences: A vision of educare. *Childrenz Issues, 8*(2), 41–44.

Duncan, J., Bowden, C., & Smith, A. B. (2005). Reviewing and rethinking parent support and parent education opportunities in New Zealand. *New Zealand Annual Review of Education, 14,* 153–170.

Duncan, J., Bowden, C., & Smith, A. B. (2006a). *Early childhood centres and family resilience.* Report prepared for the Ministry of Social Development. Retrieved from http://www.msd.govt.nz/about-msd-and-our-work/publications-resources/evaluation/early-childhood-centres-and-family-resilience/

Duncan, J., Bowden, C., & Smith, A. B. (2006b). A gossip or a good yak? Reconceptualising parent support in early childhood centre based programmes. *International Journal of Early Years Education, 14*(1), 1–13.

Duncan, J., Bowden, C., & Smith, A. B. (2006c). Aotearoa New Zealand Early Childhood Centres and Family Resilience: Reconceptualising relationships. *International Journal of Equity and Innovation in Early Childhood, 4*(2), 79–90.

Duncan, J., Dalli, C., Becker, R., Butcher, M., Foster, K., Hayes, K., ... Walker, W. (2006). *Under three-year-olds in kindergarten: Children's experiences and teacher's practices. Report prepared for the Teaching and Learning Research Initiative.* Retrieved from http://www.tlri.org.nz/under-three -year-olds-kindergarten-children%E2%80%99s-experiences-and -teachers%E2%80%99-practices

Eldridge, D. (1994) Developing coherent community support networks. *Family Matters, 37,* 56–59.

Fleer, M. (2002). *Journeying back to the roots of sociocultural theory: Rebuilding the theoretical foundations of early childhood education.* Unpublished paper, Canberra University.

Foucault, M. (1970). *The order of things: An archaeology of the human sciences.* London: Routledge.

Foucault, M. (1971). Orders of discourse. *Social Science Information, 10*(2), 7–30.

Foucault, M. (1977). *Discipline and punish* (Alan Sheridan, Trans.). London: Penguin Books.

Foucault, M. (1980). *The History of Sexuality* (Robert Hurley, Trans.). New York: Pantheon Books.

Foucault, M. (1991). Politics and the study of discourse. In G. Burchell, C. Gordon, & P. Miller (Eds.), *The Foucault effect: Studies in governmentality* (pp. 53–72). London: Harvester: Wheatsheaf.

Freeman, C., Quigg, R., Vass, E., & Broad, M. (2007). *The changing geographies of children's lives: A study of how children in Dunedin use their environment.* Dunedin. NZ: Department of Geography, University of Otago.

Giorgas, D. (2000, July). *Community formation and social capital in Australia.* Seventh Australian Institute of Family Studies Conference, Sydney.

Gordon, C. (1980). *Power/Knowledge: Selected interviews and other writings, 1972–1977: Michel Foucault.* Hemel Hempstead: The Harvester Press.

Gornick, J. C., Meyers, M. K., & Ross, K. E. (1997). Public policies and the employment of mothers: A cross-national study. *Social Science Quarterly, 79*(1), 35–54.

Martin Jenkins & Associates Limited. (2010). *Early Childhood Education Centre-based Parent Support and Development, Final Report.* Wellington, NZ: Martin Jenkins & Associates Limited.

Ministry of Education. (1996). *Te Whāriki: Early Childhood Curriculum. He whāriki mātauranga mō ngā mokopuna o Aotearoa.* Wellington, NZ: Learning Media.

Ministry of Education. (2002). *Pathways to the Future: Ngā Huarahi Arataki. A 10-year strategic plan for early childhood education.* Wellington, NZ: Ministry of Education.

Ministry of Education. (2006). *Centre-based parent support and development guidelines.* Retrieved from http://www.minedu.govt.nz

Ministry of Education. (2011). *Annual early childhood report*—July 2010. Retrieved from http://www.educationcounts.govt.nz/statistics/ece/55413/licensed_services_and_licence-exempt_groups/annual-ece-summary-report-2010

Pohatu, H. R., Stokes, K., & Austin, H. (2006). *Te Ohonga Ake o Te Reo. The re-awakening of Māori language: An investigation of kaupapa-based actions and change. Te Kōhanga Reo o Pūau Te Moananui a Kiwa. Ngā Mahi Auaha (Centre of Innovation) 2003–2006*. Auckland: Te Kōhanga Reo o Pūau Te Moananui a Kiwa.

Powell, K., Cullen, J., Adams, P., Duncan, J., & Marshall, K. (2005). *The effect of adult playcentre participation on the creation of social capital in local communities*. Report prepared for the New Zealand Playcentre Federation. Wellington, NZ: New Zealand Playcentre Federation.

Putnam, R. (2000). *Bowling alone: The collapse and revival of American community*. New York: Simon & Schuster.

Smith, A. B., Grima, G., Gaffney, M., & Powell, K. (2000). *Early childhood education: Literature review report to Ministry of Education*. Dunedin, NZ: Children's Issues Centre.

Scott, D. (2000, November). *Building communities that strengthen families: Elements of effective approaches*. Australian Institute of Family Studies Seminar Paper, at AIFS, Australia.

Tamati, A., Hond-Flavell, E., Korewha, H., & the whānau of Te Kōpae Piripono. (2008). *Ko koe kei tēnā kīwai, ko au kei tēnei kīwai o te kete (You carry your handle and I'll carry my handle, of our kete). Centre of Innovation Final Report*. New Plymouth, NZ: Te Kōpae Piripono.

Whalley, M. (2006). Leadership in integrated centres and services for children and families—A community development approach. *Childrenz Issues, 10*(2), 8–13.

Whalley, M., & The Pen Green Centre Team. (2007). *Involving parents in their children's learning* (2nd ed.). London: Paul Chapman Publishing.

Yeatman, A. (1990). *Bureaucrats, technocrats, femocrats*. Sydney: Allen and Unwin.

CHAPTER 6

Family and Community Perspectives: Voices from a Qualitative Statewide Study in the Southwest United States

Jamie Patrice Joanou, Dawna Holiday, and Beth Blue Swadener

INTRODUCTION

This chapter draws from the family and community case-study component of a longitudinal, mixed-method evaluation of a statewide initiative for children birth to age five and their families in Arizona, United States. Unlike most of the chapters in this volume, we situate family and community engagement in a different context, as we take a statewide perspective, drawing from a qualitative study of diverse families, early childhood education and care service providers, and children in an attempt to foreground their voices and perspectives in a large-scale, primarily quantitative, evaluation project. Just as many early years programs and service providers seek to involve parents in more culturally inclusive and authentic ways, the project from which data for the chapter are drawn also attempts to respect the views of parents from a wide range of backgrounds and life experiences. The narratives of nearly 70 families and 110 care and service providers and community leaders convey perspectives that can be informative to early childhood programs both in the United States and beyond. They also provide a unique window into ways in which programs serving young children and their families can be more responsive to a range of issues that families face in the current economic and socio-political climate.

An interdisciplinary research team from three public Arizona universities is conducting the overall evaluation within which this study is situated and is charged with determining the impacts of the statewide initiative over time on the educational and health outcomes for young children, birth to age five, and their families in Arizona. This initiative is also looking at how the programs and services it funds are impacting both capacity and quality in the early childhood service delivery system. Finally, the statewide initiative seeks to ensure a comprehensive answer to the overarching questions: What impact is there on the lives of young children and their families when the state supports new and expanded initiatives in early childhood care, health, and education? Are children healthy and ready for school? Do families have access to high-quality early childhood services?

Nested within the larger longitudinal evaluation, the purpose of this qualitative study is to address issues of access, cultural relevance of programs, and other more subtle issues in the availability, affordability, visibility, quality, utilization, and satisfaction with early childhood care and health services available to families across the state. This study is a key component of the overall evaluation and serves to more holistically portray the experiences of Arizona's children and their families, as well as views of providers of an array of services and support for families with young children. Qualitative research methods are employed (individual semi-structured interviews and focus groups) to elicit in-depth information from primary caregivers (including parents, guardians, and others caring for young children), providers (professionals providing a variety of services to families with young children), and children before and after they enter kindergarten. Through twice-yearly interviews, this study was designed to offer rich family and provider data that speak directly to the experiences of families in Arizona as they reach out for support in raising their young children. We believe the incorporation of qualitative methodologies, in an evaluation of this nature, is essential for contextualizing the complex variables associated with children's well-being, early learning, care, health, and various support systems (Graue & Walsh, 1998; Hatch, 2007; Merriam, 1998).

In this chapter we share examples of ways in which early childhood program evaluations, as well as other longitudinal early childhood research projects, whether small or larger scale, can better include parent and community perspectives. We touch on the study briefly, but most of the chapter focuses on what parents and providers have shared about a range of issues affecting their lives (e.g., support systems, child and health care, communication, collaboration, and a more seamless and better-funded early years system). This chapter utilizes a "funds of knowledge" perspective (Gonzalez, Moll, & Amanti, 2004; González, Wyman, & O'Connor, in press), which refers to a body of research and practices that "for two decades has engaged with the knowledge and skill sets available in the households of students" (González et al., in press, p. 481). We also resist *at risk* or *pathologizing* constructions of families (Heydon & Iannacci, 2008; Swadener & Lubeck, 1995). Taking a strengths-based approach is critical in studies such as this one, particularly given our sampling strategy to oversample under-represented populations or communities. We conclude by situating our findings in a discussion of globalized neoliberal policies in early childhood and how bringing the direct voices of primary caregivers and providers into state-level planning can address issues that matter to families and honor their funds of knowledge.

Design and Methods

The participants in this study are primary caregivers, providers, and children. "Primary caregivers" refers to those persons who are the primary source of care to their young children. The primary caregiver participants include parents (both biological and adoptive), mothers, fathers, grandparents, and guardians. Providers are those persons within the community who provide, plan, and administer services to young children and their families. The child participants in this study are the children of primary caregiver participants between the ages of four and six, who are preparing to enter kindergarten or who have just entered kindergarten. Discussion of child data is beyond the scope of this chapter. For each of these groups, we solicited and garnered participation in communities in the northern, central, and southern part of the state, including rural and urban communities, border communities, and tribal communities. We were also mindful to recruit primary caregivers from a variety of racial, ethnic and religious backgrounds, family structures (e.g., two-parent, single-parent, same-sex, grandparents raising children), and socioeconomic levels. Similarly, in a state with a large Spanish-speaking population, we recruited Spanish-speaking participants.

The participating providers were selected from six categories: umbrella agencies providing multiple services for young children and families; childcare; health care (professionals specializing in a variety of areas); early education, including programs focused on special needs; family support; and community leaders (nominated by local providers). These participants included providers affiliated both with programs funded by the initiative and with programs not receiving funding. We took care to include in our sample providers who provide services to culturally and linguistically diverse communities. Sampling plans were also sensitive to factors including representativeness (providers from programs, organizations or agencies that represent a wide range of types of services and include both small and large agencies), role of provider (e.g., both direct-service providers and program administrators), and geographic location. These providers participated in an individual interview and focus group annually.

Through the incorporation of parent, provider, and child perspectives, particularly those from groups that are typically underrepresented in research and evaluation, we sought to better listen and respond to diverse voices in our state. The participants in this study are more than research subjects, as the design for this qualitative portion of the evaluation is very much participant driven. Primary caregivers, in particular, help to determine the pertinent and salient themes that will be discussed in consecutive interviews, allowing our parent involvement in this study to be both sustained and authentic. This chapter focuses on primary caregiver and stakeholder perspectives, and does not include findings from the children's interviews.

Early Childhood Policy and Provision in the United States and Arizona

Early childhood policies and public provision for families have been described in ways that range from a *patchwork* of services to *antifamily*, reflecting the lack of universal provision for children and families seen in many welfare states of Western Europe, Canada, and Oceana. While *Head Start*, a national preschool and family support program, continues to enjoy bipartisan support, in the United States, childcare is considered by most policymakers and much of the public to be a private issue for families to solve. Given the plethora of research documenting the positive impacts of early childhood education, some of the neoliberal policies of the United States have focused on strategies to expand access to quality early learning and parent education approaches. The rationale for these initiatives are typically instrumental, reflecting a cost-benefit perspective versus a child-rights-based rationale. As the only nation over 1 million in population yet to sign the United Nations Convention on the Rights of the Child, the United States is unique in its lack of systematic provisions for children.

Within this broader context, the patchwork of early education and care in the United States includes an array of private, for-profit and non-profit childcare and preschool programs, regulated family child-care (homes), and nonregulated *kith and kin* care, in which friends, family, or neighbors care for children. There are also *wrap-around* childcare services that may start with preschool, such as *Head Start* or other part-day public programs, and extend into elementary schools as before- and after-school care. Childcare and early education are also very stratified based on class and race/ethnicity.

It is important to offer some context, both of the state and of the project, for readers less familiar with the US Southwest and the focus state of Arizona, in order to contextualize the findings summarized in this chapter. Arizona is a *younger* state than many in the United States and has a history of being on contested land, with 22 federally recognized tribal nations and having been part of northern Mexico prior to 1853. It has strong Libertarian and conservative political forces and has been described as an "epicenter of human rights," particularly immigrant rights (West, 2011). With English-only legislation and some of the harshest policies regarding immigrant detention and deportation in the United States, Arizona is also a state that has a concentrated population in only three urban centers, with the largest, Maricopa County in which Phoenix is located, housing 65 percent of the state's population. Arizona is known for its beautiful and stark desert and mountain scenery, including the Grand Canyon, and has more area than any other state that is classified as *frontier* land.

When compared to other states in the nation, Arizona falls behind in education and health care for its residents. Arizona ranks forty-ninth out of 50 states in per-pupil expenditures (Children's Defense Fund, 2011), and thirty-ninth in overall child well-being (Annie E. Casey Foundation, 2010). State budget cuts have further impacted Arizona's children, as Arizona ranked forty-seventh in the percentage of children with access to affordable health care. To exacerbate these statistics, the Department of Economic Security (DES) recently cut 10 million US dollars in childcare subsidies for fiscal year 2010–2011 and plans to cut another 23 million.

It is no surprise that Arizona's economic crisis and the recent state budget cuts in excess of 1.1 billion US dollars to education, health care, and other vital social programs affect Arizona's families in significant ways. Many options, available to assist families in finding and paying for affordable, quality care and programs for their young children, have vanished. Services that were once available to families have been cut back, eliminated, or may be more difficult to access as a result of lengthy waitlists.

Furthermore, in a state that seems to place little value on health and education for young children, primary caregivers in Arizona face significant challenges when it comes to raising their children. In fact many of the families and providers in our study spoke about these challenges at great length, some of which can be directly attributed to the current economic situation, while others are felt in more nuanced ways and are reflected in many families' inability to locate a system of support. In the following sections, we outline these struggles and highlight, in particular, the isolation felt by many of our families as they find themselves in a state that historically has placed little importance on child well-being.

Families' Need for Community

Families interviewed as a part of this study articulated a real desire to locate themselves within a greater community. Often, they expressed their desire for this to be a community of like-minded people experiencing similar struggles, joys, and challenges. The primary caregivers we interviewed related that support systems are fundamental to raising young children, and many of our families were able to locate this system of support among friends, neighbors, their immediate family members, or their faith communities.

> Yeah, we're blessed in that way [family support] because I think isolation is one of the things that probably would be the biggest impact on how I feel about doing the job that I'm doing right now.

Parents and primary caregivers expressed that they reach out for support among family, friends, neighbors, employers, and their church communities for a variety of reasons, including trustworthy childcare, information and advice, emotional and financial support, and for playmates for their children. We also found that while having a support system in place is important for all of our families, some have to work to build this for themselves in creative ways. In their second interview, for example, this mother of two children related the ways in which her family has begun to build a network of support for themselves, a task that proved difficult for them as transplants to the Phoenix area.

> We still don't have family around, but we have managed, especially in the past year, to develop a little bit more cohesive community of a few other close friends who have young kids. So, we have a little more of

a kind of regular crowd of people that we're hanging out with. All of that kind of help makes us feel more at home, even though at least six years we've lived here.

The sentiments expressed by this primary caregiver echoed the experiences of many of our participants that locating a support system can be a difficult and often daunting process.

Cultural factors also contribute to a family's access to support networks. In one indigenous community, for example, we found that many of the primary caregivers we interviewed lived with their parents, or other elderly relatives. These households benefited from a community approach to childrearing, where primary caregivers care for their parents, who in turn help care for the grandchildren. These families benefit from a support community in close proximity, where everyone lends a hand in caring for the members of that community. For one mother, her more recent return to her grandparent's home is an essential part of her ability to pursue her college education, while also being able to care for her aging grandmother.

Informal support networks are also essential as families attempt to pass down cultural knowledge and practices to their children. Three participants, for example, all of Native American descent, expressed the importance of cultural practices and language that family members, particularly grandparents, provide to their children. Additionally, these families noted the need to visit family members living on tribal land in order to effectively pass cultural knowledge down to their children. One mother explained:

My family is pretty involved. Just over the weekend we went home.... So it's just introducing him to all kinds of stuff. We're still talking to him in our tribal language, and he's beginning to speak the language too.[1]

For these families, engaging in communities where their culture is both valued and respected is an essential aspect of their parenting philosophy and practice.

EXPERIENCING ISOLATION

While it is clear that most families would like a support system, not all of them benefit from one. Several families living in the downtown area of the state's capital moved to this area for the diversity that downtown neighborhoods offer, as well as the cultural resources and easy access to services. Yet due to the higher turnover in these neighborhoods, the young parents found themselves struggling to find a community of support. One of our participants, raising two young children in a same-sex relationship, expressed:

> The reason why we chose this [neighborhood]—well, one, it's pretty diverse—it's ethnically diverse. It's income diverse, and also it has a gay population here.

Despite all that the neighborhood has to offer, finding a network of support has proven difficult for her and her partner. She continued:

> We had a network of people that we could do that with back home— and so here, finding those relationships that match and intersect in all the ways that you start to feel comfortable sharing.... Those aren't easy to develop or find them. I wish there were more opportunities or resources than that.

When a family moves to a new state, away from friends and family, they often lose this built-in network of care. Left without this support system, families find themselves much more alone, isolated, and challenged. While extended family members can offer support over the phone, this isn't the same as having them physically present. Another participant, also in a same-sex relationship raising two young children, expressed similar sentiments as she described the difficulty in finding people to reach out to. She told us, "Because in South Carolina, I had organized a family group, so we had kind of a network of people, and we got together often and did activities together, and I haven't been able to find anything like that here." Later on in her interview she elaborated on the difficulty in finding a network of support where she can confide in people about the struggles that come with raising young children:

> And that—to be honest, that's not even necessarily something that's very easy to talk to people about. It's easy to say, "Well, do you have a good pediatrician?" It's hard to say "I don't know what to do with—my child is having tantrums" or like how—I don't know how—I talk to my sister, but she's in Alaska.

Both of the same-sex families expressed isolation in this regard, as they have struggled to locate themselves within a greater community of LGBTQ (Lesbian, Gay, Bisexual, Transgender, Queer) parents raising young children. These parents find themselves excluded in a variety of ways as they encounter heteronormativity in its many and varied forms. Anne,[2] a doctoral student, elaborated on her struggle to find a support system as she articulated the necessity of finding a community of people with similar ideals:

> My sister and I talk about this a lot, about it's not just as simple as finding other families. If you want to really connect with people, you need to find families who have similar discipline and philosophies, or philosophies on life or family. At least enough that you can figure out how to be friends together.

She continued:

> There's always this kind of in the back of my mind, will those families have values that maybe are against our family structure? I'm not really interested in being hush hush about Carter has two moms. That's not something that I'm interested in doing or making him feel shameful.

Tory and Anne, as well as other same-sex parents, face challenges in addition to finding a community within which to situate themselves. These parents find themselves combating heteronormative structures at their childcare facilities, in parenting classes, and in prenatal classes. As Tory and Anne prepared for the arrival of their second child, for example, they signed up for a birthing class. Anne explained, "It was really nice. The only thing that we didn't like is they did a sibling class that we took Carter to when we were getting ready for Rachel—the whole thing was very mommy/daddy focused, so I wrote them a letter."

Sexual orientation is just one of the factors that contributes to a family's isolation and seclusion. Being an outsider in a community of insiders can further serve to isolate families. While families searching for a residential community to move into and raise their young children often turn to what appears to be a family-oriented community (larger homes, parks and community green space, good school districts, and many families with children), they may end up finding themselves isolated, as outsiders within their immediate community desperately seeking an invitation in:

> I tried some *Mommy & Me* groups; that did not go well. It was kind of—I feel like you needed like an invitation only kind of thing to participate, like you would need to, you needed to know somebody in that group first...I never felt welcomed...And that was with a couple, I tried I think two or three different ones, too.

Although families choose residential communities that they believe will provide the kinds of community support they are seeking, they find themselves outsiders when they do not share the dominant culture of that community, whether it be different religious affiliations, languages spoken, or ethnic backgrounds, therein presenting families with a complex set of circumstances and barriers to navigate. With highly mobile, transient, and fluid neighborhoods, and new residential communities that, in reality, are not really communities, parents in Arizona often struggle to find a network of support. This problem is perhaps more acute in Arizona, with its relatively high rate of immigration of families from other states and countries, than in states with stable or declining populations. Regardless, if their support system once existed but was lost, or if they never had it to begin with, when primary caregivers lack a support system, this seclusion brings a set of challenges that can make raising young children a struggle. Families who do not have a community expressed feelings of isolation and the difficulty in raising their children without this support that so many other families benefit from.

Linguistic isolation was another factor that affected the primary caregivers in our study. One of our primary caregiver participants, for example, explained how she felt excluded from her daughter's treatment after she was diagnosed with cerebral palsy. As a Spanish-speaking parent, she was unable to fully communicate with her daughter's health-care providers and take an active role in her daughter's care. "*No crea que sé mucho porque, pues la mayoría de las veces son todas las consultas en inglés*" (Don't think I know much because, well most of the time the consultations are in English). Marisol blames herself in some ways for her daughter's condition, which can be attributed to a traumatic brain injury that occurred during birth. She explained,

> *Llega a un país nuevo, entonces, uno, muchas veces por ignorancia o por temor de preguntar cosas que uno dice pues no la sabe uno, o si la sabe; pues yo no pregunté si podían hacerme una cesárea.*
>
> [When you arrive in a new country, well, many times because of ignorance or because you are afraid of asking about things you may know or not know about; well I didn't ask them to perform a c-section.]

Due to her linguistic isolation, Marisol not only carries a heavy burden of guilt surrounding her daughter's condition but is also unable to be fully invested in her treatment, which includes both physical and speech therapy. The medical providers treating her daughter fail to appreciate and take advantage of Marisol's knowledge about her daughter and her family's needs, in many ways marginalizing her from her daughter's care.

FINDING CULTURALLY RESPONSIVE SERVICES

For many of the families interviewed, an important part of educating and caring for their children was locating services that respect their family culture. These services ranged from services related to health, including birth, prenatal, and postpartum services, to services related to early care and education. Furthermore, parents look to childcare providers to not only care for their children in their absence, but to provide them with age-appropriate learning opportunities, engage them in early literacy activities, and participate in the development of their world view. Finding the right childcare provider proved to be challenging, however, for many of the families participating in this study. Again, we look to our interviews with Anne as she expressed the shock she felt when she tried to find quality care for her two young children:

> And I started asking around about like just trying to figure out like were there childcare centers that were nationally accredited and what was available here in terms of infant care and then also for preschool care, and I found out that there was almost no—very basic accountability for childcare centers, very little training required,...—just the minimal, and that was really kind of discouraging.

While not completely dissatisfied with her choice, she explained:

> I do feel a little bit like I had to settle, and that's not—I don't know that that's always what people should have to do—with their most precious thing in their lives.

Furthermore, As Tory and Anne raise their children, it is important for them to see their culture and lifestyle reflected in the curriculum of the classroom, as well as in the curriculum of their everyday social structures. "I think that's important, and we always talk about this. Carter hears people talk about stuff and even just at school, they read books, and the books are very kind of hetero-focused. They're the mommy/daddy books just like that class."

As they are confronted with various situations that do not reflect diversity but rather reinforce the heteronormative structures seen in

Carter's classroom environment, Tory and Anne find themselves even more compelled to search out a community of like-minded parents:

> Even now, as he's getting more into imaginative play, he talks about—he does mommy/daddy. That's how he sets up families, and that's fine because I know that that's one way to be a family, but I don't want him to forget that there are lots of different kinds of families and other families like our family. I don't want him to feel like we're the only ones, so that's something that we'll be kind of working on in the next year or two I guess.

Finding care that adheres to a culturally relevant pedagogy (Ladson-Billings, 1995) is essential for the families in our study. Just as Anne and Tory feel as though their son has to unlearn the heteronormative lens he is faced with at school, without an informal support system of other same-sex parents, they take on the full burden of teaching him a more accepting and open-minded world view. Yet their hard work is often negated by the strong forces at play within the curriculum of the classroom.

Furthermore, we have found in our interviews that, not surprisingly, primary caregivers possess a rich body of knowledge when it comes to understanding what families need to raise healthy young children. Our conversations with primary caregivers suggest that parents' perspectives are often not prioritized in the early care and education system, particularly if these parents are from marginalized groups, like the LGBTQ and Spanish-speaking parents cited here. In this sense, we look to a *funds-of-knowledge* perspective. This framework was developed as "a theoretical validation of the social and cultural capital of communities," more specifically marginal communities that have been historically viewed as lacking. The *funds-of-knowledge* approach "reconceptualized communities from a strength-based perspective" (González et al., in press, p. 482), a perspective we have embraced and applied in this project, as we privilege the voices of underrepresented populations.

Interestingly, as parents seek out support in raising their young children, they also recognize that the leading authorities on childrearing are frequently other parents, parents with similar ideals and values. For this reason, the primary caregivers we interviewed want easier access to other parents and to support groups within their immediate communities. Parents already understand and are putting into practice a funds-of-knowledge perspective.

Providers' Perspectives on Support, Isolation, and Culturally Responsive Programs

This section illustrates providers' (early childhood service providers' and community leaders') perceptions of the efforts to address some of the concerns expressed by primary caregivers surrounding availability, affordability, sensitivity, and quality of early childcare, education, and health services. Similar to the section on primary caregivers, many of the quotes featured are from one provider's perspective but are representative of perspectives shared by multiple providers.

At the time of these interviews public discourse was heavily focused on issues related to the economic crisis; thus the national and state recession is the backdrop that sets the stage for many of the comments and efforts of agencies at both state and local levels. Conversations with providers frequently turned to topics of funding cuts and program erasure due to federal and state decisions. Providers expressed that these decisions and the lack of investment in early childhood services have direct and indirect implications and carry with them explicit and implicit messages. The direct result is that the trickle-down effects of cuts at one level affect services and resources at other levels. More explicitly, vulnerable populations are typically the ones most affected; namely, children, low-income families, and the working poor. The implicit message that permeates the public discourse is one that suggests that these populations, particularly the working poor, should be able to take personal responsibility, suggestive of underlying beliefs in meritocracy and individualism. This perspective alludes to the belief that every family has an equal chance to flourish and as a result, it minimizes the need for government programs to assist vulnerable families in Arizona. Without question, these funding cuts and the underlying beliefs that pervade leave vulnerable populations even more vulnerable. To further complicate matters, these *vulnerable* populations at times experience multiple layers of barriers—lack of education, lack of knowledge of services, and inability to navigate a complex early childhood system.

A number of providers expressed the sentiment that the funding cuts are commonly directed to programs that impact young children, creating an unstable system for a population that urgently needs stability. As the economy takes a downward spiral, the focus is on loss of jobs and homes—economic issues—while the underlying issues, like access to quality care and support for childrearing, that impact the most vulnerable populations and their quality of life are overlooked.

A director of a preschool in an urban area expressed this concern in these words:

> Everybody [is] so focused on the parents losing their jobs and losing their homes. What about the children?...I think everybody forgets about the little ones. They say "Oh, they're just children, they don't understand." But they do understand. They're the ones that have been suffering.

Children should not have to suffer the impact of economic changes, but all too often this is the case. Furthermore, as economic difficulties increase, there is also a greater harm to vulnerable residents' well-being. The economic problems create an inhospitable landscape for these families in need of formal supports. The sheer volume of those in need has adversely affected the providers' confidence as they are confronted with families in dire situations. Simply put, the need has exceeded the provision. A director of a child and family program in a rural region summed this up by stating:

> [Families] are seeing, with the recession, a greater disparity in their income. They're seeing a greater disparity in their stability. We are also seeing that, and so it's this systemic thing that we're supposed to be the helpers and give more, and yet we are also experiencing loss.

The recession is creating widespread deficits. While some programs barely remain in full operation, other once-viable programs with multiple offerings resort to addressing only the minimum basic needs. And, there remain those who are unwillingly forced to turn families away. In smaller communities, with already fewer program offerings, the issue is compounded when programs are eliminated or budgets are cut. In a state that has eliminated public preschool programs and a host of health services, cut Medicaid services, and placed strict timelines on cash assistance, along with a variety of other cuts, it is not surprising that sustained funding for successful programs was identified as an important consideration in the early childhood education and health systems.

MEETING THE NEEDS OF FAMILIES

The response to this imbalance is to strengthen the early childhood network to better meet the needs of families. Effective collaborations and creative solutions are ways providers feel they can stitch together some of the holes created by the economic recession and budget cuts. An umbrella agency provider in a diverse rural region of southern Arizona related this sentiment:

> We know there are gaping holes that didn't use to be there, even last year, so the way we respond this year is going to look completely different.

Just as families are relying more heavily on extended family for support, providers rely on community programs and collaborations between agencies to meet the needs of families. An administrative executive of several childcare centers from an urban community illustrates how they address this problem in the quote below:

> [W]e do find that sometimes services are no longer available. They've lost funding, and we've got to help families by continuing our search. We're able to call other established places in the field saying, "Did you know this was closed? I've got a family that needs this. What do you suggest?"

This kind of networking has allowed providers to offer a more comprehensive approach by referring families to local providers. While they know they cannot support the needs of *all* of the children on their own, they know they can increase efforts and find alternative ways of addressing the gaps. One school-district-based childcare provider says:

> Department of Economic Security (DES) will cover some of them but because DES has done their cutbacks, we have really done a lot of grant research and gotten grants to pay for scholarships for kids.

The fortitude, flexibility, and willingness to seek alternative funding are testaments to the many individuals who are committed to early childhood education and care in the state of Arizona, regardless of the challenges that have arisen for them in the past few years.

Beyond economic access to programs and finding ways to support families, providers have also made efforts to address the exclusion and isolation concerns raised by the families, including isolation experienced due to remoteness and distance, which includes geographic access, racial (immigration), and linguistic divides. Our data indicate that in order for connections between families and service providers to be possible and for service provision to be maximized, families must have consistent access to transportation. In interviews, conducted with providers, they expressed that the biggest concern communicated to them by families was transportation. This lack of transportation creates a significant barrier, particularly to those families who must travel long distances to access needed services. Unfortunately, those who may normally qualify for services (*the neediest families*) are typically the ones who have no way of getting to these services, according to providers. These may include services to meet their basic needs. A director of a *Head Start* center described this challenge by commenting:

> Even [to] find food banks and clothing banks and things like that [families] sometimes have to travel a little bit of a distance.

Rather than accessing services in one location, in order to obtain the full range of resources that make up the system of services, families are often expected to visit several locations. Thus more isolated families find themselves in intensifying *isolating* situations. For some families, there are layers of factors that add to their already-difficult situations. One such group that the provider participants spoke about are those who are doubly marginalized by poverty (already an outsider) and by the fact that they are living in rural areas (geographically isolated). These groups face barriers in terms of a lack of reliable transportation and the lack of available services. And, even if services are available, those who lack reliable transportation are barred from access to critical services. These families find themselves not only isolated geographically, but also marginalized as a result of their circumstances.

Marginalization and exclusion that contribute to isolation also come in various forms. For example, when the rules (appointments, etc.) set by the providers are not met it creates an opportunity to marginalize groups who were already excluded as a result of their class condition. This is a common situation on reservations (tribal land areas) and in rural communities. Remoteness complicates mobility making accessing resources difficult and increasing the rate of missed appointments. The providers may view missed appointments by families as not respecting their time, yet the families' absence may be a direct result of lack of transportation. Recognizing this, one health-care provider from a rural community commented:

> It's not simply a cultural value, it's also the fact that maybe two or three families rely on one pickup truck. Well, that pickup truck had to

go shopping, had to take somebody to work or had to take somebody to the hospital who was sick.

In these instances, the lack of adherence to rules due to transportation limitations places families in a situation in which they are socially stigmatized, further resulting in the exclusion of already-isolated, vulnerable groups.

In one unconventional solution to meet the needs of families, a community in a rural area has come up with a way to resolve the transportation issue through their local *Head Start* program. Through transportation coordination, the center allocates several buses to connect families to appointments, which meets the transportation needs of this isolated community and helps connect providers. This agency-based transportation is one solution to the transportation barriers. These stories, however, are rarities, as the more common expectation is that families should *take personal responsibility* for finding ways to get to the service locations.

Transportation needs are simply greater in some communities, such as in rural and/or tribal communities. However, this does not mean it does not impact families in urban communities, as well as providers. A director from a family support agency speaks to the importance of providing transportation for their own operation: "I [would] probably have a zero attendance . . . if I did not drive them."

For other providers, the solution to the transportation issue is addressed by bringing mobile services into communities that lack service offices. This health-care provider, specializing in serving women and children, provided an example of ways they meet the needs of families.

> We take a mobile clinic three days a week to [a small rural community] to provide WIC and immunizations because we don't have an office there.

Providers articulated many compelling ideas for ways to establish connections between services and help families physically access these services; collaboration is the most effective because it allows providers to stay connected with fellow service providers, which can result in the ability to formally or informally refer families to services. While it may not always be seamless, provider collaboration is an excellent way to meet the multifaceted needs of families and is one catalyst to community progress. Furthermore, providers also acknowledged their role in fostering effective communication with families and other providers.

The communication process, however, can be compromised if and when providers are unable to communicate with those families whose primary language is not English.

CULTURALLY RESPONSIVE PROGRAMMING

The ways in which language acts as a barrier to communicating about services to parents and other primary caregivers was a consistent theme in interviews with providers. As one provider commented, language barriers present "one more complication" for non-English-speaking parents and children living in Arizona and for providers providing services to this population. In some instances, language differences can even serve as obstacles to quality care. This provider articulated the need for Spanish-speaking staff in order to address the needs of the families in their county:

> [T]here's a fairly high Spanish-speaking population in our county, so that can be an obstacle, but about two-thirds of the staff speak Spanish. We try to stick to that because that really helps.

Other providers have developed alternative ways to address language barriers. Several providers acknowledged that one common way around language barriers between providers and caregivers is to have bilingual children translate information. This practice does not augment or replace the need to staff agencies with people who can communicate in more than one language but serves as a solution when no other options are available. While these practices may be controversial, placing the child as translators sometimes is the only solution to filling the language gap. In research conducted by Soto (2002), she observed that bilingualism is often constructed as altruism by young children. The children in her research took pride in their ability to help children understand each other, help teachers and other children understand each other, and translate for family members and said they liked helping people as a result of being bilingual.

Clearly, service providers who serve people who do not speak English need trained bilingual staff to relay information. The ideal is to employ multilingual staff at each agency, but the reality is that there is a lack of culturally, ethnically, and linguistically diverse staff working in the system of services, which hinders the system's ability to effectively address diverse populations. The result of this is that families who need a service may not be able to access that service due to language barriers. Language thus becomes the barrier that isolates and excludes people in need of services. And, in a state with conservative policies surrounding language, the marginalization continues and an already-complicated situation worsens, for both providers and families.

Bound by state policies, providers are challenged to try to meet the diverse needs of the communities they serve. This is not an easy task, as one family support provider explained:

> The only stumbling block sometimes we have is making sure when we're translating things to be accommodating to someone's language, that we're doing it in a way that does not go against what our state policies are, but doing it to accommodate the families so that they can get the information they need.

Language barriers may on the surface not appear to be a big issue; however, one must consider that when an already-vulnerable population is forbidden to use their mother tongue it prevents them from receiving services, contributing to feelings of isolation. A director in an agency committed to early childhood education and care spoke about this reality by stating:

> [S]ome parents may not have a command of the English language and therefore feel threatened in our state. They don't want to publicly go out because they don't feel there's a value for what they have as a parent to share, especially if they carry an accent or a different language.

The politics surrounding language are not confined, but seep into larger issues of immigration, which providers expressed as a barrier to receiving services. In Arizona, immigration policies negatively impact both undocumented and documented immigrants, reflecting the restrictive landscape within which providers must navigate. As providers have expressed, sometimes it is not the policies that create the problem but the attitudes toward perceived immigrants and the social climate of fear that acts as the barrier. This happens even when the provider does not need to verify citizenship for participation in a program, as in the case of private or federally funded programs:

> [E]ven if we say, "Everybody's eligible. You don't have to provide citizenship," they might be fearful to go and apply.

Aware of the intense emotional impact of immigration policy on families in the community, some providers, particularly this family support agency director, find ways to try to make services more accessible by focusing on the need rather than the status:

> I think that we are working very hard to be supportive of families and their circumstances [by considering] what does this child need and how can we support this family with any kind of legal issues they may be having.

How are providers to meet the needs of linguistically, ethnically, and culturally diverse families in a politically charged climate? Unfortunately, in the current political climate, some providers find it essential to support the undocumented immigrant families they serve prepare for the worst. One provider, an administrator of a family support agency identified a few key questions that she believes undocumented families must consider:

> What's going to happen if you're picked up? What will happen with your kids? What will you do? What's your plan?

The immigration policies have not only negatively affected families who are undocumented but have also impacted the services that those who have legal citizenship could benefit from. This umbrella agency provider from an urban community spoke to how culturally relevant programs are impacted as a result of policies (immigration) that dictate what providers can and cannot do:

> Well, we take [cultural relevancy]...very seriously and certainly target recruiting staff who can provide services...more culturally relevant services. We keep running into a brick wall with the State departments that...money can't (be used to translate) English and Spanish or other languages, which is ridiculous.

Clearly, increased communication with families who have concerns about the state's immigration policy is the one real concrete solution to dealing with the new state policy. Increased communication is one way to give opportunities to children whose families may otherwise not seek out services, even though they may qualify.

CLOSING THOUGHTS

Situating our findings in the nested contexts of globalized neoliberal policies, persistent national economic recession, and the conservative politics of our state, the voices of parents and providers shared in this chapter shed light on how policies, funding cuts, persistent biases, and even public attitudes toward childcare and early education affect the daily lives of families and communities. An irony of the study is that it is part of documenting impacts of a major and much-needed new state initiative for children birth to age five and their families, which was fully launched just as the height of the national recession was hitting and many early childhood and health programs were absorbing deep funding cuts. Meant to supplement and complement existing programs, this initiative has a funding stream separate from the general funds and has been pressured to fill gaps created by statewide and local budget cuts. As the gap widens even more dramatically between rich and poor in the United States, families face a range of forced or limited choices in finding health and childcare and overall support in childrearing. The reputation of the United States as having one of the least child- and family-friendly set of social policies is evident in many of the family and provider narratives.

In applying our findings to the themes of this volume, which includes ways of rethinking parent and community involvement in early years programs and practice, we have shared some of the roles that larger-scale qualitative studies can play in contributing to literature on family-/community-focused early childhood program planning and practice. For example, the multiple ways in which parents and providers alluded to isolation sheds light on ways in which families can experience forms of exclusion. The theme of isolation was both physical (e.g., long distances to limited services in rural areas or lack of transportation in urban settings) and metaphorical (e.g., the social exclusion felt by religious minorities or same-sex parents in their immediate communities).

Language and citizenship also formed markers for various forms of exclusion, in an English-only state that had recently enacted harsh anti-immigrant legislation that has instilled fear in many families who are undocumented residents and risk arrest and deportation. Parents' fears of seeking out services for their children spoke volumes about the social climate, as well as economic constraints, in our state.

Another trend in our many interviews with families and providers was the preference that many parents had for care provided by family members or more informally by trusted neighbors, or *kith and kin* care. This trend echoes literature showing that families of infants and toddlers, as well as Latino and African American families in general, prefer kith and kin to center-based care. Concerns of safety, changing childcare staff, language and cultural issues, and shared childrearing

beliefs have all been cited by parents as factors in choosing nonregulated care or keeping young children at home. These findings also
have implications for regulated childcare, including centers and family
childcare homes. The need for more, culturally sensitive, affordable,
and home-like care, are among the implications.

Throughout this ongoing study, we have attempted to take a
strengths-based approach to listening to parents and other primary
caregivers of young children. We have drawn from a *funds- of-knowledge*
perspective that attempts to honor and understand the life experiences,
aspirations, and perspectives of diverse families as well as the views of
community members whose lives are spent trying to address the needs
of families in our state. Funds of knowledge can provide a "forum
to acknowledge complexity without invoking deficit or culture-based
discourses," resulting in "deeper understandings of communities' cultural capital" (González et al., in press, p. 489). We have much to learn
from parents as well as early childhood providers about raising young
children and the ways in which state and local services can support
them. We have shared one way that research, evaluation and an early
childhood system of services can begin to listen and help to redefine
parent involvement and partnerships.

Notes

All research and analysis activities were funded by a grant from the Arizona
Early Childhood Development and Health Board. We also acknowledge
the contributions of the Family and Community Case Study team, particularly Melinda Hollis.

1. This quote is from a primary caregiver with tribal membership living
   off tribal land.
2. All names used in this chapter are pseudonyms.

References

Annie E. Casey Foundation (2010). *2010 Kids count data book: State profiles
of child well-being.* Baltimore, MD: Annie E Casey Foundation. Retrieved
from: http://datacenter.kidscount.org/DataBook/2010/Default.aspx

Children's Defense Fund. (2011). *Children in Arizona fact sheet.* Retrieved
from http://www.childrensdefense.org/child-research-data-publications
/data/state-data-repository/cits/2011/children-in-the-states-factsheets
.html

González, N., Moll, L., & Amanti, C. (Eds.). (2004). *Funds of knowledge:
Theorizing practices in households, communities, and classrooms.* Mahwah,
NJ: Lawrence Erlbaum Associates.

González, N., Wyman, L., & O'Connor, B. H. (in press). The past, present and future of "funds of knowledge," in B. A. U. Levinson & M. Pollock (Eds.). *A companion to the anthropology of education* (pp. 481–494). West Sussex, UK:Blackwell Publishing Company.

Graue, M. E., & Walsh, D. (Eds.) (1998). *Studying children in context: Theories, methods & ethics.* Thousand Oaks, CA: Sage.

Hatch, J. A. (2007). *Early childhood qualitative research.* New York: Routledge.

Heydon, R. M., & Iannacci, L. (2008). *Early childhood curricula and the de-pathologizing of childhood.* Toronto, ON: University of Toronto Press.

Ladson-Billings, G. (1995). But that's just good teaching! The case for culturally relevant pedagogy. *Theory into practice, 34*(3), 159–165.

Merriam, S. B. (1998). *Qualitative research and case study applications in education.* San Francisco, CA: Jossey-Bass.

Soto, L. D. (Ed.) (2002). *Making a difference in the lives of bilingual/bicultural children.* New York: Peter Lang.

Swadener, B. B., & Lubeck, S. (Eds.) (1995). *Children and families "at promise": Deconstructing the discourse of risk.* Albany, NY: State University of New York Press.

CHAPTER 7

Beyond Heteronormativity: Hospitality as Curriculum

Debora Lee

INTRODUCTION

This chapter examines ideas about hospitality for all in Early Childhood Education and Care (ECEC) in Aotearoa New Zealand. ECEC has a unique relationship with hospitality through *te ao Māori* (the Māori [indigenous New Zealander] world view) and *manaakitanga* (looking after people). Although *Te Whāriki,* Aotearoa New Zealand's early childhood education curriculum (Ministry of Education, 1996), espouses a *kaupapa* (philosophy) of welcome through the *Whānau Tangata Principle* (Family and Community), most ECEC environments tend to be heteronormative (Gunn & Surtees, 2004). Heterosexuality is therefore pervasively established as the only option for adult sexual and life partnerships. Research suggests that, for those who are Lesbian, Gay, Bisexual, Transgender, Queer/Questioning (LGBTQ), hospitality in educational settings can be in short supply (Allen & Elliot, 2008). In 2006, I conducted a study of the experiences of a group of gay mothers in a range of ECEC centers. In this chapter I argue that, despite the heteronormative[1] nature of ECEC settings (see Gunn & Surtees, 2004; Robinson, 2005), some teachers demonstrated an authentic hospitality to these families.

The involvement of families and *whānau* (extended family) in ECEC requires teachers to have a commitment to ethical practice and democracy. Meaningful collaboration provides opportunities for teachers to listen, and to make space for the *Other* (Dahlberg & Moss, 2005). My study showed that hospitality has the potential to confront and disrupt the pervasive presence of heteronormativity. I begin this chapter by describing the context for LGBTQ and ECEC in Aotearoa New Zealand, followed by an examination of relevant constructs of hospitality. I then briefly outline my research project and share and discuss stories from my study with reference to two key ideas about hospitality: *hospitality as hosting* and *hospitality as curriculum.*

THE NEW ZEALAND CONTEXT

Aotearoa New Zealand has a history of promoting social justice for LGBTQ people. A range of legislation such as the Homosexual Law Reform Act (1986), the Human Rights Act, (1993), and the Status of Children Amendment Act (2004) suggests that Aotearoa New Zealand society is welcoming and accepting of diverse sexualities. However, research evidence points to a possible mismatch between the legislative direction and the experiences of many, especially young LGBTQ people (Henrickson, 2005; Rossen, Lucassen, Denny, & Robinson, 2009). Despite efforts by some to address LGBTQ equity concerns, there still appears to be a strongly heteronormative climate in both the social and educational structures of the country (see Allen & Elliot, 2008; Carpenter & Lee, 2010; Gunn & Surtees, 2009; Lee & Duncan, 2008).

ECEC in Aotearoa New Zealand has a complex history. Kindergartens, beginning in 1889, were initiated to address inequalities and poverty. Later nurseries, or crèches, were established. These childcare facilities prioritized children's safety and well-being and did not demonstrate any desire for partnerships with families. In 1948, playcentres began and challenged the indifference to parents and *whānau* that had previously been demonstrated in ECEC (May, 2009). Playcentres have been based on families and *whānau* as vital to the provision of quality care and education for children. Changes in views about early education in the 1960s and 1970s created debate and challenge, and women's rights became a focus of the campaign for childcare (May, 2001). Later in the twentieth century ECEC continued to stimulate discussion and dissension, with a potential tension between the rights of the child and the rights of families and, more particularly, mothers (May, 1992). Current challenges and debates include the rights of all children, *whānau,* and families to access to affordable, high-quality, and culturally congruent ECEC (May & Mitchell, 2009)

The number of children attending ECEC has increased exponentially over the last 20 years. In 2010, figures released by the Ministry of Education suggest 58.7 percent of children from birth to five years of age attended a licenced ECEC. These figures increase as children grow older, with 95.1 percent of children turning five years of age will have regularly attended ECEC before commencing compulsory schooling (Education Counts, 2010). There is currently a diverse range of settings that children can attend and these include public kindergartens, private and community-based ECEC centers, playcentres, *Te Kohanga Reo* (Māori language immersion centers), *Pasifika* (Pacific language immersion centers), and playgroups. Teachers in each of these settings are expected to demonstrate a philosophical and pedagogical commitment to meaningful engagement with families and *whānau* and this expectation is mandated by many policy documents (Ministry of Education, 2002, 2005). The early childhood curriculum *Te Whāriki* is, arguably, influenced by the principles of social justice alongside fundamental Māori values such as *manaakitanga* (Ministry of Education, 1996).

In ECEC, families and *whānau* are seen as within the teacher's circle of responsibility and as recipients of an ethic of care and hospitality, or *manaakitanga*. According to Macfarlane (2004) the Māori cultural construct of *manaakitanga* refers to an ethic of a caring community and includes cultural expectations that provide for people's safety in a myriad of ways. This socially constructed lens views care as a duty or an obligation. In Aotearoa New Zealand teachers have a responsibility to "establish honest, open and respectful relationships" with families and *whānau* (New Zealand Teachers Council, 2007, p. 1) and to "engage in ethical, respectful, positive and collaborative professional relationships with *whānau* and other carers of *ākonga* (children or students)" (New Zealand Teachers Council, 2005, p. 1). Ideally, this hospitality is visible in the day-to-day interactions and relationships between teachers and children, family, and *whānau* within an ECEC community.

Research in Aotearoa New Zealand suggests that collaborative partnerships with families and *whānau* can be problematic. Families' and teachers' expectations and perceptions of family involvement in ECEC settings are likely to differ (Billman, Geddes, & Hedges, 2005). Mitchell (2008) found that teachers tended to overestimate the degree of involvement of families and *whānau* in comparison to what the families themselves reported. Meade and Podmore (2002) argue that in order for meaningful collaborative relationships to develop, a sociocultural stance is necessary. A position taking into account the complex sociocultural implications of family-teacher collaboration would entail an understanding of the possible power relations inherent in such partnerships. In Australia MacNaughton (2005) emphasizes the tendency of teachers to privilege those families whose lived realities sit comfortably alongside those of the dominant groups. She acknowledges that these lived realities are unlikely to be the same for those who identify or are seen as *Other*: "single parents, lesbian and gay parents, parents with a disability, indigenous parents and so on" (MacNaughton, 2005, p. 45). Heteronormativity is therefore likely to strongly influence the level of hospitality offered to gay mothers and their families.

HOSPITALITY: THE FIRST RULE OF HUMAN CONDUCT

To move beyond heteronormativity requires a paradigm shift in how hospitality is viewed. Kant's use of hospitality suggested responsibility to a common humanity (Bauman, 2008). Hospitality can be viewed as necessary for a civil society, and, in fact, as a moral imperative. Bauman (2008, p. 227) states: "Indeed, if ethics is a work of reason, as Kant wished it to be, then hospitality is—must be, or must sooner or later become—the first rule of human conduct." In a diverse world to be *hospitable* creates complexities for teachers. Hospitality in itself requires a statement of *ownership* that perhaps counteracts the possibility of an authentic welcome. Derrida and Dufourmantelle's (2000) exploration of the construct of hospitality suggests that the term is, of itself, a contradiction. When offering hospitality people actively assert their place and their power within that place. The *host* provides a welcome, but it is a welcome that is at the whim of the host and therefore perhaps not a *true* welcome at all. Is it merely as Kant (1796, p. 28) regarded in his *Third Definitive Article for a Perpetual Peace*: "The right a stranger has of not being treated as an enemy"? What constitutes hospitality in the twenty-first century? Bauman (2008) challenges us to consider the implications of shared spaces, public places, and the fluid boundaries of these in a global society. Derrida and Dufourmantelle's (2000) supposition suggests that the construct of hospitality requires an assertion of ownership. Graham and Slee (2008) argue similarly that the term *inclusion*, as it is used in relation to people with disabilities, raises the question: "included by whom and into what?" Hospitality, and the resultant seamless inclusion into the ECEC setting, is important for gay mothers and their families to avoid *Othering*, or being viewed and treated as less important than the *norm* of the heterosexual-headed family.

The construct of hospitality is significant when addressing collaborative partnerships with *whānau* in ECEC. *Te Whāriki* (Ministry of Education, 1996, p. 42) asserts that: "The curriculum builds on what children bring to it and makes links with the everyday activities and special events of families, *whānau,* local communities and cultures." Many policies and government documents stress the vital role of family in the educational lives of their young children (Ministry of Education, 2002, 2005; New Zealand Teachers Council, 2007). Therefore the *kaupapa* of early childhood care and education in New Zealand supports hospitality and *manaakitanga*.

Findings from my research demonstrate that there are many ways that teachers can, and do, offer hospitality. Their actions varied from overt and visible to more subtle. Some of these actions may be regarded as *wise practice*, or long-practiced and accepted means of making families and *whānau* feel welcome in an ECEC setting. However, some teachers showed a deeper level of commitment to diversity than others, a commitment that did not expect the families to downplay their differences.

GAY MOTHERS AND ECEC: MY RESEARCH

My research project aimed to find out about the experiences of a group of 17 gay mothers from 12 lesbian-parented families who had children enrolled in ECEC centers in two major cities in Aotearoa New Zealand (Lee, 2008). I am both a lesbian mother and early childhood teacher educator, so this project was of personal and professional interest to me. The study was advertised in gay social spaces and gay media. Prospective participants were invited to contact the researcher. Some snowballing occurred with women who had agreed to take part contacting their friends and suggesting that they also become involved. The study used a qualitative approach, with interviews involving open-ended questions as the only data-gathering technique. Each participant was interviewed on one occasion, with the interview lasting up to one and a half hours. Several couples chose to be interviewed together. Privacy and confidentiality were respected at all times throughout the research process, and in later publications and conference presentations.

A strongly reflective and critical approach combined with peer supervision was used to ameliorate possible bias. The following stories are from 4 of the 12 interviews I conducted and I believe that they exemplify some of the possibilities for teachers to demonstrate hospitality toward gay mothers and their families in ECEC settings. These stories narrate a *welcoming in* that is on the terms of those receiving the welcome, not on the terms set by the host. I consider that each of the stories presents evidence that the teachers in these ECEC centers showed a deep level of hospitality and, in so doing, broke out of the traditional mold of a conditional and heteronormative hospitality. The participant mothers are referred to by the pseudonyms used in the research: *Sue* and *Laura, Kerry, Gabrielle,* and *Fern.*

SUE AND LAURA

Sue and Laura chose the ECEC center their daughter attended because the teacher-child ratios for the very young children were good (one adult to every three children); the building was light and airy; there were plenty of resources; it had a *homely* feel about it; and, it was a workplace center for a targeted community which meant the families had a lot in common.

Sue stated:

> They [the teachers] fell in love with her [our child] right away and they gave her individual attention. And that happens with other kids too, but because there is a good teacher-to-child ratio it means they can spend that quality of time with them and that's really important to us.

Initially Sue and Laura had described themselves to the teachers as mothers rather than explicitly explaining their family. Sue said: "We just assume that they are going to pick it up and we don't necessarily introduce ourselves or make a point of making sure that they know." The structure of the family was understood by some of the teachers, however, as one teacher, with a long-standing relationship with them, had asked them how they had conceived their child.

There were also some practices teachers employed that Laura and Sue felt supported a sense of community and belonging for all families. One of these practices was the use of photo boards, where family photos were displayed. Sue and Laura happily shared family photos. Another practice was a teacher asking how the child referred to each of the mothers. The teachers, who worked closely with the family, were also interested in the child's weekend activities, and these were shared with the teaching team to allow a greater depth of understanding and connection between the home and the center. Sue and Laura appreciated that the teachers did not limit children's play by gender or stereotype, and the relaxed and communicative atmosphere was highly valued. Sue spoke about enjoying and sharing humorous stories with teachers:

> In our baby group one of the mums was saying:
> He is not saying "mamma" yet but he says "dada." And I said: "[Our daughter] says 'dada' too and [there is] no father in the house!" So I told them the story…[and] they were laughing about the whole thing. (Sue)

KERRY

When Kerry and her partner chose an ECEC center for their child they believed that conversations about the form their family took could take place at a later time. When they shared with the teacher, fielding their initial questions, that they were a lesbian-headed family, she responded with thoughtful and sensitive questions such as "What do the children call each of you?" indicating her acceptance of them as a family. Kerry and her partner, like Sue and Laura in the previous story, found this approach welcoming. For Kerry a highlight of this conversation was that the teacher could "say the word lesbian, so they got marks for that!" Although Kerry believed that the teachers could have done more to support her family she spoke positively about a range of practices that she appreciated and that helped build relationships and assisted her child's sense of belonging.

Relationships between the families in the ECEC center and the teachers were reinforced by the center's primary caregiver[2] approach. The primary caregiver of Kerry's child was open to ideas to better support the family. For example, when Kerry's three-year-old daughter chose to use the term *mum-dad* to name her social mother, the teacher accepted this without question. Kerry said: "I was sort-of worried that [the teachers] would think it was odd or something, but they…were fine.…Things have moved on and now she is very proud of the fact that she's got two mums." The teachers always remembered her and her partner's name and greeted them both warmly. When they were expecting their second child they were asked by the teachers how this pregnancy had come about. Rather than feeling that this question was an intrusion on their privacy, Kerry saw it as an attempt to get to know the family better: "Not in a nosey or an *odd situation* kind of way, but actually as a genuine curiousness."

Two of the teachers at the ECEC center were undertaking postgraduate study and Kerry saw these teachers as "quite open to new ideas and to change." Kerry has an interest in children's books and had taken a number of books with gay or lesbian content into the center. Three books in particular that she had recommended had been purchased by the center. She appreciated that the teachers read these books to the children and that they were part of the revolving library available to the children.

Kerry and her partner continued to feel supported by the teachers as they developed relationships with other families in the center. When Kerry gleaned from one of the teachers that other family members been asking inquisitive questions about her family, she and her partner believed that the teachers' response had been supportive and almost protective. It appeared to Kerry that the other children in the center had come to accept their family over time: "When they [reach] about three or four [years old] they start asking questions and asking who else lives at the house and things like that. But I think because we have been there so long, it's just ordinary."

Gabrielle

The ECEC center Gabrielle and her partner chose was the only one that they looked at because when they walked in they liked it straightaway, and their daughter felt at home there. Gabrielle said that when they first visited the center: "They were just really welcoming and I liked the way they were with the kids." Gabrielle's response to a warm welcome mirrors the feelings of Sue and Laura, and Kerry and her partner, and the sense that their families were accepted was also a significant factor in their choice of center.

When she made the initial approach, Gabrielle told the teachers about the nature of her family and felt accepted and welcomed immediately.

Later, Gabrielle was to discover that there were two lesbian teachers working at the center, but she believed that this would not have influenced her choice. There were extensive opportunities for the family to let the teachers know about any aspects of their family that were important or unique. One of the practices of this center was that home visits were organized to allow teachers to develop close relationships with the children and their families. Soon after Gabrielle's daughter started to attend the center, two of the teachers visited Gabrielle's home, and she saw this as extremely beneficial for her child. Her daughter had been extremely delighted at being able to host her teachers, and Gabrielle believed that this visit had a positive influence on the developing relationships with the center.

Other practices that Gabrielle recalled were the use of scrapbooks for each family, including family photos. These books allowed the family to highlight special features about the family, such as the names the children used for the mothers. The importance of recognizing specific family nomenclature was also emphasized by Sue, Laura, and Kerry. The scrapbooks also eased communication about the involvement of donor fathers and significant special events such as the *Big Gay Out* (an annual gay pride day in Aotearoa New Zealand's major cities). These scrapbooks were readily available for the children to share with the other children and to take home if they wished. The information was therefore readily shared with others and provided links between both environments.

Gabrielle spoke with respect of the work that the teachers did in the ECEC center and their acceptance of diversity. Children with disabilities were readily included in all aspects of this center's program. The ethnic, cultural, and linguistic backgrounds of the children were also integrated into the curriculum in a respectful manner. One of Gabrielle's children has a different ethnic and cultural background from Gabrielle, through her donor father. The teachers were sensitive to this and included aspects of the child's culture and language in the program to enrich her understanding and cultural competence. These practices allowed greater connections to be forged between the teachers and Gabrielle's large family.

Extended family was a valued part of Gabrielle's life. At the time of the research there were 11 grandmothers actively involved with Gabrielle's family. One of Gabrielle's three children had a donor father who was very present in her life and visited the home frequently. When her daughter was about three years old her donor underwent gender realignment. The change was managed in a considered manner, and the family was careful to explain the situation accurately to the children. Gabrielle reported that her daughter's understanding of gender was very sophisticated and that she spoke openly about her family at the ECEC center. Gabrielle's daughter had been heard to state that: "Some girls have penises and some boys have penises, and some girls have vaginas and some boys have vaginas." Gabrielle reported that the teachers had no difficulty accepting her daughter's valid understanding and interpretation of gender: "They have been happy to work with us and . . . if they hear her dealing with that with other children, to back up what we are saying. So that's been pretty good".

FERN

Fern spoke highly of the teachers at her daughter's kindergarten and was deeply appreciative of their commitment and professionalism. She commented that the teachers had an understanding of difference, as they had both raised children in sole-parent households: "They know that [we] are not part of the *normal* equation so things need to occur differently, or be accommodated differently."

When Fern spoke of a connection that had been made with another gay family who attended the kindergarten she could not remember how the contact had been made, and recognized the possible sensitivity of such facilitation. "I don't know how you broker that into terms of confidentially and privacy, but...if you make it known, or there is some kind of questioning process that the teacher can kind of say: 'Would you be interested in knowing there was another gay couple?'" The family had now been introduced to this other family, and enjoyed the friendship with them. This introduction had turned out well; however, Fern acknowledged that being gay is not a guarantee that families will be compatible.

Communication with the families was described as a strength of this kindergarten. Fern was impressed that, where parents had separated, newsletters were sent to separate houses:

> There are a lot of kids whose mum and dad live in separate houses.... They run off numbers of newsletters so that the little fella can take home two newsletters. One which might go with them to their dad's place for the weekend and one which stays with them at their mum's place. So they are already thinking quite clearly.

The teachers' understandings about the complexities of families were evident in a variety of ways. Fern reported that the teachers welcomed the father of her child, and her parents, when the occasion arose. The warm atmosphere, and the friendly and engaging teachers, Fern believed, meant that both adults and children were likely to feel at home. The recognition of the teacher's role in establishing a welcoming environment is consistent with what Sue, Laura, Kerry, and Gabrielle reported as being significant for them and their families. Fern stated that: "The culture of the place is such that I think anyone would feel welcome, and you would be hard pushed not to feel welcome."

For Fern, leadership was a factor in the success of the kindergarten and she saw leadership as vital within the kindergarten. The head teacher's ability to manage her role and to consistently demonstrate a warm and welcoming demeanor to all families was seen to contribute to the inviting atmosphere: "The head teacher is very much the person who will be holding the culture of that [kindergarten] and she does a fabulous job of it. She does a really, really fabulous job."

The head teacher's ability to accommodate the many different families and identities represented in the kindergarten was another strength that Fern admired. She appreciated the challenge of managing groups of diverse people and ensuring that all feel included: "The [kindergarten] accommodates any and all of those identities really easily." She believed that the teachers were highly competent at professionally and sensitively dealing with diversity and working for the best outcomes for all the children and their families. They achieved these outcomes by being constantly available, demonstrating warmth and caring, and facilitating opportunities for families to be fully involved in the kindergarten, both on a day-to-day basis and through regular social events. Fern summed up her thoughts when she said: "If you get a right for kids, you get a right for everybody…if you get a right for gay families; you get a right for everybody."

The broader political nature of ECEC was of concern to Fern and she acknowledged that, for her, a government commitment to diversity was an imperative. She saw the danger of the word *diversity* being seen only as *window-dressing* yet understood that its use in policy documents affirmed that those responsible for the wording had at least considered the *Other*. Fern wondered if legislation was necessary to encourage all teachers to take steps to be inclusive of gay families, and said:

> Naming things is really important…so the key strategic documents that guide the development and work of the early childhood sector [should make sure] that it is named and people have to be measured, and have to demonstrate effectiveness at working alongside gay families.

Summary

The stories that I have shared from my study are the unique voices of five gay mothers explaining aspects of their experiences as mothers of children in ECEC settings in Aotearoa New Zealand. These mothers saw the relationships the children developed with teachers as paramount to their children's well-being. For all of the mothers in my study, as for most mothers, the welfare of their children was of critical importance. Each of the 17 mothers in my study made positive statements about the teachers in the ECEC centers. The four stories I chose highlighted practices that showed acceptance, openness, and a willingness to engage with difference. These practices demonstrated hospitality and *manaakitanga* and challenged the discursive practices of heteronormativity.

Discussion

There were two key ideas about hospitality that emerged from the stories: the construct of *hospitality as hosting* in order to provide for the *guest*, and the broader understanding of hospitality as an opportunity for learning, and for moving beyond heteronormativity: *hospitality as curriculum*.

Hospitality as hosting

There are many examples of warm and caring interactions and practices in the stories. Fern's assertion that "If you get it right for gay families you get it right for everyone" declares a position in keeping with the widely recognized view that many LGBTQ people want to be seen as part of the wider community rather than wishing to be treated differently (Bernstein & Reimann, 2001; Bos, van Balen, & van den Boom, 2004; Cross & Epting, 2005). The welcoming practices that occurred for the families in my study are valued as part of developing collaborative partnerships. What appeared significant about these practices were some key factors that influenced the atmosphere in the center and contributed to the mothers feeling welcome. These factors were: *leadership* and *a sense of community*.

Leadership

Leadership is a highly significant factor in how hospitality is conceptualized in ECEC centers. Traditionally a *top-down* approach has been common; however, Fasoli, Scrivens, and Woodrow (2007) call for leadership approaches that incorporate ethics, hopefulness, caring for others, and action for social justice. Leadership through activism in ECEC can mean advocating for children and their families, as well as for social justice (Curtis & Carter, 2008). Gabrielle admired the teachers for their ethical commitment to children with disabilities. Warmth, positivity, and caring were qualities that were appreciated by all the families. Teachers have a responsibility to maintain a positive, and hopeful, outlook (Halpin, 2003). Fern specifically mentioned that the head teacher at the kindergarten her daughter attended did a *fabulous job* in providing a warm atmosphere that catered to all of the families and children. Sue, Laura, and Kerry believed that the primary care arrangement promoted by the leadership of the ECEC centre provided the best possible care for their child. Other actions that show inspired leadership included the generosity inherent in sending home newsletters to all who are part of the immediate family. Leadership was evident also in Kerry's center, where two teachers were involved in postgraduate study. Research findings confirm that qualifications are a feature of effective ECEC in Aotearoa New Zealand (May, 2001). Another factor in quality ECEC identified by Aotearoa New Zealand research is the importance of belonging to a community (Duncan, Bowden, & Smith, 2006).

Sense of community

There are legislative, policy, and curriculum expectations for establishing a sense of community in any ECEC environment in Aotearoa New Zealand. Communities of practice, where a common vision and commitment to a cause are present, are seen as a desirable (Fasoli et al., 2007). A sense of community develops when there is genuine interaction and reciprocal concern. The following teacher actions acted to build and strengthen community:

1. warm and reciprocal interactions with children;
2. home visits by the teachers;
3. welcoming new babies to the family;
4. family evenings at the centers;
5. successful participation of children with disabilities;
6. inclusion of appropriate cultural knowledge and languages;
7. parent-teacher meetings;
8. the learning and consistent use of both of the mothers' names.

Home visits and social events have been used successfully to establish greater understanding of families (Hedges & Gibbs, 2005). Responsive and reciprocal relationships with children, the inclusion of culturally familiar curriculum content, and use of home languages are highly valued in *Te Whāriki* (Ministry of Education, 1996). The teacher practices listed above demonstrated hospitality to the mothers as unique individuals in the ECEC community, and also offered opportunities for learning about difference.

Hospitality as curriculum

Teacher education has the potential to play a vital role in challenging heteronormativity. The teacher education curriculum, however, is viewed as conservative and unlikely to adequately prepare teachers to address issues related to sexual diversity (Carpenter & Lee, 2010; Quinn & Meiners, 2010). The term *curriculum* is defined in ECEC as "The sum total of the experiences, activities and events, whether direct or indirect, which occur within an environment designed to foster children's learning and development" (Ministry of Education, 1996, p. 10). Therefore, curriculum includes learning that occurs for children that is not necessarily planned or intentional. There are many messages in, for example, teachers' genders, backgrounds, cultures, ethnicities, languages, sexualities, and in the messages made explicit through their values, dispositions, and discursive practices. Despite the perceived lack of preparation for teachers to appropriately deal with heteronormative practices, the families in my study provided examples of insightful hospitality, and at times what Taylor and Richardson (2005) might call a *queering of the curriculum* in the areas of *visibility*, *discourse* and *dignity*.

Visibility

In this context, the term *visibility* refers to the extent to which diverse family structures were visible in the ECEC environment. The Centre for Equity and Innovation in Early Childhood (CEIEC) (2004) argues that there are three rationales for a greater visible presence of LGBTQ in ECEC settings. Every person will, at some time in their lives, come into contact with LGBTQ; a child may have a family member who is LGBTQ; or the child may later come to the realization that they are LGBTQ. Visibility of sexual diversity in the early years of life can assist in the acceptance of difference. Children from nontraditional families have been found to be more accepting of all types of difference than children from heterosexual-headed families (Casper & Schultz, 1999). The four mother's stories identified practices that *queered the curriculum* by making the families visible in the ECEC environment. These practices included scrapbooks, photo boards, and using children's literature that included same-gender relationships. These practices harvested the learning opportunities made available by difference and upheld the rights of the families.

Visibility is an area of advocacy for those interested in LGBTQ rights. *The Lesbian and Gay Taskforce Report on Quality Childcare* in the United States project (Dispenza, n.d.) advocates for the visible presence of gay and lesbian families and teachers in ECEC. This report suggested using inclusive language and resources, posters, and photographs of diverse families. Images are critical to confronting discrimination: "Dominant groups tend to entrench their hegemony by inculcating an image of inferiority in the subjugated. The struggle for freedom and equality must therefore pass through a revision of these images" (Taylor, 1994, p. 66). Without the conscious effort of teachers, children are unlikely to see any LGBTQ presence represented in the education environment, or hear terms that provide an alternative to heteronormativity.

Discourse

Another way of *queering the curriculum* is through discursive practices and the use of language. Discourse is a tool of the powerful and acts to privilege dominant groups (Cannella, 1999). While information is shared through language there occurs also a simultaneous transmission of attitudes and values (Hyland, 2005). Foucault (1972) saw discourses as creating frameworks that can control people's understandings of social phenomena. These frameworks result in narrow classifications that can lead to the disempowerment of others (Miller & Eleveld, 1999). Disempowerment also occurs with the silencing of the LGBTQ voice through the privileging of heteronormative discourses. An awareness of the power of language is vital if teachers are to interrupt the discursive practices of heteronormativity.

In my study the mothers noticed how teachers used words and named family roles. Several of the mothers described a teacher's use of language that they experienced as affirming of their families. Queer researchers, for example, Jackson (2009), advocate for the necessity to move beyond labels like *gay, lesbian,* and *bisexual* because of their prescriptive nature. However, a teacher's use of the word *lesbian*, without embarrassment, was of particular significance to Kerry. Previous research suggests that social mothers, those who did not birth the child, are likely to be denied a visible presence in the child's life (Hequembourg, 2007). Several mothers were delighted when teachers asked how to refer to each mother. Kerry also appreciated her child's teacher using the composite word *mum-dad* that her child had devised. Swainson and Tasker (2006) argue that one of the challenges for LGBTQ families is the absence of appropriate language. This child, with the support of her family and teacher, managed the situation successfully. Sue and Laura loved that the teachers could engage in good humoured discussions about their child's first recognizable sound being *dada* in an all-women household. Each of these examples shows atypical use of discourses in an ECEC environment. The readiness with which the teachers showed acceptance of individual children's lived realities demonstrated leadership, an ethic of care and a level of hospitality that kept the dignity of the families intact.

Dignity

I have chosen to use the word *dignity* to express a depth of acceptance that is more than the equity that legislation requires. By dignity, I mean the moral acceptance and freedom to be true to self. In his vision for LGBTQ people, Cuomo (2007, pp. 85–87) noted:

> Where free expression and diversity are allowed to flourish, the sort of consciousness-raising and familiarity that promotes mutual respect for dignity across difference becomes more possible, and the harsh judgments of stereotypes and prejudice have less power.

Dignity for LGBTQ is one of the human rights protections affirmed in a recent report by the New Zealand Human Rights Commission (2010). Dignity is implicit in a broader definition of curriculum, one where the experiences of the families are a part of the learning environment for all children. It was dignity, I believe, that was preserved for the families in the stories when the acceptance and hospitality they experienced was unconditional and showed an understanding of difference.

Members of communities who do not fit the norm appreciate the opportunity to meet with people they have something in common with. The teachers sensitively put Fern and her partner in touch with another gay family at the kindergarten. Skattebol and Ferfolja (2007) consider that facilitating relationships between families is one of the important roles that teachers should take. Gabrielle spoke of attending *The Big Gay Out*. The teachers recognized this event as an important occasion in the children's lives. Herquembourg (2007) recognized the importance of gay pride events and reported that the mothers in her study attended these if they had access to them. Spending time within a safe community builds the resilience needed to manage potentially difficult situations.

Questions about family composition arose at times in the ECEC settings. Consistent with a healthy community the teachers appeared to protect the interests of Kerry and her family when inquisitive questions were broached by other heterosexual-headed family members within the ECEC setting.

Kerry saw the teachers fielding of other families' questions about her and her family as supportive. Heteronormativity allows those who belong to the dominant heterosexual group to make judgments about those who are non-heterosexual (Sedgwick, 1991) and Kerry felt that the teachers had acted ethically. Two of the mothers described having been asked by teachers about the formation of their families, and to them this was a very human and trusting connection. Gay mothers have been found to be far more open about alternative insemination options than heterosexual mothers (Golombok, 2000). Gunn (personal communication, July 2006) describes the question regarding the formation of gay families as "the elephant in the room." In both the cases where the mothers had been asked about how they came to have children, the mothers had developed a relationship with the teachers whereby they felt the question was appropriate. The questions gave the families and teachers an opportunity to discuss the nature of the families in a manner that may not have been possible otherwise.

Gabrielle's daughter shared her experiences of the complexities of gender in the ECEC center. The teachers accepted her as having expert knowledge and supported her conversations with other children. This situation is a queering of curriculum to an extent that is unusual in the traditionally conservative space of ECEC. Robinson (2005) argues that, in most ECEC settings, teachers view children as *innocent* and unable to comfortably manage notions of sexuality diversity or challenges to heteronormativity. The teachers at Gabrielle's center moved beyond fears of disrupting childhood innocence and showed the utmost respect for Gabrielle's daughter as a "competent and confident learner(s) and communicator(s)" (Ministry of Education, 1996, p. 9).

CONCLUSION

Te Whāriki (Ministry of Education, 1996) advocates for learning communities where families receive hospitality and where children's backgrounds are acknowledged and respected. One of the challenges to these grand aims is the powerful and pervasive presence of heteronormativity. Heteronormativity can render the daily lives of LGBTQ people invisible and silence their voices. The experiences of families described in this chapter demonstrate that there are teachers who manage the complexities of sexual diversity with a rich array of skills, and an open and accepting approach to difference. I interpreted these practices used by the teachers as *hospitality as hosting*, that is, generating a warm and welcoming atmosphere. As hosts providing for the families, the teachers showed leadership and worked to develop a sense of community in their ECEC settings. The sense of community generated by the teachers' actions meant that the intentions of *manaakitanga* were likely to be realized for these families.

Hospitality as curriculum involved a recognition of the learning potential of difference. The teachers worked to make visible all the families in the centers and challenged the dominant discourses to make room for a queering of curriculum. Furthermore the teachers showed an ethic of caring and a genuine commitment to honoring the dignity of the families.

ACKNOWLEDGMENTS

My warmest thanks go to the mothers who generously shared their stories with me. The project on which this chapter is based is from my master's thesis, and I was ably supervised by Associate Professor Judith Duncan and Megan Gollop from the Children's Issues Centre at the University of Otago. I am grateful to the University of Auckland, Faculty of Education, and the University of Otago for funding that allowed me to complete this work.

NOTES

1. The pervasive presence of heterosexual discourses and the expectation that everyone is heterosexual.
2. Describes the formal arrangement. Children are allocated a particular teacher to take responsibility for the majority of their care and education; predominantly used in infant and toddler settings.

REFERENCES

Allen, L., & Elliot, K. (2008). Learning and teaching sexualities in Aotearoa New Zealand. In V. Carpenter, J. Jesson, P. Roberts., & M. Stephenson (Eds.). *Ngā kaupapa here: Connections and contradictions in education* (pp. 168–178). Melbourne, AUS: Cengage Learning.

Bauman, Z. (2008). *Does ethics have a place in a world of consumers?* Cambridge, MA: Harvard University Press.

Bernstein, M., & Reimann, R. (2001). Queer families and the politics of visibility. In M. Bernstein., & R. Reimann (Eds.). *Queer families and queer politics: Challenging culture and the state* (pp. 1–17). New York: Columbia University Press.

Billman, N., Geddes, C., & Hedges, H. (2005). Teacher-parent partnerships: Sharing understandings and making changes. *Australian Journal of Early Childhood, 30*(1), 44–48.

Bos, H., van Balen, F., & van den Boom, D. C. (2004). Minority stress, experience of parenthood and child adjustment in lesbian families. *Journal of Reproductive and Infant Psychology, 22*(4), 291–304.

Cannella, G. S. (1999). *Deconstructing early childhood education: Social justice and revolution.* New York: Peter Lang.

Carpenter, V. M., & Lee, D. (2010). Teacher education and the hidden curriculum of heteronormativity. *Curriculum Matters, 6,* 99–119.

Casper, V., & Schultz, S. (1999). *Gay parents/straight schools.* New York: Teachers' College Press.

Centre for Equity and Innovation in Early Childhood. (2004). *Lesbian mothers on "Playschool"—what's the fuss?* Retrieved from http://www.edfac.unimelb.edu.au/ceiec/documents/lesbians.pdf

Cross, M., & Epting, F. (2005). Self-obliteration, self-definition, self-integration: Claiming a homosexual identity. *Journal of Constructivist Psychology, 18,* 53–63.

Cuomo, C. (2007). Dignity and the right to be lesbian or gay. *Philosophical Studies: An International Journal for Philosophy in the Analytic Tradition, 132*(1), 75–85.

Curtis, D., & Carter, M. (2008). *Learning together with young children: A curriculum framework for reflective teachers.* St. Paul, MN: Redleaf Press.

Dahlberg, G., & Moss, P. (2005). *Ethics and politics in early childhood education.* London: Routledge Falmer.

Derrida, J., & Dufourmantelle, A. (2000). *Of hospitality.* Stanford, CA: Stanford University Press.

Dispenza, M. (n.d.). *Our families our children.* Seattle, WA: The Lesbian and Gay Child Care Task Force.

Duncan, J., Bowden, C., & Smith, A. (2006). *Early childhood centres and family resilience.* Wellington, NZ: Centre for Social Research and Evaluation, Ministry of Social Development.

Education Counts. (2010). *Education statistics of New Zealand.* Retrieved from http://www.educationcounts.govt.nz/publications/ece/2507/80221

Fasoli, L., Scrivens, C., & Woodrow, C. (2007). Challenges for leadership in Aotearoa/New Zealand and Austaralian early childhood contexts. In H. Hedges & L. Keesing-Styles (Eds.). *Theorising early childhood practice: Emerging dialogues* (pp. 231–253). Castle Hill, NSW: Pademelon Press.

Foucault, M. (1972). *The archaeology of knowledge.* London, UK: Tavistock Publications.

Golombok, S. (2000). *Parenting: What really counts?* London, UK: Routledge.

Graham, L., & Slee, R. (2008). An illusory interiority: Interrogating the discourse/s of inclusion. *Educational Philosophy and Theory, 40*(2), 277–293.

Gunn, A., & Surtees, N. (2004). Engaging with dominance and knowing our desires: New possibilities for addressing sexualities matters in early childhood education. *New Zealand Journal of Educational Leadership,* *19,* 79–91.

Gunn, A., & Surtees, N. (2009). *We're a family: How lesbians and gay men are creating and maintaining family in New Zealand.* Wellington, NZ: Families Commission.

Halpin, D. (2003). *Hope and education: The role of utopian imagination.* London, UK: RoutledgeFalmer.

Hedges, H., & Gibbs, G. J. (2005). Preparation for teacher-parent partnerships: A practical experience with a family. *Journal of Early Childhood Teacher Education, 26*(2), 115–126.

Henrickson, M. (2005). Lavender parents. *Social Policy Journal of New Zealand, 26,* 68–83.

Hequembourg, A. (2007). *Lesbian motherhood: Stories of becoming.* NY: Harrington Park Press.

Homosexual Law Reform Act. (1986). *The Statutes of New Zealand, 1986, No. 033.*

Human Rights Act. (1993). *The Statutes of New Zealand, 1993, No. 082.*

Human Rights Commission. (2010). *Human Rights in New Zealand.* Wellington: The Human Rigths Commission.

Hyland, K. (2005). *Metadiscourse.* London, UK: Continuum.

Jackson, J. (2009). "Teacher by day. Lesbian by night": Queer(y)ing Identities and teaching. *Sexuality Research & Societal Policy, 6*(2), 52–70.

Kant, I. (1796). *Project for a perpetual peace. A philosophical essay By Immanuel Kant, professor of philosophy at Koningsberg.* Retrieved from // find.galegroup.com.ezproxy.auckland.ac.nz/ecco/infomark.do?&conten tSet=ECCOArticles&type=multipage&tabID=T001&prodId=ECCO& docId=CB127597134&source=gale&userGroupName=auckland_ecco& version=1.0&docLevel=FASCIMILE>

Lee, D. (2008). *We are family: Gay m/others and early childhood education* (Unpublished Masters thesis). The University of Otago, Dunedin, NZ.

Lee, D., & Duncan, J. (2008). On our best behaviour: Lesbian-parented families in early childhood education. *Early Childhood Folio, 12,* 22–26.

Macfarlane, G. (2004). *Kia hiwa ra! Listen to culture.* Wellington, NZ: New Zealand Association for Research in Education.

MacNaughton, G. (2005). *Doing Foucault in early childhood studies: Applying poststructural idea*s. London, UK: Routledge.

May, H. (1992). *Minding children, managing men: Conflict and compromise in the lives of postwar pākehā women.* Wellington, NZ: Bridget Williams Books.

May, H. (2001). *Politics in the playground.* Wellington, NZ: Bridget Williams Books & New Zealand Council for Educational Research.

May, H. (2009). *Politics in the playground: the world of early childhood education in New Zealand.* (2nd ed.). Dunedin: Otago University Press.

May, H., & Mitchell, L. (2009). *Strengthening community-based early childhood education in Aotearoa New Zealand.* Wellington, NZ: NZEI Te Riu Roa.

Meade, A., & Podmore, V. (2002). *Early childhood education policy co-ordination under the auspices of the Department/Ministry of Education: A case study of New Zealand (no. 1)*. Paris: UNESCO.

Miller, G. D., & Eleveld, M. R. (1999). On "having differences" and "being different" from a dialogue of difference to the private language of indifference. In S. F. Steiner (Ed.). *Freirean pedagogy, praxis and possibilities: Projects for the new millennium* (pp. 87–100). NY: Garland.

Ministry of Education. (1996). *Te Whāriki: He whāriki mātauranga mō ngā mokopuna o Aotearoa*. Wellington, NZ: Learning Media.

Ministry of Education. (2002). *Pathways to the future: Ngā huarahi arataki*. Wellington, NZ: Learning Media.

Ministry of Education. (2005). *Kei tua o te pae, Assessment for learning: Early childhood exemplars*. Wellington, NZ: Learning Media.

Mitchell, L. (2008). *Assessment practices and aspects of curriculum in early childhood education: Results of the 2007 NZCER national survey for ECE services*. Retrieved from http://www.nzcer.org.nz/pdfs/16544.pdf.

New Zealand Teachers Council. (2005). *Code of ethics for registered teachers*. Wellington, NZ: New Zealand Teachers Council.

New Zealand Teachers Council. (2007). *Graduating teacher standards: Aotearoa New Zealand*. Wellington, NZ: New Zealand Teachers Council.

Quinn, T., & Meiners, E. R. (2010). Teacher education, struggles for social justice, and the historical erasure of lesbian, gay, bisexual, transgender, and queer lives. In A. F. Ball & C. A. Tyson (Eds.). *Studying diversity in teacher education* (pp. 135–151). New York: American Educational Research Association.

Robinson, K. H. (2005). "Queering" gender: Heteronormativity in early childhood education. *Australian Journal of Early Childhood, 30*(2), 19–28.

Rossen, F. V., Lucassen, M. F. G., Denny, S., & Robinson, E. (2009). *Youth '07 The health and wellbeing of secondary school students in New Zealand: Results for young people attracted to the same sex or both sexes*. Auckland, NZ: The University of Auckland.

Sedgwick, E. (1991). *Epistemology of the closet*. New York: Harvester Wheatsheaf.

Skattebol, J., & Ferfolja, T. (2007). Voices from an enclave: Lesbian mothers' experiences of child care. *Australian Journal of Early Education, 32*(1), 10–18.

Status of Children Amendment Act, 18 (2004).

Swainson, M., & Tasker, F. (2006). Genograms redrawn: Lesbian couples define their families. In J. J. Bigner (Ed.). *An introduction to GLBT family studies* (pp. 89–109). Binghamton, NY: The Haworth Press.

Taylor, A., & Richardson, C. (2005). Queering home corner. *Contemporary Issues in Early Childhood, 6*(2), 163–174.

Taylor, C. (1994). The politics of recognition. In A. Gutman (Ed.). *Multiculturalism: Examining the politics of recognition* (pp. 25–73). Princeton, NJ: Princeton University Press.

CHAPTER 8

Creating Community through Connections in SPACE

Sarah Te One[1]

INTRODUCTION

This chapter is about a unique Aotearoa New Zealand early childhood program that originated within a community-based, parent-cooperative early childhood service—the Playcentre. Supporting Parents alongside their Children's Education (SPACE) is an innovative program designed predominantly for first-time parents with newborn babies. SPACE programs provide new parents with an opportunity to develop friendships with other parents and to forge links with a range of family-oriented community organizations and service providers.

In late 2004, the SPACE program at Te Marua/Mangaroa Playcentre (hereafter referred to as the Playcentre) was selected as a Centre of Innovation[2] and funded by Aotearoa New Zealand's Ministry of Education to undertake three years of participatory action research. Based in a semirural community, the Playcentre is licenced to run on a sessional basis, five mornings a week. During the research period (2005–2007), the SPACE program at the Playcentre ran sessions for one afternoon per week. The Playcentre has an established culture of being hands-on and grounded in current theory as well as the New Zealand playcentre philosophy. It also has a climate of cooperative collaboration that is valued by the parents, grandparents, and other associated community members.

The research (Podmore & Te One, 2008; Podmore et al., 2009) found that the Playcentre's SPACE program created a sense of community for first-time parents by promoting a culture of care. Sociocultural theories (e.g., Lave & Wenger, 1991; Rogoff, 2003; Rogoff, Baker-Sennett, Lacasa, & Goldsmith, 1995; Rogoff, Matusov, & White, 1996; Rogoff, Mistry, Goncu, & Mosier, 1993) propose that through participation in everyday cultural processes, members (children and adults) come to understand the values and mores of specific communities. This dynamic process contributes to a constantly evolving understanding of what community means in particular contexts. Community-based collaborative support for parent participants in the Playcentre SPACE program had the dual effect of increasing parental efficacy: first, parents developed more confidence as parents; and second, parents evidenced a newfound respect for themselves and each other as parents, and as families.

Relationships within the community were strengthened during the SPACE sessions, where guest speakers from a range of community-based services (health, education, recreation, and welfare) encouraged group members to actively engage with them. Sociocultural constructs, such as *community of learners, community of practice,* and *community of inquiry,* were relevant to both the process of the research and to the findings. Both sociocultural and ecological theories were used to interpret data generated over two action research cycles between 2005 and 2007. This chapter begins with a brief overview of the SPACE program followed by an explanation of the Aotearoa New Zealand early childhood context (and the playcentre service). A more in-depth explanation of the theoretical ideas precedes the final section and concluding discussion.

What is the Supporting Parents alongside their Children's Education (SPACE) program?

The SPACE program is based on the premise that parents are the most important educators of their children. Infants joining a new SPACE session are usually between two weeks to three months of age. There are sometimes opportunities for older infants to join an existing SPACE or playcentre session depending on the availability of places. Facilitators run weekly sessions for parents and infants in a relaxed and baby-friendly environment, usually a playcentre (described below). These sessions provide a forum for parents to meet and get to know one another in a facilitated group setting. Parents who enroll in a SPACE program are offered support and encouragement from other participants in the group by two facilitators (one trained and one in-training) who guide the group as they share the journey through their child's early months. Facilitators hold recognized early childhood qualifications and have completed the SPACE Facilitators Training program. Facilitators are encouraged to reflectively evaluate their sessions with their support person. Ongoing support for facilitators is provided by the SPACE New Zealand (NZ) national office staff. Facilitators receive a training manual with up-to-date resources to use in SPACE programs.

Spread over 30 to 40 weeks, SPACE sessions provide parents and infants with a range of play experiences to support infants' learning and development alongside group discussions. In response to group-initiated topics, facilitators and community-based guest speakers provide information on child development and parenting topics.

A typical SPACE session runs for up to two and a half hours, and begins with a welcoming and settling-in time, a thought for the session, often a Māori *whakatauki* (proverb), followed by an ice-breaker or sharing time. In keeping with Aotearoa New Zealand's cultural traditions, SPACE sessions always include either morning or afternoon tea. Sessions conducted during the first three to six months tend to focus more on relationship building and attachment between parent and infant through discussion topics such as *Getting to know you and your baby*, *Heuristic play*, and *Natural movement* (influenced by Magda Gerber, 2002). SPACE facilitators use music and stories to encourage playfulness between parent and infant (Te One et al., 2007). Discussion topics, sometimes with a guest speaker from the community, characterize the SPACE sessions. These discussion topics are decided on by the group and can reflect current concerns, for example, sleep or immunization. Later sessions introduce traditional early childhood areas of play such as blocks, water play, painting, and sand (Somerset, 1976), and a short course covering an orientation to Aotearoa New Zealand early childhood education and care services.

SPACE Programs in the Aotearoa New Zealand Early Childhood Context

Increasingly, first-time parents can experience feelings of isolation and loneliness in their new role. The gradual demise of traditional community-based networks, where neighbors knew one another and extended family (*whānau*) lived nearby, can make it difficult for new parents to find support. The literature reviewed as part of the research identified two key points. First, there had been a significant drop in the number of first-time parents and infants enrolled in playcentres; and second, there was a need for a support and education program for new parents and their infants based in a group setting (Podmore & Te One, 2008). Duncan and Bowden (2004) found that family engagement in early childhood services of good quality enhanced resilience, particularly among vulnerable populations, by building on a sense of belonging to a community. Universally provided services, such as those funded by the state, are a nonstigmatizing strategy, which improve, intervene, and strengthen "families, *whānau* and communities, and [improve] interagency co-ordination, collaboration and communication" (Ministry of Social Development, 2006, p. 4). The notion of an early childhood center as a hub is a collaborative strategy reflecting research, which suggests that targeting single risks in isolation is relatively ineffective (Clarkin-Phillips & Carr, 2009; Duncan, Bowden, & Smith, 2006a, 2006b; Gray, 2001; Whalley, 2006).

Based in communities, working out of early childhood education services, the SPACE program supports a vision that New Zealand children "have the best start in life, flourish in early childhood, and are supported to reach their potential" (Ministry of Education, 2002, p. 1). Several Ministry of Education policies and projects support increased participation in good-quality early education based on evidence that this may improve social and educational outcomes for children (Dixon, Widdowson, Meagher-Lundberg, Airini, & McMurchy-Pilkington, 2007; Ministry of Education, 2002; Mitchell & Hodgen, 2008). Furthermore, involving parents in educational experiences at a local, community level has positive ongoing benefits (Clarkin-Phillips & Carr, 2009; Te One, 2010a). Research evidence has demonstrated "that two-generational programmes that combine parent education and support and ECEC can raise child outcomes and are more effective than solely parent-focused or child-focused programmes alone" (Ministry of Social Development & Ministry of Education, 2004, p. 1). SPACE programs are intergenerational and operate from within group settings (playcentres) that, by definition, have the potential to alleviate isolation and promote community wellness as parents and their infants participate together in the sessions.

PLAYCENTRES

Playcentres are a parent-/*whānau*-led cooperative early childhood service unique to Aoteoroa New Zealand. Publicly funded playcentres are licenced by New Zealand's Ministry of Education, the body responsible for enforcing the early childhood regulatory framework to ensure that minimum operational requirements such as staffing ratios, group size, and qualifications are in place. Like all other licenced services, playcentres follow the national curriculum guidelines of *Te Whāriki* (Ministry of Education, 1996). Playcentre parents adhere to a philosophy of child-initiated, free (spontaneous) play. Historical accounts of the New Zealand Playcentre movement note that progressive educational ideas such as free play and parent involvement broke new ground (May, 2007; Somerset, 1976). The benefits of play and empowering parents through an emergent leadership education program remain integral to the playcentre philosophy to promote adults' active involvement in children's learning (Densem & Chapman, 2000; May, 2007; Somerset, 1976). Consistent with this philosophical approach, the SPACE program at the Te Marua/Mangaroa Playcentre was the venue for parents to meet and discuss a wide range of issues concerning infants and parenting as well as learning about community-based services.

Research: Theory, Design, and Method; A Collaborative Experience

The facilitators at the Playcentre's SPACE program and two university-based researchers formed a team to investigate how their innovative practices influenced learning and teaching. The research addressed two key research questions:

1. How does the SPACE program, implemented at the Playcentre for new parents and infants, support and foster their learning?
2. How does the SPACE team and program, together with the Playcentre, network and support collaborative relationships?

Two cycles of action research were completed between 2005 and 2007. Action Research Cycle 1 addressed the first research question and Action Research Cycle 2 explored the second. Researchers used observations, parent interviews, facilitator reflections, and cross-sectoral consultations (interviews and a focus group) (Borgia & Schuler, 1996; Cardno, 2003). In Action Research Cycles 1 and 2 there were between 15 and 17 parent participants and 16 to 17 infants (one set of twins in Action Research Cycle 1), making a total of 32 parents and 33 children across both action research cycles. Parent participants were drawn from several sources—antenatal groups, midwives' referrals, and recommendations from family members. The infants' ages

ranged from three weeks to five and a half months at the commence-
ment of the program. The parents' ages ranged from mid-20s to
early-40s. Most families included two parents, but three were single-
parent families. Participants were mainly *Pākeha* (non-Māori) New
Zealand mothers; however, there were four new immigrant mothers.
One father participated in the latter stages of Action Research Cycle
2 because the mother returned to work.

During Action Research Cycle 2, seven community members from
a range of health professional services, community support services,
and education services participated in a focus group interview to
investigate how the SPACE program supported collaborative networks in the community. Guest speakers (12 in total) were a feature of the program, and these included health professionals, music
advisors, psychologists, and sociologists. Researchers interviewed two
guest speakers and three health professionals.

The research team submitted two detailed applications to the relevant human ethics committees: one where the two university-based
researchers were employed (this covered the research team, facilitators, and parents who consented as well on behalf of their infants);
and one to a health provider whose employees were interviewed either
individually as guest speakers or as part of the focus group interview.
Sensitivity to infants' rights (Hedges, 2002; Te One, 2010b), cultural
appropriateness, and inclusiveness were important ethical considerations, and representatives from local Māori *iwi* (indigenous tribes),
early childhood services, health professionals, researchers, and parents formed an advisory group to guide the research team.

SOCIOCULTURAL AND ECOLOGICAL THEORIES

Since the mid-1990s, the New Zealand Ministry of Education has
supported a diverse approach to learning and development in early
childhood (Ministry of Education, 1996, 1998, 2005, 2006) that
retains an alliance with developmental psychology, yet at the same
time creates a new paradigm to incorporate ecological theory and
recent interpretations of sociocultural theories of development
(Anning, Cullen, & Fleer, 2008; Smith, 1998). This research used
sociocultural theoretical constructs (Cullen, 2004; Lave & Wenger,
1991; Rogoff, 2003; Rogoff et al., 1993) and ecological concepts
(Bronfenbrenner, 1979, 2005) to interpret how parents' participation
in the SPACE program changed (or transformed) over time as they
became more familiar with their role as parents and as their relationship with their children deepened. Ecological perspectives provided

insights into how participation in the SPACE program promoted collaborative networks for parents across different settings (systems), including homes, the Playcentre, and the wider community. Both sociocultural and ecological theoretical traditions acknowledge the centrality of socially mediated activity to human development and learning. Development and learning are a consequence of participation in social and cultural processes, taking into consideration both internal development and the cultural, social, and political influences on that development.

COMMUNITIES OF LEARNERS, COMMUNITIES OF PRACTICE, COMMUNITIES OF INQUIRY

Sociocultural theories propose that through participation in cultural processes, members come to understand the values and mores of specific communities. In other words, children and adults develop and learn as a result of their participation in communities. This dynamic process contributes to a constantly evolving understanding of what community means in particular contexts.

The *community of learners* model is based on principles of collaboration that encourage shared endeavors based on certain principles: the process is learner centered; knowledge is co-constructed and interwoven with common, shared understanding; and facilitators aspire to meaning making (Bartel, 2005). Rogoff (2003, p. 52) observed that "development is a process of *people's changing participation in sociocultural activities of their communities*" (italics in the original). According to Wenger (1998), communities of practice show how individuals, communities, and organizations learn together through shared participation. Members of the community need to make abstract concepts become workable tools. As part of the research journey, the research team increasingly became a "community of inquiry" (Wells, 2001; Wells & Claxton, 2002) as they reflected, questioned, and reviewed the action research processes and findings.

Sociocultural and ecological theories provided a framework for analysis. Two key themes emerged during an inductive analysis process of both action research cycles. The first theme was collaborative support, with subthemes of the impact of the environment, respecting parents, and valuing families and communities; and the second theme was communication across sectors, which included referrals to SPACE programs from other agencies, interactions across settings, and cross-sectoral content (Podmore & Te One, 2008). The remainder of this chapter focuses on the first theme, collaborative support, and how the different theoretical constructs of community contributed to understanding the overall effect of the SPACE program on infants, parents, and the research team.

How SPACE Built a Sense of Community

Observations of the SPACE sessions recorded the impact of the physical environment on the social environment and revealed that simple changes encouraged interactions between parents, infants, and the facilitators. Initially, a deeper engagement with one another led parents to a sense of belonging to a community of learners.

Facilitators actively supported parents to participate in the program through a range of strategies designed to set the group at ease. Although informal, the structure of the sessions offered a sense of predictability. Parents knew that sessions would begin with a *whakatauki* and that there would be music and food and drink. The environment was set up to ensure comfort for the parents and infants, and to support interactions (Elam, 2005). For example, an observer noted that

> due to the number of babies being put onto the rug, the environment has become quite cluttered [with] babies [and]car seats [on the rug], making it harder for parents to get around during an icebreaker. (Observation, Action Research Cycle 1)

Further analyses led to facilitators removing chairs and replacing these with a comfortable couch and large cushions, which encouraged parents to sit on the floor. The same observer commented that the room was now "very open and inviting." Adapting the environment continued in the second action research cycle:

> Environment set up differently which allows for more infant:infant, parent:infant interactions and is feeling more open/spacious—e.g., fewer chairs are available, tables have been folded away so the rug area is larger, large cushions are on the floor. Most parents choose to sit on the cushions with their babies so lots of babies [have been put] straight onto the rugs today. [Parents] are arranging themselves...bringing cushions over to the group area—moving between the floor and the chairs to feed/play. (Observation, Action Research Cycle 2)

The overall effect of these changes in the environment was threefold: first, parents were observed to interact more with their infants; second, there were increasing numbers of interactions between parents and others' infants; and finally, the infants being in closer proximity to one another facilitated infant-to-infant interactions:

> The babies on rugs were able to observe much more of the group/environment than in their car seats. They were physically active and free with their bodies. (Facilitator's reflection, Action Research Cycle 1)

The SPACE sessions were designed to strengthen relationships through facilitated group learning where parents could safely explore their experiences as they adjusted to their new role. Changes to the environment created new possibilities for parents and infants to establish a learning community in a relaxed, informal way. Another example of a simple but effective environmental change was to alter the shape of the seating arrangements:

> So that parents were sitting in more of a square/circular shape, rather than a rectangular format. Before this change, facilitators and guest speakers were sitting at the top of the "rectangle." It was conscious change, to say "this is a discussion, not facilitators as teachers at the top." (Facilitator's reflection, Action Research Cycle 1)

A subtle geometric alteration shifted the balance of power. Facilitators, observers, and guest speakers all noted how changes to the physical environment improved social interactions for everyone within the group.

Observations during the first action research cycle showed infants and parents being stepped over/across. In view of Māori cultural considerations it was important to avoid this:

> Traditionally in Māori culture women and girls are encouraged to sit with discretion. Women and girls do not step over other people's bodies or legs. They move or walk around so that they do not need to step over others. Awareness of this can mean others can be sensitive and move so as not to make it difficult for them. (Report to the New Zealand Playcentre Federation from the Working Party on Cultural Issues 1990, cited in Podmore & Te One, 2008)

An awareness of cultural practices therefore influenced how the environment was set up, and facilitators placed the rugs so there was walking space around them. After making these changes, the need for them seemed obvious. Overall, evidence suggested that changes to the physical environment enhanced the social environment, which contributed, in the longer term, to establishing a sense of belonging to the group for the parents attending the SPACE sessions.

Emotional safety is an important consideration in group dynamics at any age (Elam, 2005). During both action research cycles, researchers observed numerous incidents of parents sharing concerns about their personal experiences which indicated a degree of comfort within the group.

> Several of the parents who hadn't contributed to the earlier discussion do so now and [facilitator] shares her own experiences with the group. The parents enjoy sharing their experiences and there is a great deal of laughter as they listen to each other. (Observation, Action Research Cycle 2)

Parents recognized that their experiences were common across the group, and through discussions it was evident that the nature of parental participation had transformed:

> I've learnt a lot, with the other new mums, who are often going through the same sort of things—you know, like nappy rash, or teething—or all that sort of stuff. (Parent interview, Action Research Cycle 1)

Facilitators' on-going reassurance to parents was critical to frank and open discussion within SPACE sessions. Opportunities to share within the group allayed common fears all parents seem to have about their infants:

> It's been a huge support, because you really [are] fumbling your way around when you're a new parent—well, that's how you feel like you're doing—you're guessing a lot of the time and learning about new instincts that you didn't know you had and things like that. I've really enjoyed that when we chat things through with [facilitators] or just another mum. You realize you're not the only one. That's been a really great support. (Parent interview, Action Research Cycle 2)

Facilitators encouraged thoughtful reflection, which promoted the well-being of the parents participating in the SPACE program, but this was not always comfortable for them:

> [I find] it really hard to listen to some conversations where parents are offering advice which I find that I do not agree with and trying not to state my opinion, but to rather question them on theirs....I don't feel that they are expecting us to be the expert, rather more of an

information-sharing opportunity. However, when the advice is questionable, and possibly not correct—that is a challenge. (Facilitator's reflection, Action Research Cycle 2)

Nonjudgmental listening, respecting confidentiality, quietly observing, and modeling alternative ways of interacting with infants were part of the skill-set facilitators used to establish trust within the group. They consciously created opportunities for parents to raise questions and share their experiences, which were then incorporated into the SPACE sessions. These cultural processes characterize communities of learners, practice, and inquiry. In the above example, the facilitator was a contributor to the *community of learners*, but was part of a different *community of practice*. Facilitators' critical reflections shifted the focus beyond the immediate research questions, thus creating a *community of inquiry*. This was explained by one of the researchers as follows:

> As a SPACE session formed, i.e. the parents and babies started bonding as a group with the facilitators, the researchers embarked on the process of gathering data and analyzing them. We saw two things happening—the SPACE group became a community of learners that *shared understandings* during the SPACE sessions. They transformed their participation through shared understanding. At the same time, the researchers and the research associates formed another *community of learners*. As we engaged in this collaborative activity (discussing and analyzing the data), we underwent a further transformation of participation, which led us to an even deeper level of contribution, collaboration and understanding. We became a community of inquiry. In this community participants feel confident and secure to source or contribute additional levels of involvement, which in turn transforms to a deeper shared understanding. We thought of ourselves as a community of inquiry because we were asking questions beyond the original research question, and looking at how what we had learnt in one setting (the Playcentre's SPACE sessions), influenced our practices in another (developing new resources for SPACE, like training facilitators and introducing sociocultural theories). Our resulting community of learners looked very different from the original one, having undergone many transformations and reached many shared understandings on their journey. This process occurred numerous times, in multiple contexts within the SPACE setting, and with a variety of participants. (T. Dingemanse, personal communication, June 4, 2007)

This process was interpreted metaphorically as a spiral shell (figure 8.1) and used by the research team for explicating both action

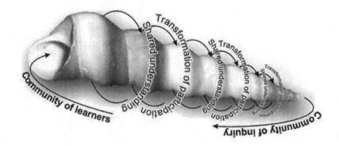

Figure 8.1 Transformation of participation: A conceptual model by Truus Dingemanse

Source: Podmore & Te One, 2008, p. 7.

research as a method, and a growing sense of collaboration, which transformed understandings of community of practice beyond the research questions towards those reflecting the traits of a community of inquiry.

The stated aims of the SPACE program value parents and parenting skills, and by establishing a collaborative climate that nurtured and valued first time parents' experiences, the research team members observed a deep respect for the experiences these participants were encountering. Data from the focus group interview and guest speaker interviews evidenced respect for parents as a contributing factor in collaborative support offered during SPACE sessions:

> You can see from the discussions [during SPACE sessions] they're valuing the role of parents in a world which is more and more work-oriented, and more and more the identity of the person is through their working life as opposed to their parenting life. (Focus Group interview, Action Research Cycle 2)

> Yeah, and telling them they have got the most important job, not only are they the best at it, but it's the most important role. And I don't think we say that enough and I don't think we give parents enough…support and education to be good parents. (Guest Speaker, Action Research Cycle 2)

Guest speakers, too, formed a community of practice with facilitators. Their role was educative and, to some extent they advised parents about their area of expertise. Their contributions informed the community of learners operating within the SPACE sessions.

Valuing Family and Community

Research on family resilience suggests that participation in community activities, or, in theoretical terms, cultural processes, is fundamental to well-being (Duncan & Bowden, 2004; Duncan et al., 2006a, 2006b). The long-term benefits of supporting parents and families as contributing to community and societal well-being were acknowledged by focus group participants representing agencies involved in education (primary and early childhood), child health, and social development:

> It's filled a big gap...If you were a young mum, you know, there's [*sic*] not a lot of places to go. There was a gap...there's a real gap that's being filled by SPACE. (Focus Group Interview, Action Research Cycle 2)

Furthermore, there were positive comments from participants in the SPACE program, the guest speakers, and the wider community about the value of the program for families:

> Good parenting always has an impact in society, which is why I'm interested in anything that goes into helping parents in any way when children are young. The ramifications are 50 years down the track, aren't they? They're for life. (Focus Group Interview, Action Research Cycle 2)

Nevertheless there was important affirmation for SPACE as a center-based group program, for drawing families from the community together as a group. One participant in the focus group commented:

> It seems to be such an individual world at the moment. Everybody's off doing their own surviving. And to have that—time just to be part of a community—of people doing the same thing, similar thing [that's so important]. (Focus Group Interview, Action Research Cycle 2)

Collaborative support in the SPACE program at the Playcentre nurtured a culture of care, respected parents, and valued families in communities. Focus group participants were enthusiastic:

> [SPACE] is just a neat support. There's not a lot of support for mums out there in the community. You go down any street and everybody's at work. It's not like 30 to 40 years ago when people were at home and you had a neighbour, you could have the support; and it really is

> a time when [first-time mothers] need it. . . . [The SPACE program is] an education *and* a support. (Focus Group Interview, Action Research Cycle 2)

Theoretically, interpretations of the focus group data reveal a wider macrosystem level of support for the SPACE program. Arguably, the focus group participants formed a *community of practice* (albeit temporary), which offered the research team insights into the influence of SPACE sessions on parents and infants. Like the facilitators' community of practice, there were elements of shared understanding about the purpose and benefits of the SPACE program for first-time parents.

SPACE in the Wider Community

Through multiple data sources, communication across sectors emerged as a major theme contributing to building community. Duncan and Bowden (2004) reported four key themes, identified by participants in their research, which supported their parenting and the resilience of their families:

> Being there; meeting the holistic needs of the children; assisting parents to be involved in their children's lives; and negotiating and facilitating family contacts with other agencies and families. (p. 42)

These themes were also apparent in the research at the Playcentre, as community-based agencies recognized the value of the SPACE program for first-time parents and consequently referred them on. Interestingly, evidence of referrals to SPACE also came from within the group as they communicated their perceived benefits with one another and to their wider family and community networks.

Referrals to SPACE from Inside and Outside

The nested imagery of Bronfenbrenner's Russian dolls became apparent once referral data were analyzed. SPACE participants were recruited from Plunket, a New Zealand child and maternal health service offered nationally to all parents of newborn infants, and from midwives, either attached to maternity units in hospitals, to a general medical practice, or working independently. Playcentres in other areas of New Zealand also referred prospective participants to the national SPACE co-coordinator, who then teamed them up with a program in a nearby playcentre. Other referrals came from government social service agencies dealing with children and families. These agencies recommended the SPACE program for clients. Education services, both early childhood and primary (elementary school), also referred individuals to SPACE. As the SPACE research progressed, it became possible to disseminate the emerging findings, and this generated interest locally, regionally, and nationally, leading to an increased demand for programs, which in fact, became problematic at the time due to a lack of skilled, trained facilitators. Prior to the SPACE research, the referrals were typically word-of-mouth and relied on the reputation of the messenger or the organization. For example, Plunket nurses are generally well-respected infant health professionals with an interest in maternal health as well. The majority of referrals from outside came from either Plunket nurses, or midwives who ran antenatal groups:

> I was advised by my midwife and Plunket nurse to come along.... Everyone I seemed to come across they showed the SPACE pamphlet, so I figured it was a good idea. (Parent, Action Research Cycle 1)

As external agencies, Plunket nurses and midwives played a key role in connecting families to SPACE programs and facilitated contact initially through antenatal groups and then as part of their role as community-based child health professionals. The expertise of these community-based professionals was informed by exosystem policies and activities. They recognized the positive impact of SPACE for first-time parents, particularly in creating a sense of community that enhanced family well-being as a direct result of participation in the SPACE program. Their actions occurred at a macrosystem level, and at the same time, were an example of how a community of practice supported communities of learners.

Interactions between Different Community Groups

The focus group data were particularly revealing because they drew on the expertise of professionals from diverse disciplines: education, social services, and health (e.g., a Plunket nurse and a local general practitioner). In their capacity as representatives of their respective sectors, several community-based personnel reflected on the numerous services available in the community and how these could offer mutual support to first-time parents. The potential of the SPACE program to offer extended support was a dominant theme. An experienced Plunket nurse noted:

> Once again, it's the [SPACE program's] support thing and that really impresses me. You get a girl in there who's inclined to be a bit postnatally depressed [*sic*] and [the SPACE] group just really rally round her and support her. Especially for the people who are new to the country—for them it's just a wonderful because home sickness when you've had a baby is probably the worst thing that can happen and it's just so supportive…and relaxed. (Focus Group Interview, Action Research Cycle 2)

One antenatal educator commented:

> We've made that initial contact but then SPACE can follow up, because we often have little contact with the mums once their babies…thinking about [enrolling mothers in SPACE] while they get over that initial "I'm really tired with a brand new baby," six, seven weeks down the track when they're ready to be involved with a group. (Focus Group Interview, Action Research Cycle 2)

Another health professional observed:

> In many ways the [Name of a parenting program] offers a similar sort of program really. What I understand about SPACE is that it has a lot more detail to it whereas [Name of a parenting program] is just a 12-hour course. (Focus Group Interview, Action Research Cycle 2)

A further comment about the SPACE program implied that the community group setting of the playcentres removed any stigma from the referral process, which in the case of the social workers, was often due to perceived vulnerabilities of the parents. One commentator noted that some of the other parenting programs were targeted, elitist, exclusive, and even in competition with one another, but not so the SPACE programs:

> [Parenting Group 1] run their own program. I think there is strong opposition from a very strong [Parent Group 2] who do a lot of parent education as well. They are geared more to your middle class, affluent person—I mean it's hundreds of dollars to enroll. [SPACE] caters for everybody across the board. There's no social standing at all…you're all trying to do the same job. (Focus Group Interview, Action Research Cycle 2)

The SPACE program was regarded as a sustainable community model that recognized the benefits of support for parents, highlighting the low status parenting was perceived to have:

> People do need to know about parenting—lots of people! With this programme, these people that come from SPACE are out in the community [and they are] good role models for people to follow and will be confident in what they are doing. (Focus Group Interview, Action Research Cycle 2)

A local primary school principal commented further on the benefits of the SPACE program for one of her staff members who had returned to work part-time with her infant after taking maternity leave:

> [Parent's name] is to me the most wonderful example of a brilliant mum. She uses such great techniques with her daughter, and she's in the classroom with her daughter for part of the day, and the children see first-hand, really good parenting. I think for some of them it might be the only time. For me, I'm a grandma, so I'm interested from that point of view as well. As I said, I think good parenting makes a difference, and I think these days, it's so hard sometimes to find good role models for good parenting. (Focus Group Interview, Action Research Cycle 2)

Observations by professionals prompted some discussions about the SPACE program in wider community forums:

> I think that when you're in a [SPACE] group that's being facilitated in a way, that's about the sharing of knowledge, the sharing of parenting knowledge, just the process itself, rather than "Well I learned this about blah, blah, blah," just the process of working together....And realizing that someone else's worries are the same as yours....That's the feedback from our [health and social services] groups. That it's really neat to just have this time to share. Rather than just to hear from [experts], but share among themselves, and work out things that have worked for this person, and not worked for that person....Again, [it's] community building—mother to mother. (Focus Group Interview, Action Research Cycle 2)

The powerful impact of the SPACE program was recognized as a contributing factor in building confidence for first-time parents. Furthermore, the nonstigmatized delivery in a group setting facilitated parents' participation in the SPACE sessions and enabled them to establish useful networks as members of a community of learners.

Connecting with Community Services

An intention of the SPACE program was to link participants to community-based services. Sessions were responsive to participants' interests and invited guest speakers from a range of agencies and sectors, such as, for example, midwives and other health professionals. Early childhood education services and other community-based services formed an integral part of the program as well as introducing a new dynamic to the group. This meant that the content was adapted to suit the interests of the participants, and drew on community resources and speakers, as well as on expertise within the group (Podmore & Te One, 2008). Guest speakers and topics were decided through group discussions, questionnaires about potential topics, and through the facilitators' reflections. Participants reflected that, even if the topic information was not new to them, they were now looking at things from a parent's perspective:

> I'm a trained nurse and I've done child development, but when it's your own kid [sic] you just forget all that stuff....Because you don't know what to expect, and so it was nice to have [guest speakers] come along and talk about those things. (Parent, Action Research Cycle 2)

Guest speakers were conscious of the group dynamics' impact on participants. The group as a *community of learners* was observable to invited guests:

> I think the learning from each other is really powerful. And the networking with each other and I don't see that networking with other organisations and agencies...I can see [the mothers] getting support from each other and that they're learning from each other and that they are seeing there is lots of different ways of being a parent that are all OK. And getting that level of support—that's what I see. And it gives [parents] the confidence to go home and be good parents—that's definitely what I see. (Guest Speaker, Action Research Cycle 2)

During the SPACE sessions, guest speakers from different community service agencies provided information about health, welfare, and social services, as well as ECEC services. The topics addressed by guest speakers adapted to the interests and requests of the group members. This open agenda occasionally raised controversial issues that created ethical dilemmas for facilitators. For example, one facilitator commented:

> A parent rang me who had concerns about the new immunization schedule and wondered if we could have a discussion on session.

I spoke to [another facilitator] about it and we agreed that it was such a personal decision that this forum would not be appropriate—we referred her to other avenues to source more information and reassured her that then she would be able to make an informed decision. (Facilitator's reflection, Action Research Cycle 2)

The SPACE sessions offered these parents a venue for a range of activities that deepened their connectedness to community-based networks, reduced social isolation, and affirmed participants' new role as parents (Podmore & Te One, 2008). Data from parent exit interviews, facilitators' journals, and observations as well as the focus group interview provided evidence that communication across sectors was strengthened by referrals from the community and within the SPACE program, interactions among participants, and the influence of guest speakers. When regarded as a whole, these data illustrate that, over time, the parents and their infants, the facilitators, and the research team developed a shared understanding that transformed participation in the respective communities of learning (for parents and infants), of practice (for facilitators), and of inquiry (for the research team).

Conclusion: Creating Community through SPACE

The SPACE program is an Aotearoa New Zealand educational innovation, which supports first-time parents and their infants. This research revealed how the SPACE program at the Te Marua/Mangaroa Playcentre supported and fostered learning among the participating parents, their infants, and the research team. Sociocultural and ecological theoretical constructs across a range of data sources (observations of SPACE sessions, exit interviews with participating parents, reflections of SPACE program facilitators) revealed how several processes and strategies contributed to creating a sense of community. As one of the advisory group members commented:

To me SPACE is about connections and communities. The [research] project has forged a web of powerful and hopefully enduring connections between families, children, facilitators, the playcentre, and the researchers themselves. I believe a lack of the sense of belonging that a community creates is one of contemporary society's biggest weaknesses and one of the prime reasons for our increasing problems of abuse, violence and crime. SPACE builds communities, and the importance of that cannot be overestimated. (Podmore & Te One, 2008, p. 178)

Throughout the course of the three-year research period (2005–2007) the researchers recognized theoretical constructs of community. Parents, guided by skilled facilitators, formed their own community of learning as they shared their experiences of parenting with one another. Over time, they became acculturated to their new role and emerged as confident and competent participants within their SPACE group. The research team, which included facilitators (some of whom were also parents involved in the Playcentre) and university-based researchers, experienced a transformation from a community of practice to a community of inquiry as they jointly challenged and interrogated the data and the analyses.

Since the researchers began disseminating their research findings, there has been an increased demand for SPACE programs in Aotearoa New Zealand (Leanne Dawson, NZ SPACE Trust, personal communication). SPACE programs can operate from within existing ECEC services. Evidence from the SPACE program indicated that the programs empowered parents; they provided a forum for parents to seek information about social services, health, and education; and, most importantly, SPACE programs enhanced community well-being for those parents.

ACKNOWLEDGMENTS

The author acknowledges that the New Zealand Ministry of Education funded the Centre of Innovation research that forms the basis of this chapter. Comments or views expressed do not reflect government policy or the views of the New Zealand Ministry of Education. The author is particularly grateful to the SPACE NZ Trust; the research team for the *Te Marua/Mangaroa* Playcentre Centre of Innovation; the advisory group; and, the community members, families, and children who voluntarily participated in this research.

NOTES

1. With thanks for the help of Val Podmore, Leanne Dawson, Truus Dingemanse, Jeanette Higham, Justine Jones, Kathy Matthews, and Sue Pattinson.
2. The *Centre of Innovation* program funded selected early childhood services to undertake research into innovative practices that promoted quality early childhood education. The program ran from 2003 to 2009.

References

Anning, A., Cullen, J., & Fleer, M. (2008). Research contexts across cultures. In A. Anning, J. Cullen & M. Fleer (Eds.). *Early childhood education: Society and culture* (2nd ed., pp. 1–24). London: Sage.

Bartel, V. B. (2005). Learning communities: Beliefs embedded in content-based rituals. *Early Childhood Education Journal, 33*(3), 151–154.

Borgia, E. T., & Schuler, D. (1996). Action research in early childhood education. *ERIC Clearinghouse on Elementary and Early Childhood Education.* Retrieved from www.ericfacility.net/ericdigests/ed401047.html

Bronfenbrenner, U. (1979). *The ecology of human development: Experiments by nature and design.* Cambridge, MA: Harvard University Press.

Bronfenbrenner, U. (Ed.). (2005). *Making human beings human. Bioecological perspectives on human development.* Thousand Oaks, CA: Sage.

Cardno, C. E. M. (2003). *Action research: A developmental approach.* Wellington, NZ: New Zealand Council for Educational Research.

Clarkin-Phillips, J., & Carr, M. (2009). *Strengthening responsive and reciprocal relationships in a whānau tangata centre: An action research project.* Retrieved from http://www.tlri.org.nz/assets/A_Project-PDFs/9249_finalreport.pdf

Cullen, J. (2004). Adults co-constructing professional knowledge. In A. Anning, J. Cullen & M. Fleer (Eds.). *Early childhood education: Society and culture* (pp. 69–79). London: Sage Publications.

Densem, A., & Chapman, B. (2000). *Learning together: The playcentre way.* Auckland, NZ: New Zealand Playcentre Federation.

Dixon, R., Widdowson, D., Meagher-Lundberg, P., Airini, & McMurchy-Pilkington, C. (2007). *Evaluation of promoting early childhood education (ECE) participation project.* Wellington, NZ: Ministry of Education.

Duncan, J., & Bowden, C. (2004). Promoting stress-resilient families, positive parenting practices and experiences: A vision of Educare. *Childrenz issues, Journal of the Children's Issues Centre, 8*(2), 41–44.

Duncan, J., Bowden, C., & Smith, A. B. (2006a). *Early childhood centres and family resilience.* Report prepared for the Ministry of Social Development. Retrieved from www.msd.govt.nz

Duncan, J., Bowden, C., & Smith, A. B. (2006b). A gossip or a good yak? Reconceptualising parent support in early childhood centre-based programs. *International Journal of Early Years Education, 14*(1), 1–13.

Elam, P. (2005). To teach as Magda taught or mutual respect and trust: The role of the mentor in RIE. In S. Petrie & S. Owen (Eds.). *Authentic relationships in group care for infants and toddlers—Resources for infant educarers (RIE). Principles into practice.* (pp. 113–126). Philadelphia, PA: Jessica Kingsley Publishers.

Gerber, M. (2002). *Dear parent: Caring for infants with respect. Resources for Infant Educarers (RIE).* Los Angeles, CA: Resources for Infant Educators.

Gray, A. (2001). *Family support programs: A literature review.* (Prepared for the Ministry of Education). Wellington, NZ: Ministry of Education.

Hedges, H. (2002). Beliefs and principles in practice: Ethical research with child participants. *New Zealand Research in Early Childhood Education, 5,* 31–47.

Lave, J., & Wenger, E. (1991). *Situated learning: Legitimate peripheral participation.* Cambridge, UK: Cambridge University Press.

May, H. (2007). *Politics in the Playground. The world of early childhood in postwar New Zealand.* (2nd ed.). Dunedin, NZ: Otago University Press.

Ministry of Education. (1996). *Te Whāriki. He whāriki mātauranga mō ngā mokopuna o Aotearoa: Early childhood curriculum.* Wellington, NZ: NZ Learning Media.

Ministry of Education. (1998). *Quality in action. Te mahi whai hua. Implementing the revised statement of desirable objectives and practices in New Zealand early childhood services.* Wellington, NZ: NZ Learning Media.

Ministry of Education. (2002). *Pathways to the future: Ngā huarahi arataki. A 10-year strategic plan for early childhood education.* Wellington, NZ: Ministry of Education.

Ministry of Education. (2005). *Kei tua o te pae. Assessment for learning: Early childhood exemplars.* Wellington, NZ: NZ Learning Media.

Ministry of Education. (2006). *Ngā arohaehae whai hua. Self-review guidelines for early childhood education.* Wellington, NZ: NZ Learning Media.

Ministry of Social Development. (2006). *Early years service hubs* Discussion Paper. Wellington, NZ: Ministry of Social Development.

Ministry of Social Development, & Ministry of Education. (2004). *ECE centre based parent support.* Overview paper. Wellington, NZ: Ministry of Social Development.

Mitchell, L., & Hodgen, E. (2008). *Locality-based evaluation of Pathways to the Future-Ngā Huarahi Arataki-Stage 1 Report.* Wellington, NZ: Ministry of Education

Podmore, V. N., & Te One, S. (2008). *Nurturing a culture of care for infants and first-time parents: The SPACE programme at Te Marua/Mangaroa Playcentre early childhood centre of innovation (Round 2). Final research report for the Ministry of Education.* Wellington, Ministry of Education.

Podmore, V. N., Te One, S., with, Dawson, L., Dingemanse, T., Higham, J., Jones, J.,...Pattinson, S. (2009). Supporting parents alongside children's education at Te Mārua/Mangaroa Playcentre: Relationships, environment and collaboration. In A. Meade (Ed.). *Generating waves. Innovation in early education* (pp. 53–62). Wellington, NZ: NZCER Press.

Rogoff, B. (2003). *The cultural nature of human development.* Oxford and New York: Oxford University Press.

Rogoff, B., Baker-Sennett, J., Lacasa, P., & Goldsmith, D. (1995). Development through participation in sociocultural actvity. In J. J. Goodnow, P. J. Miller & F. Kessel (Eds.). *Cultural practices as contexts for development* (pp. 45–65). San Francisco, CA: Jossey-Bass.

Rogoff, B., Matusov, E., & White, C. (1996). Models of teaching and learning: Participation in a community of learners. In D. Olsen & N. Torrance

(Eds.), *The handbook of education and human development* (pp. 388–414). Cambridge, MA: Blackwell.

Rogoff, B., Mistry, J., Goncu, A., & Mosier, C. (1993). Guided participation in cultural activity by toddlers and caregivers. *Society for Research in Child Development, 58*(8), 1–174.

Smith, A. B. (1998). *Understanding children's development: A New Zealand perspective* (4th ed.). Wellington, NZ: Bridget Williams.

Somerset, G. (1976). *Vital play in early childhood.* Auckland, NZ: New Zealand Playcentre Federation.

Te One, S. (2010a). "You're allowed to play": Children's rights at playcentre. *New Zealand Research in Early Childhood Education Journal, 13*, 5–16.

Te One, S. (2010b). Advocating for infants' rights in early childhood education. *Early Childhood Folio, 14 (1)*, 13–17.

Te One, S., Podmore, V. N., with Dawson, L., Dingemanse, T., Higham, J., Jones, J.,…Pattinson, S. (2007). Relationships and interactions: A research project on supporting parents alongside children's education (Hutt SPACE National) programme in a Playcentre. *Early Childhood Folio, 11*, 10–14.

Wells, G. (2001). *Action, talk and text: Learning through inquiry.* New York: Teachers College Press.

Wells, G., & Claxton, G. (2002). *Learning for life in the 21st century: Sociocultural perspectives on the future of education.* Oxford, UK: Blackwell Publishers.

Wenger, E. (1998). *Communities of practice: Learning, meaning and identity.* Cambridge, New York, and Melbourne: Cambridge University Press.

Whalley, M. (2006). Leadership in integrated centres and services for children and families—A community development approach. *Childrenz issues, Journal of the Children's Issues Centre, 10*(2), 8–13.

CHAPTER 9

Disturbing Cultures of Incarceration: The Struggle for Normality and the Imprisoned Family

Liz Jones, Rachel Holmes, and Maggie MacLure

INTRODUCTION

In this chapter we examine the ways a prison-based Mother and Baby Unit (MBU) is managed as it strives to develop innovative ways of working with diverse family cultures so as to extend and consolidate family resilience and family well-being. The chapter draws on data that were collected while undertaking an evaluation of an MBU. We begin with a brief description of the methods used before offering both a succinct history of MBUs in the United Kingdom and more specific contextual details in relation to the MBU where we undertook the evaluation. Examples of data are introduced that, when read within a Foucauldian framework, foreground some of the tensions between the philosophy and practices of the MBU and the locations of *prison, prisoner, mother,* and *child*. It is by opening up these tensions that we are able to interrogate the discourses that are in circulation and in so doing make a space for renewed discussions that relate to both early childhood education as well as to what might constitute the resilient family.

EVALUATING A MOTHER AND BABY UNIT

Schwandt and Abma (2005) describe evaluation as "a professional social practice concerned with determining the value (merit, worth, significance) of a program, policy or project" (pp. 105–106). They distinguish a number of different purposes of evaluation, which, although not necessarily mutually exclusive, include:

- evaluation to improve performance and accountability;
- evaluation for knowledge building;
- evaluation for development;
- evaluation for understanding;
- evaluation for social critique and transformation.

Given that our remit was to conduct an inquiry that identifies aspects of the MBU that appear to be working well, and consider ways these can be further developed to meet the best interests of children and families, it is clear that our endeavors centered more on areas of knowledge building, development, and understanding rather than on performance and accountability. It is also clear that in trying to identify the *best interests* in relation to children and their families, the evaluation would also have to offer critique as a necessary precursor for transformative change.

The study took place over a four-month period. There were two researchers involved in data collection and a third involved in data analysis. One researcher made a total of 14 visits to the MBU, during which time she met informally with the mothers and babies; undertook focus groups and semi-structured interviews, and collected auto-biographical accounts from the mothers; attended a Thanksgiving Service in the chapel; had a tour of the prison; observed mothers and babies playing together in the crèche facilities; and attended the meetings of two admission boards and one separation board. The second researcher made intermittent visits to the MBU to examine documentation on the mothers and their babies, to interview MBU and prison service staff, and to meet with other related professionals that service the MBU. While we did gather data that illuminated how the fathers of children and wider family members were involved and implicated in the overall care of the babies and toddlers, our specific focus within this chapter is on the interrelationship among practitioners, mothers, and the children.

The ethical implications of undertaking research activities within an MBU are complex. Permission was sought from all the practitioners and mothers who were directly involved with the evaluation project. The use of recording equipment had to be negotiated both with the prison authorities and with the participants themselves. When the mothers expressed anxiety toward such equipment, their views were respected and the use of recording machines was abandoned. All participants involved in the research have been anonymized.

As the research period progressed, the three researchers sporadically came together to discuss data and emergent themes, ideas, and areas for potential development of practice. The theoretical framework underpinning the evaluation was informed by discourse analysis and poststructuralist theory (Butler, 2004; Foucault, 1977; MacLure, 2003) and particularly by work in early childhood (Brown & Jones, 2002; Burman, 2007; Davies, 1994; Holmes, 2010; James & Prout, 1997; Walkerdine, 1999). Discourse-based approaches conceptualize subjectivity as produced in the discursive practices that make up the social world. As Britzman (2000) reminds us,

> Discourses authorize what can and cannot be said; they produce relations of power and communities of consent and dissent, and thus discursive boundaries are always being redrawn around what constitutes the desirable and the undesirable and around what it is that makes possible particular structures of intelligibility and unintelligibility. (p. 36)

We were interested, then, in the ways that *communities of consent and dissent* emerged in the MBU, and how they operated to sustain, for instance, the *(un)desirable mother* or the sorts of practices within the MBU that were harnessed so as to produce *intelligible structures*. The evaluation also incorporated insights from Conversation Analysis (CA), a methodology that allows for fine-grained analysis of the specifics of interaction (Drew & Heritage, 1992). A CA perspective on identities assumes that both "'children' and 'adults' are cultural events that members make happen" in and through their interactions (Watson, 1992, p. 262). CA allowed us to trace the ways in which tacit and overt assumptions about what, for instance, constitutes the *good mother* or *proper conduct* and so on were actualized in the interactions through which the staff, the mothers, and their babies interpret, categorize, recognize, and judge one another.

However, while we have drawn upon the above theories and ideas so as to assist us in the ways in which we have interpreted data, it should be stressed that there are of course alternative ways of interpreting the data.

Situating MBUs within the UK Context

If, as it is commonly assumed, justice is about acquitting the innocent and punishing the guilty, "why then," asks Shaw (1992), "are the innocent children of imprisoned parents often penalised?" (p. ix). In part, the establishment of MBUs within Her Majesty's prisons can be understood as going some way to ameliorate a penal system in which the imprisonment of parents inflicts punishment on children. The principle of the MBU recognizes that the stability of the mother-child relationship is crucial for the child's subsequent development (Belsky et al., 2007; Bretherton, 1992; Brooks-Gunn, Sidle-Fuligni, & Berlin, 2003; Melhuish, 2004; Prior & Glaser, 2006; Rogoff, 2003). Yet, in spite of MBUs being understood as a response to the plight of innocent victims, their history has been overshadowed by controversy. During the latter part of the 1990s and the early 2000s, MBUs were deeply impoverished environments that were unacceptably dirty with an absence of stimulating décor for children (Her Majesty's Inspectorate of Prisons [HMIP], 2006; Owers, 2004). There were instances of babies found lying inert for long periods of time on play mats, toddlers were strapped in their buggies in front of videos, and there was little space for babies to do anything but be static. Additionally, breastfeeding was at that time discouraged, and babies were fed according to the clock. Ethnic differences in child rearing were frowned upon. Crèches were run by fellow prisoners and overseen by prison staff who had minimal experience in caring for children. There were no facilities for mothers to cook for their children, and the diet for both the mothers and their young children was lacking in fresh fruit and vegetables (Department of Health, 1992; Dillner, 1992). Moreover, as Farrell notes, the day-to-day organization of MBUs was structured around archaic prison regimes where the philosophy of incarceration, the modes of containment, and the prison rules and regulations ran "counter to the actual range of needs of incarcerated mothers and their young children" (Farrell, 1996, p. 2; see also the Ministry of Justice: Corston Report, 2007). While Farrell was commenting on prisons within an Australian context, her observations are pertinent to the UK context as well.

However, since 2006, shifts in policy have meant that women who are pregnant or who have young children are to be imprisoned only as a last resort when there are no suitable alternatives to custody (Ministry of Justice, 2008). There have also been shifts in the structural organization of female prisoners so as to ensure that mandatory and auditable standards of the gender-specific needs of women are met (Her Majesty's Prison Service Order [HM PSO], 4800, 2008). Further significant shifts have also occurred in terms of the overall ethos of MBUs so as to ensure that they are child centered and that the babies' progress and best interests are reviewed regularly (HM PSO, 4801, 2009).

Following these shifts in policy, the MBU, which is the focus for this chapter, came under external management. One of the incoming organization's first actions was to temporally close the MBU so as to create an opportunity to reorganize its provisions, providing wider health-care and education services. The organization also began working toward taking on many of the responsibilities and duties that had previously been performed by prison officers.

The MBU provides a 24-hour, 365-day service to mothers and babies. The regular staff falls into three groupings—parent support workers, nursery-nurse crèche workers, and a business support officer. All nursery staff are appropriately qualified; two have undertaken a practice qualification in addition to a Bachelor of Arts (Honors) Early Childhood Studies degree. Consequently the MBU practitioners have knowledge of child development, observation, and assessment for learning. A number of additional people, such as the Health Visitor and Pastor, make visits as and when necessary. Clear attempts have been made to soften the prison environment in which the MBU is located. There are, for example, no metal bars over the nursery windows.

The Good Mother

Although all pregnant women who are given custodial sentences are encouraged and supported to fill in an application form for a place in the MBU, this process does not always result in the woman being offered a place. For various and often complex reasons, many women are not afforded opportunities or the right to be with their babies. Because of the nature of the MBU, the only women offered places are those who are able to demonstrate to the satisfaction of gatekeepers exemplary behavior in terms of no drug use, the ability to parent successfully, nonviolent or nonaggressive behaviors or attitudes, and an aptitude to work with professionals. These conditions are deemed necessary prerequisites because

> they are around, not only their own baby, but also six, seven, eight, nine other babies. So they have to be women who have demonstrated that—they may well be women who are in for a violent offence—but they have to be women that have demonstrated that there are reasons why that happened or that they are suitable or that they have moved forward or that they have changed. (Interview with MBU Parent Support Worker)

Thus, to take up a place on the MBU, the mothers have to demonstrate

> a level of parental responsibility and parenting capacity, that they can manage their child and they can make sensible decisions in that way. (Interview with MBU Parent Support Worker)

Notions of being a *suitable mother* and having *the potential to parent successfully* are sets of ideas that circulate both in and outside of the prison context. As several commentators note, what does or does not constitute "the good/suitable mother" has undergone a number of modifications. Johnston and Swanson (2006) highlight how during significant parts of the twentieth century the *good mother* was defined as being "full-time, at home, white, middle class, and entirely fulfilled through domestic aspirations" (Johnston & Swanson, 2006, p. 54; see also Boris, 1994). Such a construct has been challenged on a number of fronts, not least because it carries patriarchal assumptions (Chang, 1994); excludes women of color (Collins, 1994; Dill, 1988; Glenn, 1994); excludes mothers who are single (Duncan & Edward, 1999), gay (Lewin, 1994), or are teenagers (Hays, 2003), or who work outside the home (Elvin-Nowak & Thomsson, 2001); and ignores class variations (Baca Zinn, 1990, 1994; Collins, 1991, 1994; Glenn, Chang, & Forcey, 1994; Stack & Burton, 1993).

To understand the relation between the condition of being a good/suitable mother in an MBU and the lived experience of being a good/suitable mother in an MBU, it is necessary to examine what subject positions are created within specific practices and how actual subjects are both created in and live those diverse positions (Walkerdine, 2001). To illustrate this we draw on the following observation, which was undertaken in the crèche, an integral part of the MBU. With the exception of items that are considered a security risk (e.g., pliable dough and scissors), this room has been equipped with most of the usual items of educational furniture, including wooden blocks, books, toys, and so on that one would customarily find in a kindergarten classroom:

> "I don't know how Josh got rid of so much water," says one of the practitioners to Lorna (Josh's mother) as she poured the remaining water out of a low tray into a washing up bowl. "I put two bowls of water in there and you spilt it all didn't you, you little rascal," says the practitioner, softly rubbing Josh's cheek. "I know he loved it, didn't you baby," replied Lorna. Josh was still splashing the remnants of water on the plastic mat, laughing. "Come on you, do you want a sleep before

tea?" said Lorna as she picked Josh up. "Why don't you read him one of those stories?" asked the practitioner as Lorna stands up to leave the room. "You could take one of those books. He'll like that. Read it to him tonight." Lorna goes over to the books and kneels down with Josh on her hip. "Which one Josh? Shall we take one of these?" she says. She picks up the book, puppet, and little hessian bag she was looking at and leaves the room with Josh. (Data from field notes)

This extract is useful because it allows us to catch glimpses of the ways in which each of the participants—the practitioner, the mother, and her baby—are inscribed in a number of discourses. First, let's consider Josh. In the above scene we find him affectionately described as a *little rascal* because he has managed to splash and spill the water. *Rascals* are invariably boys who are mischievous, playful, and have irreverence for rules. In effect, Josh, through language, is being called into a subject position. It is, as MacLure (2003) points out, "through their entry into language that children get their sense of what it is to be a person, of the possibilities of self-hood" (p. 17). *Rascal* effectively works in two significant ways. It configures and confirms Josh as a *boy* and it imbues him with a *natural* disposition. But, as Walkerdine (2001) notes, the "nature" of the child is not "discovered." Rather, it is "produced" in "regimes of truth" that are *"created in those very practices that proclaim the child"* (p. 23, our emphasis). While *rascal* works at proclaiming Josh as a playful, roguish boy, to his mother, he is "baby," one who "loves" splashing water. Positioning Josh as "baby" works at confirming Lorna's own position as "mother," a situation that is reflected in Elvin and Thomsson's (2001, p. 407) statement that "the child creates the mother, and the mother exists for the child." So while the practitioner is able to account for the bowlfuls of water that have been spilled by Josh, the mother displays (natural) knowledge and an appreciation of Josh's inner self, including his visceral response to water play and his need for a nap. We can see how both adults are busy conjuring a bit of the world for Josh. They name it (e.g., rascal and baby) and invest actions with purpose and reason (e.g., a practitioner who provides water play; a "rascal" who spills water; a mother who knows it will soon be nap time). It is through such practices and interactions that Josh is invited to "consider his place within the world," where he will be learning "what the world will be for him" and "what will be the identity, scope for action and obligations of a person in such a world" (MacLure, 2003, p. 18).

Foucault's (1979) concept of "pastoral power" is useful when examining the short interaction between the practitioner and Lorna in relation to borrowing a book. The concept of "pastoral power" resembles in a metaphoric sense the devotional shepherd where "everything the shepherd does is geared to the good of his [*sic*] flock. That's his constant concern. When they sleep, he keeps watch (Foucault, 1979, n.p.). Foucault continues:

> The theme of keeping watch is important. It brings out two aspects of the shepherd's devotedness. First, he acts, he works, he puts himself out, for those he nourishes and who are asleep. Second, he watches over them. He pays attention to them all and scans each one of them. He's got to know his flock as a whole, and in detail. Not only must he know where good pastures are, the seasons' laws and the order of things; he must also know each one's particular needs. (Foucault, 1979, n.p.)

These are interesting ideas to take across to the data where it becomes possible to perceive the practitioner as exercising her power not through coercion, but through professional kindness and expertise As a consequence of careful and ongoing observations she will be scanning Josh, and it is through such processes that she will know that both playing in the water and reading will *nourish* him. This knowledge comes from her own immersion in the discourse of developmentally appropriate curricula, a widely applied set of curriculum theories that correlates activities, lessons, and so on within a sequence of capabilities (Fendler, 2001). Josh's mother must also read to him because within contemporary *order of things* a direct line has been drawn between *good parenting* and subsequent developmental outcomes. As Arendell (1999) makes clear, there are "long-standing social processes in which mothers are held accountable for such things as children's behavior, mental and physical health, school performance, character and developmental outcomes" (p. 44, see also Barnard & Martell, 1995; Caplan, 1998; Phoenix, Woollett, & Lloyd, 1991). Further emphasis on the *order of things* is evident within the United Kingdom's recently elected coalition government rhetoric:

> It is within the family that children develop—psychologically, physically, emotionally and socially—and this is the foundation for children reaching their potential. Children who grow up in stable families have a better start in life—from educational attainment to mental health to future employment prospects—than their peers who experience fractured, chaotic, or dysfunctional home environments. And it is not only individuals who benefit; there are economic and societal benefits when a supportive family environment in childhood is reflected in adulthood. (Secretary of State for Work and Pensions, 2011, p. 3)

Lemke (2000) notes that a policy for making individuals or families "responsible" necessitates shifting the responsibility for social risks such as illness, unemployment, poverty, and so on, and for life in society, "into the domain for which the individual is responsible and transforming it into a problem of 'self-care.'" He goes on:

> One key feature of the neo-liberal rationality is the congruence it endeavors to achieve between a responsible and moral individual and an economic-rational individual. It aspires to construct responsible subjects whose moral quality is based on the fact that they rationally assess the costs and benefits of a certain act as opposed to other alternative acts. As the choice of options for action is, or so the neo-liberal notion of rationality would have it, the expression of free will on the basis of a self-determined decision, the consequences of the action are borne by the subject alone, who is also solely responsible for them. This strategy can be deployed in all sorts of areas and leads to areas of social responsibility becoming a matter of personal provision. (Lemke, 2000, p. 12)

The task of acting sensibly, responsibly, and so on has particular poignancy within the MBU, where it is a criterion for securing and maintaining a place within the MBU. Borrowing a book will be understood as an integral part of good parenting that will benefit Josh's progress. But as Street (1995) highlights, while there is a prevalent view that sees literacy skills as a benign gift to be given to people, it can nonetheless be understood within the wider context of institutional purposes and power relationships. A further layer of complexity arises from the fact that both mother and child are situated within what Bialostok (2004, p. 131) refers to as "narratives of risk." Risks, however, can be defended against if prevailing literacy practices and ideologies are adopted that "both depend on and reinforce notions of personal autonomy and independence that conform to the needs of late-modern capitalism (Bialostok, 2004, p. 131). The "pedagogicalization" (Popkewitz, 2003, p. 35) of Lorna is a necessary precursor in ensuring that Josh makes a shift from a narrative of *risk* to one of *salvation*.

Inevitably, the practitioners, the mothers, and the children at the MBU are caught within relations of power. In the MBU the mothers occupy two significant positions: they are both mothers and prisoners. Likewise the practitioners have dual roles in that they are simultaneously early years professionals and quasi prison-workers. This situation casts multifarious hues in terms of how relations of power play out between the mother/prisoner and practitioner/prison-worker, particularly in relation to compliance and noncompliance. In returning to Lorna's interaction with the practitioner and the issue of borrowing a book, we could understand Lorna's acceptance of the book as either situational compliance or as committed compliance. In other words we can question whether her acceptance of the book is because she has at some level internalized the values of the practitioner (i.e. committed compliance) or whether she takes the book as a means of being polite or perhaps as a way of executing an exit from the crèche. In this latter sense Lorna would have no internal commitment to the norms of the practitioner and her actions are simply a form of situational compliance (Kochanska & Askan, 1995). Foucault's notion of *pastoral power* can also be hitched to the complexities that lie between compliance and noncompliance. It will undoubtedly be in Lorna's best interest for her to take the book. Such an act will, for instance, demonstrate that she is a good mother and a model prisoner, one who demonstrates *an aptitude to work with professionals*, and moreover she can make *sensible decisions*. As such she is both the compliant mother and the compliant prisoner who acts for both the practitioner and herself. It is a form of self-governance undertaken out of a sense of her well-being and self-interests. This is *pastoral power* at work, where it is neither oppressive nor does it bear down "on individuals from above, smiting them with prohibitions of this or that." Rather, it is "a set of relations that is unbalanced" (Foucault, 2000, p. 341) where the practitioner can act upon Lorna and she in turn allows herself to be acted upon.

Discussion

In this chapter we have taken an example of data that for many of us who work in the field of early years education would be regarded as both ordinary and unexceptional. A child playing with water and a mother being encouraged to read to her child are instances of practices that are mirrored in countless settings across the United Kingdom. Within the MBU such practices are undertaken to ensure that the babies and toddlers have sets of experiences that are "as usual or as normal as what they would experience if they were in the community" (Manager, MBU). The manager of the MBU continues:

> So, in terms of experience and environment, something that is quite, I don't want to use the word *normal*, but that is quite usual and normal for babies to be in. The fact that it's placed within the prison doesn't impact on the child either psychologically or physically, and that it's

a safe environment that encourages positiveness in all areas, in their development, in their well-being, in their parenting, in their long-term outcomes, in the planning, that looks forward not backwards.

We want to suggest two things. First, in hesitating over the word *normal* the MBU manager has some reservation toward it as a descriptor. Second, we suggest that this hesitation can constitute a starting point for critical discussions in relation to the children, mothers/prisoners, and practitioners/prison-workers within the MBU.

Interrupting how we think about both the (normal) *child* and the (normal) *mother* is of course rendered particularly challenging because both are inscribed within cultural frames that confine them in ways that for all sorts of reasons are intransigent. For female prisoners who come into the MBU, an opportunity is afforded for them to become *good mothers.* As we discussed previously, what constitutes the *good mother* is contentious. Hays suggests that "good mothering" now equates with "intensive mothering" (Hays, 1996, p. 132), where the mother is always "on the job." Coupled with "intensive mothering" is deep-rooted cultural ambivalence toward mothering behaviors that exist outside of ideological canons.

Employment and *intensive mothering* constitutes one particular flashpoint (Hays, 1996). Here the realities of life, that is having to work to bring in money, or choosing to do so for personal fulfillment or other reasons, clashes with the discourses surrounding being an *intensive mother,* leading to all sorts of tensions, not least mother guilt and mother blame. Feeling guilty is never a comfortable experience, but to feel guilty within the MBU is particularly complex given that this is a specific arena where an individual has the chance to redeem herself, to show that despite committing a crime she can be *good.* *Mother blame,* as we explained previously, assumes that mothering that is impaired or inadequate has long- reaching effects in terms of the child's social, emotional, and psychological development.

In returning once again to the data, we can appreciate that for the practitioner the question "Why don't you read him one of those stories?" is perfectly intelligible. It is after all part of her professional remit to offer guidance and advice, particularly as it will benefit Josh's long-term life chances. And, while the practitioner does suggest, "Read it to him tonight," the injunction to borrow a book comes fast on the heels of Lorna's question to Josh, "Come on you, do you want a sleep before tea?" By inference, a child that is sleeping is going to demand little from his mother. Lorna then proceeds to borrow not only a book but also a puppet, which makes us wonder whether she senses her own lack of not being fully *on the job* in offering Josh the opportunity to nap and that she self-corrects this by borrowing both a book and a puppet. By reading to Josh and instigating puppet play she will be intensifying her own immersion in *intensive mothering.*

If it is difficult to see *mothers* outside of discursive and ideological frames, the task of trying to see *children* in any sense that is different is equally complex. The discursive frame of developmental psychology, for instance, indicates what is (or is not) normal in terms of a child's age and his or her developmental stage. Aligned to this are curriculum guidelines that the practitioner will have to address so as to plan appropriate activities for the babies and toddlers. It is within these frames that the child is made intelligible, knowable, and hence normal. On the one hand, we can understand these discursive frames as making enormous sense in that they are "structures of intelligibility" (Britzman, 2000, p. 36). On the other hand, as Fendler (2001) warns, these discursive frames, while instigating constructions of *normality,* also by default create other behaviors or possible actions as "not normal." So the meaning of *normal* carries greater connotations and has greater effect than say, for example, *ordinary* or *usual.* "Normal" also carries meanings of "correct, right, ideal, healthy, and moral" (Fendler, 2001, p. 138).

While part of the penal system, the MBU's first priority is the young and innocent children. The wretched and ignominious early beginnings of MBUs in the 1990s have been replaced by standards of care in this particular MBU that have been publicly recognized. The MBU has undoubtedly made progress and brought about radical changes. To effect *change,* staff at the MBU must have dismantled or disturbed those discursive regimes that held in check and supported previous discursive practices. Put a little differently, as a team they are already practiced in upsetting or disturbing previously accepted *normal* practices and routines (e.g., being fed *by the clock* so as to *suit* the prison regime), and in so doing, they have created a forum for change. Is it therefore possible to use the inevitable uncertainties and confusion around what counts as *normal* within a prison context so as to enable the child and her mother to be seen outside of normative boundaries?

References

Arendell, T. (1999). *Hegemonic motherhood: Deviancy discourses and employed mothers' accounts of out-of-school time issues.* Working Paper No. 9, April 1999 (pp. 1–30). University of California, Berkeley: Center for Working Families.

Baca Zinn, M. (1990). Family, feminism, and race. *Gender & Society, 4*(1), 68–82.

Baca Zinn, M. (1994). Adaptation and continuity in Mexican-origin families. In R. Taylor (Ed.). *Minority families in the United States: A multicultural perspective* (pp. 69–94) Englewood Cliffs, NJ: Prentice Hall.

Barnard, K. E., & Martell, L. K. (1995). Mothering. In M. H. Bornstein (Ed.). *Handbook of parenting, Vol. 3: Status and social conditions of parenting* (pp. 3–26). Mahwah, NJ: Erlbaum.

Belsky, J., Burchinal, M., McCartney, K., Vandell, D., Clarke-Stewart, K. & Owen, M. T. (2007). Are there long-term effects of early childcare? *Child Development, 78*(2), 681–701.

Bialostok, S. (2004). Literacy and risk: An analysis of one middle-class parent's taken-for-granted understandings of independence and freedom. *Journal of Early Childhood Literacy, 4*(1), 65–83.

Boris, E. (1994). *Home to work: Motherhood and the politics of industrial homework in the United States.* New York: Cambridge University Press.

Bretherton, I. (1992). Attachment and bonding: From ethological to representational and sociological perspectives. In V. B. Van Hasselt & M. Herson (Eds.). *Handbook of social development* (pp. 133–155). New York: Plenum.

Britzman, D. (2000). 'The question of belief': Writing poststructural ethnography. In A. St. Pierre, & W. Pillow (Eds.). *Working the ruins: Feminist poststructural theory and methods in education* (pp. 27–40). New York: Routledge.

Brooks-Gunn, J., Sidle-Fuligni, A., & Berlin, I. J. (Eds.). (2003). *Early child development in the 21st century: Profiles of current research initiatives.* New York: Teachers College Press.

Brown, T. & Jones, L. (2002). *Action research and post-modernism: Congruence and critique.* Buckingham, UK: Open University Press.

Burman, E. (2007). *Deconstructing developmental psychology* (2nd ed.). London: Routledge.

Butler, J. (2004). *Undoing gender.* London & New York: Routledge.

Caplan, P. J. (1998). Mother-blaming. In M. Ladd-Taylor & L. Umansky (Eds.). *Bad mothers: The politics of blame in twentieth-century America* (pp. 158–178). New York: New York University Press.

Chang, G. (1994). Undocumented Latinas: The new "employable mothers". In E. Glenn, N. Glenn, G. Chang, & L. Forcey (Eds.). *Mothering: Ideology, experience and agency* (pp. 258–271). New York: Routledge.

Collins, P. H. (1991). *Black feminist thought: knowledge, consciousness, and the politics of empowerment.* Boston, MA: Unwin Hyman.

Collins, P. H. (1994). Shifting the center: Race, class, and feminist theorizing about motherhood. In D. Bassin., M. Honey, & M. M. Kaplan (Eds.). *Representations of motherhood* (pp. 56–74). New Haven, CT: Yale University Press.

Corston, J. (Baroness). (2007). *Review of women with particular vulnerabilities in the Criminal Justice System. Home Office.* Retrieved from http://www.homeoffice.gov.uk/about-us/news/corston-report

Davies, B. (1994) *Poststructuralist theory and classroom practice*. Geelong, Aus.: Deakin University Press.

Department of Health. (1992). *Inspection of facilities for mother and babies in prison*. London: HMSO.

Dill, B. T. (1988). Our mother's grief: Racial ethnic women and the maintenance of families. *Journal of Family History, 13*(1), 415–431.

Dillner, L. (1992). Keeping babies in prison. *British Medical Journal, 304* (6832), 932–933.

Drew, P., & Heritage, J. (Eds.). (1992). *Talk at work: Interaction in institutional settings*. Cambridge: Cambridge University Press.

Duncan, S., & Edward, R. (1999). *Lone mothers, paid work and gendered moral rationalities*. New York: Palgrave MacMillan.

Elvin-Nowak, Y., & Thomsson, H. (2001). Motherhood as idea and practice: A discursive understanding of employed mothers in Sweden. *Gender and Society, 15*(3), 407–428.

Farrell, A. (1996). The experience of young children and their incarcerated mothers: A call for humanly-responsive policy. *International Journal of Early Childhood, 26*(2), 6–12.

Fendler, F. (2001). Educating flexible souls: The construction of subjectivity through developmentality and interaction In K. Hultqvist & G. Dahlberg (Eds.). *Governing the child in the new millennium* (pp. 119–142). New York: RoutledgeFalmer.

Foucault, M. (1977). *Discipline and punish*. Harmondsworth: Penguin.

Foucault, M. (1979*). Towards a criticism of political reason. The Tanner Lectures on Human Values*, delivered at Stanford University, October 10 and 16, 1979. Retrieved from http://foucault.info/documents/foucault .omnesEtSingulatim.en.html

Foucault, M. (2000). The subject and power. In J. D. Faubion (Ed.). *Michel Foucault: Power 1* (pp. 303–320). New York: The New Press.

Glenn, E. N. (1994). Social constructions of mothering: a thematic overview. In E. N. Glenn, G. Chang, & L. R. Forcey (Eds.). *Mothering: Ideology, experience and agency* (pp. 1–32). New York: Routledge.

Glenn, E. N., Chang, G., & Forcey, L. R. (Eds.). (1994). *Mothering: Ideology, experience and agency*. London: Routledge.

Hays, S. (1996). *The cultural contradictions of motherhood*. New Haven, CT: Yale University Press.

Hays, S. (2003). *Flat broke with children: Women in the age of welfare*. Oxford: Oxford University Press.

Her Majesty's Prison Service. (2008). *Female Prisoners*. Retrieved from http://www.hmprisonservice.gov.uk/advicesupport/prison_life /femaleprisoner/

Her Majesty's Inspectorate of Prisons. (HMIP). (2006). *Women in prison: A literature review*. London: HMIP.

Her Majesty's Prison Service. (2008). *Women prisoners. Prison Service Order 4800*, last updated April 2008.

Her Majesty's Prison Service. (2009). *The management of mother and baby units*, Prison Service Order 4801.

Holmes, R. (2010). Cinemaethnographic specta(c)torship: Discursive readings of what we choose to (dis)possess. *Cultural Studies, Critical Methodologies, 9* (6), 221–237.

James, A. & Prout, A. (Eds.). (1997). *Constructing and reconstructing childhood: Contemporary issues in the sociological study of childhood* (2nd ed.). London: Falmer.

Johnston, D. & Swanson, D. (2006). Constructing the "good mother": The experience of mothering ideologies by work status. *Sex Roles 54*(7/8), 509–519.

Kochanska, G. & Askan, N. (1995). Mother-child mutually positive affect, the quality of child compliance to requests and prohibitions, and maternal control as correlates of early internalization. *Child Development, 66,* 236–254.

Lemke, T. (2000, September). *Foucault, governmentality, and critique.* Paper presented at the Rethinking Marxism Conference, University of Amherst (MA).

Lewin, E. (1994). Negotiating lesbian motherhood: The dialectics of resistance and accommodation. In E. Glenn, N. Glenn, G. Chang, & L. Forcey (Eds.). *Mothering: Ideology, experience and agency* (pp. 333–353). New York: Routledge.

MacLure, M. (2003). *Discourse in educational and social research.* Buckingham, UK: Open University Press.

Melhuish, E. (2004). Child benefits: The importance of investing in quality childcare. *Facing the Future: Policy Papers.* London: Day Care Trust.

Ministry of Justice. (2007). *The Corston report: Women in the criminal justice system.* Retrieved from http://www.justice.gove.uk/publications/corston-report.htm.

Ministry of Justice. (2008). *Mother and Baby Units in Prisons.* Retrieved from www.justice.gov.uk/ publications /docs/mother-baby-units.pdf.

Owers, A. (2004). *Inspection report.* Retrieved from http://www.homeoffice.gov.uk/justice/prisons/inspprisons

Phoenix, A., Woollett, A., & Lloyd, E. (Eds.). (1991). *Motherhood: Meanings, practices, and ideologies.* Newbury Park, CA: Sage Publications.

Popkewitz, T. (2003). Governing the child and pedagogicalization of the parent: A historical excursus into the present. In M. Bloch, K. Holmlund, I. Moqvist, & T. Popkewtz (Eds.). *Governing children, families and education* (pp. 35–62). New York: Palgrave Macmillan.

Prior, V., & Glaser, D. (2006) *Understanding attachment and attachment disorders: Theory, evidence and practice.* London and Philadelphia, PA: Jessica Kingsley.

Rogoff, B. (2003). *The cultural nature of human development.* Oxford: Oxford University Press.

Schwandt, T., & Abma, T. (2005). The practice and politics of sponsored evaluations. In B. Somekh & C. Lewin (Eds.). *Research methods in the social sciences* (pp. 105–112). London: Sage.

Shaw, R. (1992). *Prisoner's children: What are the issues?* London: Routledge.

Secretary of State for Work and Pensions. (2011). *Strengthening families, Promoting parental responsibility: The future of child maintenance.* London: Her Majesty's Stationary Office. Retrieved from www.dwp.gov .uk/policy/child-maintenance

Stack, C. B. & Burton, L. M. (1993). Kinscripts. *Journal of Comparative Family Studies, 24,* 157–170.

Street, B. (1995). *Social literacies: Critical approaches to literacy in development, ethnography and education.* Essex: Pearson Education.

Walkerdine, V. (1999). Violent boys and precocious girls: Regulating childhood at the end of the millennium. *Contemporary Issues in Early Childhood 1*(1), 3–23.

Walkerdine, V. (2001). Safety and danger: Childhood, sexuality and space at the end of the millennium. In K. Hultqvist & G. Dahlberg (Eds.). *Governing the child in the new millennium* (pp. 15–34). New York: RoutledgeFalmer.

Watson, D. R. (1992). Ethnomethodology, conversation analysis and education: An overview. *International Review of Education, 38*(3), 252–274.

CHAPTER 10

Collaborative Play as New Methodology: Co-constructing Knowledge of Early Child Development in the CHILD Project in British Columbia, Canada

Hillel Goelman and Jayne Pivik

The more we get together, together, together,
The more we get together, the happier we'll be.
'Cuz my friends are your friends and your friends are my
  friends.
The more we get together the happier we'll be.

Traditional children's nursery song

INTRODUCTION

The Consortium for Health, Intervention, Learning and Development (CHILD) Project was a longitudinal program of research on early child development based in British Columbia (BC), Canada, from 2003 to 2008. It drew together a wide range of university-based biomedical and social scientists, community-based professionals, and government officials and policymakers. During the five years of data collection and the subsequent period of data analysis and interpretation, the CHILD Project examined the interaction and impacts of biological and social influences on early child development. Some of the studies focused on marginalized or disadvantaged populations and others focused more on universal programs of research that considered the needs of all children. As part of this program of research, the CHILD Project examined the benefits and challenges of interdisciplinary inquiry by weaving together the ontologies, epistemologies, and methodologies of different disciplines (Shonkoff, 2000) and by including community professionals as research partners in the ten collaborative research studies under the CHILD umbrella. In this way, the CHILD Project became a community of discourse of community-based professionals, university researchers, and graduate students in order to ensure that the research questions, methods, and outcomes of the ten studies were relevant to children and families.

We begin with a description of the political, social, and cultural contexts that framed the worlds—and the words—of early learning and care in Canada while the CHILD Project was being conducted. We then discuss the theoretical orientation and design of the CHILD Project. We conclude with some of the major findings of the CHILD Project, especially as they relate to parents and communities of practice. We explore the ways in which early childhood practice and research in Canada are framed by what one of our colleagues referred to as "the power of words and the words of power."

Early Learning and Care in Canada: The Contexts for the CHILD Project

At the time of data collection, Canada had a population of 30,007,094 with a child population (0–6 years) of 2,076,240. In BC the total population was 3,907,738 and the child population was 252,060. Canada is a federated state comprising ten provinces and three territories, with fairly clear delineations of the federal and provincial/territorial responsibilities and powers. Broadly speaking, the federal government is responsible for foreign, defense, and monetary policy, while the bulk of human services—education, health, and social services—are almost exclusively the responsibility of the provinces and territories (Beach, Friendly, Ferns, Prabhu, & Forer, 2009). For this reason, it is impossible to discuss *Canadian* early childhood policy because there are tremendous variations across the provincial/territorial borders. Quebec is the only jurisdiction that has universal and affordable childcare programs. Some jurisdictions offer free preschool programs while others do not. During the time frame that the CHILD Project was conducted, most but not all jurisdictions offered free half-day kindergarten programs for five-year-olds as part of the public education system. Almost all of Saskatchewan's childcare programs were offered by non-profit societies, while the majority of

Alberta's programs were run by private childcare operators. Training of early childhood professionals ranged from short 100-hour courses to four-year Bachelor of Arts programs.

The province of BC had its own confusing mosaic of early childhood programs. As mentioned, public kindergarten programs for five-year-olds were offered through the Ministry of Education while childcare, mental health, and early intervention programs were offered through the Ministry of Children and Family Development; public health services were offered through the Ministry of Health. Many of these community-based programs were not run by the province directly but were funded by contracts granted primarily to non-profit societies in the province. Programs for indigenous children in BC were largely funded by the federal government but had to conform to provincial regulatory standards. There was no consistent policy or programmatic framework to lend a sense of cohesion or coherence to this diverse array of programs.

The CHILD Project recognized this complex diversity and attempted to include a range of programs and community-based organizations in order to capture a representative, although not comprehensive, cross-section of programs that served children, parents, and families in BC. The CHILD Project took place during a unique confluence of political, economic, and cultural factors at the federal, provincial, and local levels. The Canadian government in 2003 was controlled by the *federal* Liberal Party of Canada, which had over the years addressed increased attention to early childhood matters. While the federal government was traditionally limited in terms of programs and services, beginning in 1997, the federal Liberal Party issued a *National Children's Agenda,* which began to articulate a vision of national priorities to support and enhance the development of young children. In 2003, it instituted the *Multilateral Framework on Early Learning and Child Care* in order to support funding for early child development programs that adhered—in a general way—to four underlying *QUAD* principles.[1] The programs under this *Multilateral Framework* had to be considered of high *quality*; they had to be available on a *universal* basis to all children;,they had to be *accessible* to all children; and they had to have a *developmental* focus. These bilateral agreements were used to create and support local programs that met provincial/territorial childcare priorities and commitments. While the *Multilateral Framework* did not create a national system of any kind or a consistent set of programs across provincial/territorial boundaries, it did represent a first step in partnership agreements between the two senior levels of government (Goelman, Pivik & Guhn, 2011).

Part of the federal interest in early childhood programs was expressed through the funding program that granted the CAD$2.5 million for the CHILD Project. We should note, however, that with the Canadian Federal elections of 2006, this major federal investment in early child development was severely cut back, a development that is discussed in detail below.

There was, however, a specific challenge in BC at precisely the same time. The governing *provincial* Liberal Party of British Columbia—which has no relationship to the federal party of the same name—was in the process of making massive cuts to existing education and social service programs, including to childcare and early learning programs. The province was more than happy to accept federal funds for certain programs, but at the same time was forcing program reductions or closures in areas that did not receive federal funding. Thus, at the same time that the research for the CHILD Project was being funded by the federal government, the community-based programs that served as partners in the CHILD Project were facing massive cuts and staff layoffs. This created tensions and challenges to the kind of collaboration that had to be addressed during the five years of the CHILD Project. The federal and provincial discourses on early child development were in conflict during this period, and this conflict reflected itself in the research conducted through the CHILD Project.

While the CHILD Project took place in one province and largely in one geographic area of that province, the project as a whole was informed and influenced by a number of issues and themes that impacted on children and families during this time frame (Goelman, Pivik, & Guhn, 2011). For many international audiences, Canada is (mis)perceived in two very specific ways (Goelman, 1992; Lipset, 1990). First, since we share North America with the United States, Canadian child and family policy is thought to be identical to that found in the United States. The second misperception is virtually the opposite: because Canada has a European-style universal system of health care, Canada is thought to be *Sweden-like*, governed with the same kinds of social-democratic policies found in Scandinavia and elsewhere. In a sense, both misperceptions carry some weight, since Quebec styles many of its health and social welfare policies on the European experience and Alberta's style looks more like that of the United States. However, there are important and perhaps subtle factors that differentiate Canada from both the United States and Europe and which in their own ways emerged as themes in the CHILD Project.

Until recently, Canadian history spoke of *two founding peoples*, the English and the French. The rights and legitimacy of the original Aboriginal inhabitants of what is now Canada are recognized in a growing (but still incomplete) body of legislation and social policy.[2] Canada's diversity has also been fed by immigration from all over the world; in contrast to the U.S. vision of a *melting pot*, the more common perspective in Canada is that of a *mosaic state* where national cultural, ethnic, and religious origins are recognized, respected, and celebrated. Multiculturalism is an official federal policy, and any study of children and families must recognize the multicultural fabric of Canada. While income disparity between the wealthiest and the poorest Canadian citizens is still large, the gap between rich and poor is much smaller than that in the United States. Recognizing the devastating effects of poverty, especially on children, the Parliament of Canada, in 1989, voted unanimously to end child poverty by the year 2000. While this goal has not been achieved, it remains on the agenda of many federal, provincial, and municipal governments and of a number of non-government organizations (NGOs) and non-profit societies. As we hope to show in this chapter, the research questions and methodologies of the ten studies in the CHILD Project attempted to be cognizant of various forms of diversity, to include focused work on Aboriginal Canadians, and to address the causes and outcomes of child poverty in this country.

The Theoretical Framework of the CHILD Project

The CHILD Project was guided in large part by Urie Bronfenbrenner's (1979) ecological model of early child development (see figure 10.1), a theoretical research framework that situates the development of young children within the family, social, economic, neighborhood, and policy contexts that impact on the developing child. Bronfenbrenner's framework has contributed to conceptual and empirical advances in the study of early child development within and across disciplinary boundaries.

The field of early intervention (Ramey & Ramey, 1997), for example, has developed the concept of bio-social developmental contextualism—a way of conceptualizing the interaction of a child's biological status within the social environment in which he or she develops. Similarly, advances in neuroscience have acknowledged the interaction of neurobiological aspects of the child's development with the environment, which plays the role of *pruning* or shaping

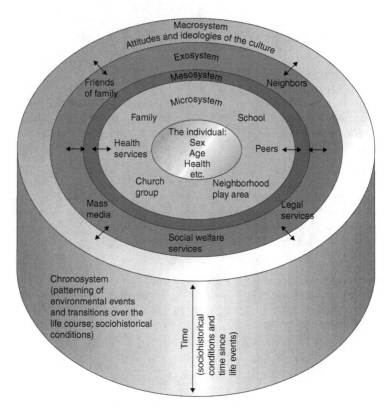

Figure 10.1 Bronfenbrenner's model of the ecology of human development

the physiological development of the brain (Cynader & Frost, 1999). A related thrust in developmental psychology and early childhood education (Goelman, Ford et al., 2011) has looked at the ways in which early childhood programs impact upon developmentally challenged children in different communities. Social geographers have begun to study the ecology of child development through community asset mapping, which visually displays the relationships between social determinants in communities and differing socioeconomic characteristics. These approaches have contributed to an emerging understanding of the interrelationships of individual, familial, community, and policy factors that impact early childhood development.

Bronfenbrenner's work has spawned a number of theoretical and methodological innovations in the study of early child development, which have in turn guided and inspired the work of the CHILD

Project. Shonkoff and Phillips' (2000) "neurons to neighborhoods" and Hertzman's "cell to society" (Barer & Evans, 2006; Keating & Hertzman, 1999) also emphasize the importance of integrating research findings from the medical, biological, health, and social sciences in order to provide greater explanatory power to the multiple contexts of early development. Research rooted more in the *cell* end of this continuum would include, for example, studies of childhood asthma in different socioeconomic contexts (Chen, Fisher, Bacharier, & Strunk, 2003), the production and influence of cortisol in children in childcare settings (Dettling, Gunnar, & Donzella, 1999; Watamura, Donzell, Alwin, & Gunnar, 2003), and the relationship between smoking and injury among adolescents and their socioeconomic status (Chen, Matthews, & Boyce, 2002). Working more from the *society* end of this continuum, Willms (2002) has studied the impact of "social gradients" upon child development outcome measures. Drawing upon population-level social, demographic, and economic data and national surveys of children's early educational achievement in different countries, Willms calculated social gradients as a means of understanding the amount and distribution of social capital in those countries and the impacts of the gradients upon both school readiness and subsequent school performance.

The CHILD Project, then, adopted a "neurons to neighbourhoods" approach (Shonkoff & Phillips, 2000) to include biomedical and social determinants in order to generate new knowledge and new perspectives on early child development. A number of studies in CHILD focused on children whose biological characteristics and compromised birth outcomes created a set of circumstances that severely limited their physical, social, motor, emotional, and intellectual development. Children with disabilities and children without disabilities are also strongly affected by the family contexts in which they are reared, and the CHILD Project included studies that attempted to understand the impacts of different kinds of family structures and family dynamics on the developing child. Studies of social and emotional development increasingly focus on the importance of peer contexts in development. It is in these friendships and relationships that children learn about the culture of childhood, about social bonds, and about emotional contingencies. Peer interactions begin to exert more powerful effects as children begin to participate in the programs and activities of preschool, childcare, play groups, drop-in centers, and other socializing contexts. In these programs children learn about the context of their own needs and desires in the contexts of the needs and desires of other children. It is in these settings that children also begin to be influenced by the different professionals who conduct or facilitate these programs. The availability, accessibility, quality, and affordability of such programs often vary across the boundaries of different neighborhoods and communities, and the variability in these factors can impact on the variability in children's development. The availability of such programs depends to a very large extent on legal, regulatory, or policy contexts that provide financial or professional support for them; these factors determine where programs exist, whether trained professionals are available for support and consultation, and whether programs and professional services are accessible and provided at reasonable costs to parents, families, and children. The discourse around children, children's services, and child development is largely influenced by the multiple contexts and discourses generated by different professions and academic disciplines.

The CHILD Project attempted to resolve some of the dichotomies that contextualized and influenced programs and services for young children. These dichotomies included the federal/provincial split in responsibilities and funding; the *neurons* versus the *neighborhoods* approaches to early development; universal versus targeted approaches to children's services; quantitative versus qualitative orientations to research; academic and community-based perspectives on research; and Aboriginal versus non-Aboriginal children. These challenges and tensions characterized what the CHILD Project set out to do, how the members of the project communicated with one another, and the broader constituencies and stakeholders in government, in non-governmental organizations (NGOs), among parents and professionals.

The Design of the CHILD Project

The ten studies in CHILD were grouped into four somewhat overlapping thematic clusters: early identification and screening; the effectiveness of early childhood intervention programs; the implementation and impact of governmental income assistance policy and childcare policy on children and their families; and the health and development of Canadian indigenous children. Elsewhere we discuss these four thematic clusters in detail (Goelman et al., 2011). In this chapter, however, we find it more useful to discuss the ten studies in two general groupings that span these four categories. Some of the studies in the CHILD Project focused on targeted groups of children who might be considered to be *at risk* for compromised development due to, for example, birth outcomes, diagnosed disabilities, poverty,

Table 10.1   Targeted and Universal Studies in the CHILD Project

Targeted Studies	Academic Disciplines	Community Partners	Thematic Cluster
The Income Assistance Study To assess the impact of changes in income assistance policy on lone-parent families with young children.	Sociology and Anthropology; Community and Regional Planning; Women's Studies	Social Planning and Research Council of BC; Canadian Centre for Policy Alternatives	*Cluster 1:* Policy Studies in Early Child Development
The Indigenous CHILD Study To obtain the perspectives of Indigenous communities on child development and measurement.	Child and Youth Care	Four on-reserve Indigenous communities	*Cluster 2:* Early Childhood Development in Indigenous Communities
The HIPPY in Aboriginal Communities Study To explore the "Home Instruction for Parents of Preschool Youngsters" program as implemented in Indigenous communities.	Early Childhood Education	Three on-reserve Aboriginal communities; HIPPY Canada	*Cluster 2:* Early Childhood Development in Indigenous Communities
The Developmental Pathways Study To follow the long-term development of highly at-risk infants.	Neonatology; Developmental Pediatrics	Infant Development Program of BC; BC Centre for Ability	*Cluster 3:* Early Identification and Screening Studies
The Infant Neuromotor Study To explore the effectiveness of two types of training models for the early identification of children with neuromotor delays.	Rehabilitation Sciences; Nursing	Infant Development Program of BC; BC Centre for Ability	*Cluster 3:* Early Identification and Screening Studies
The Outdoor Play Spaces Study To analyze how outdoor play spaces are utilized by children, and to investigate any differences that emerge.	Landscape Architecture; Policy Analysis; Child Development	City of Vancouver; BC Council for Families	*Cluster 4:* Early Childhood Intervention Programs
The Parent Counseling Study To assess the impact of counseling on parents whose children are at risk for apprehension by child protection authorities.	Social Work and Family Studies	Family Services of Vancouver	*Cluster 4:* Early Childhood Intervention Programs

Continued

Table 10.1 *Continued*

Universal (Nontargeted) Studies	Academic Disciplines	Community Partners	Thematic Cluster
The Child Care Policy Study To investigate the impact of childcare policy changes on communities, childcare facilities, families and children.	Early Childhood Education; Policy Analysis; Measurement and Evaluation	City of Vancouver Social Planning Department; Westcoast Child Care Resource and Referral	*Cluster 1*: Policy Studies in Early Child Development
The Community-Based Screening Study To determine the effectiveness of a universal, community-based, developmental screening program.	Nursing; Child Development	Public Health Nurses in Chilliwack, BC	*Cluster 3*: Early Identification and Screening Studies
The Outdoor Play Spaces Study To analyze how outdoor play spaces are utilized by children, and to investigate any differences that emerge.	Landscape Architecture; Policy Analysis; Child Development	City of Vancouver; BC Council for Families	*Cluster 4*: Early Childhood Intervention Programs
The Safe Spaces Study To examine the short- and long-term effectiveness of a preschool antibullying program.	Child Development	Westcoast Child Care Resource and Referral	*Cluster 4*: Early Childhood Intervention Programs

or Aboriginal status. Other studies focused on issues that applied to the entire population of young children, for example, childcare policy, outdoor play spaces, social development or community-based screening projects. Table 10.1 summarizes the ten studies in these two groups and describes the major objectives of each study, the community and research partners collaborating on the study, and the thematic cluster to which each study belonged.

THE TARGETED AND UNIVERSAL STUDIES

This section provides a brief description of each study and a summary of their findings (references for more detailed reports are provided). While each study had its own *life cycle* of consultation, design, implementation, analysis, and reflection, they all began in the first year of the CHILD project and terminated in the fifth year.

The Targeted Studies

The BC infant mortality rate has fallen by 50 percent in the last 20 years from eight to four per 1,000 live births (Goelman, Ford et al., 2011). In the early 1990s, survival rates were 20–36 percent (Canadian Coalition for the Rights of Children, 1999; Canadian Council on Social Development, 2001; La Pine, Jackson & Bennett, 1995; Moster, Lie & Markestad, 2008; Resnick et al., 1998). However, more recent reports give survival rates of 71–89 percent (e.g., Hack, Friedman, & Faranoff, 1996; Lorenz, 2001). Improved survival comes at cost. For example, cerebral palsy rates are 3–12 percent in very low-birth-weight survivors (birth weight < 1,500 grams) (Sauve, Etches, Robertson, Christianson, & Jain, 2004), compared to 0.1 percent in all babies born at term. Extreme premature infants score lower than healthy controls on intelligence tests (Riley, Roth, Sellwood, & Wyatt, 2008). Higher percentages of low-birth-weight infants have lower IQ scores than healthy controls, and 60–70 percent of children with birth weights less than 1,000 grams have special education needs, requiring a modified program or teaching aids in the classroom. In comparison to healthy full-term infants, preterm infants have higher rates of attention deficit disorder (23 percent versus 6 percent), generalized anxiety (8 percent versus 1 percent) and psychiatric disorders (28 percent versus 10 percent) (Hoekstra, Ferrara, Couser, Payne, & Connett, 2004). In BC, two studies reported that 14 percent of children who weighed less than 800 grams at birth had multiple disabilities and a higher incidence of attention problems (33 percent versus 4 percent) and learning disabilities (47 percent versus 18 percent) compared to classroom peers at school age (Grunau, Whitfield, & Davis, 2002; Whitfield, Grunau, & Holsti, 1997).

These targeted studies focused on children's biological or environmental vulnerabilities within the broader family, neighborhood, community, and policy contexts of the children's lives. The *Developmental Pathways Study* examined the developmental trajectories of children who were treated in Neonatal Intensive Care Units (NICUs) at birth in BC (Goelman et al., 2011). While the survival rate of these low-birth-weight and preterm babies has improved significantly from 46 percent to 69 percent over the last 20 years, the incidence of major disabilities in this group has remained at about 30 percent, resulting in the need for a wide spectrum of specialized multidisciplinary support services (Houbé, Lisonkova, Klassen, Synnes, & Lee, 2005; Synnes, Lisonkova, Houbé, Klassen, & Lee, 2004).

Approximately 535,000 Canadian children and youth from 0 to 18 years have an activity-limiting disability. Of these, 4 percent are described as "severely" disabled, 11 percent are *moderately* disabled, and 85 percent are *mildly* disabled (Canadian Council on Social Development, 2001). Over 6 percent of such children have a chronic long-term condition, such as a learning disability; nearly half cannot participate in school sports; over 10 percent are limited by long-term mental health or neurological disability; and over 17 percent of these children require hearing aids, or other medically prescribed devices. In BC, 2 percent of all 0- to 4-year-olds (3,980) had a reported disability, compared to 4.4 percent of 5- to 9-year-olds (9,460) and 4 percent of 10- to 14-year-olds (13,080).

The *Infant Neuromotor Study* assessed the validity and reliability of a new measure designed to identify neuromotor delay in infants and toddlers children. The study also developed face-to-face and Web-based teaching materials to instruct a wide range of professionals and parents in the use of this instrument (Goelman et al., 2011; Harris & Daniels, 1996, 2001; Hayes, Harris, Megens, & Backman, 2004).

The *Parent Counseling Study* involved 35 parents (31 mothers, 4 fathers) who were considered to be at high risk for abuse or neglect and were referred to a parenting program by child-welfare authorities. Most of the families were characterized by low levels of formal education and income, and substance abuse by the parents. The program was part of a *Family Preservation and Reunification Service,* and the intervention included a combination of home visiting and group programs at a parent counseling center. Participants were provided with transportation, meals, and age-appropriate activities for their children. Individual and group programs were provided for parents. The individual and group counseling sessions focused on parental strengths, accessing community resources, and the development of positive and safe parenting strategies. The results revealed varying degrees of program impact on these parents; some demonstrated improved parent skills, while others were still found to have inadequate or marginal parenting skills and faced the possible placement of their children in the care of social services or continued child-protection monitoring (Russell, 2011; Russell, Harris, Gockel, 2008a, 2008b).

Of the total child population of 252,060 in BC, 55,250 were Aboriginal children; of these, 16,195 were in the 0- to 4-year-old age bracket, 18,005 were in the 5- to 9-year-old age bracket, and 21,050 were in the 10- to 14-year-old age bracket. While the Aboriginal birth rate was 22.4 percent, the non-Aboriginal birth rate was 3.4 percent.

The indigenous CHILD Study in the CHILD Project focused on the perceptions and beliefs in indigenous communities regarding the nature and use of early childhood assessment practices. The study documented many of the extremely negative experiences of First Nations people, including culturally inappropriate standardized child development procedures, reported as oppressive and authoritarian. Many of the test administrators who conducted the assessments also demonstrated a lack of respect for the children they tested and showed no respect for, or interest in, the parents' own experiential, cultural, and intuitive knowledge of their children (Ball, 2004, 2005).

The *Aboriginal HIPPY Study* examined the impact of an adaptation of the *Home Intervention for Parents of Preschool Youngsters (HIPPY) Program,* a home-based program that has successfully promoted school readiness for *at-risk* preschoolers in different parts of the world (Westheimer, 2003). Findings have demonstrated that the program has empowered parents as the primary educators of their children in their children's lives. Taken together, these factors have been found to contribute to the positive development of the children's indigenous identities (Ball & LeMare, 2011; Beatch & Le Mare, 2007).

Of the child population of 252,060 in BC at the time of data collection, 21.9 percent of children 0- to 2-year-olds, 25.6 percent of 3- to 5-year-olds, and 21.1 percent of 6- to 12-year-olds lived in families below the Low-Income Cut-Off Rates (LICO), the official designation of the *poverty line.* The overall child poverty rate in BC was 21.9 percent compared to the national average of 15.8 percent. The *Income Assistance Study* examined the ways in which low-income lone-mother families in urban and rural areas are affected by provincial policy changes that have reduced social assistance and enforced paid work obligations for assistance recipients. Findings from the rural areas suggest that the experience of lived poverty by these mothers is characterized by powerful feelings of isolation and alienation, which for many, result in serious mental health issues. Rigorous monitoring of adherence to income-assistance regulations conveys a negative sense of being the subject of ongoing government surveillance, and the lack of affordable and accessible childcare further exacerbates an already-difficult situation (Fiske & Gervais, 2006; Kershaw, 2004, 2005; Russell, 2011).

The Universal Studies

The *Developmental Surveillance Study* conducted a population-based screening program designed to identify children with developmental difficulties. In addition to providing important results on the screening instruments, the study also demonstrated how a universal screening process can facilitate enhanced communication among early child development, education, and health professionals (Anstett & the MCFI Training Group, 2002, 2003; Dahinten et al., 2004; Dahinten, Ford, & Lapointe, 2004; Goelman et al., 2011).

The *Safe Spaces Study* examined the implementation and outcomes of a bullying-prevention and social-skills-enhancement program for preschool-aged children. The study was conducted in eight different childcare centers with children aged three to five years. The program included a number of different arts and crafts, role-playing, and story-book-reading activities. The results revealed high levels of consistency in the implementation of the intervention across many sites and positive social and emotional outcomes for the children (Pivik, Herrington, & Gummerum, 2011; Schonert-Reichl, Smith, Jaramillo, & Zaidman-Zait, 2004; Schonert-Reichl & Jaramillo, 2005)

The *Outdoor Play Spaces Study* worked with 16 childcare centers in order to address the following question: "What are the outdoor physical factors that contribute to early child development in Vancouver, and to what degree do these factors exist in these childcare centers?" Interviews with childcare staff and observations of children's play patterns revealed that childcare centers exceeding their child-to-space densities had more child aggression in their outdoor play spaces, and that child aggression in these play spaces increased when there were no materials that could be manipulated by the children. The researchers also found that contact with plants and animals increased developmental opportunities for children and that the children themselves consistently expressed a desire for more *soft spaces* in both their indoor and outdoor play spaces (Herrington & Lesmeister, 2006; Pivik et al., 2011).

There was—and is—a serious shortage of registered childcare spaces in BC. Only 18.3 percent of all children who were in need of a childcare space could be accommodated, during the time of the CHILD project. Given this shortage, the *Child Care Policy Study* focused on the implementation and effects of major provincial and federal government childcare policies and programs. Data analyses were based primarily on large national and provincial databases. These data showed that inconsistency and underfunding by government has resulted in highly unstable, inaccessible, unaffordable, and low-quality childcare in the province. The data also show dramatic turnover rates, where approximately 30 percent of all licensed childcare centers and 50 percent of licensed family childcare homes closed within five years, creating an unstable supply of quality childcare (Goelman et al., 2006; Kershaw, 2004; Kershaw, Forer, & Goelman, 2005).

The Power of Words and Words of Power

We found that much of what we learned through both the process and the outcomes of the CHILD Project could be understood through the lenses of power, language, and discourse. We first discuss some of the ways in which language and discourse issues framed and guided the ways in which we conducted and communicated our research within the CHILD Project and then proceed to explore the ways in which the power of words and the words of power helped us to understand our data better within the current context of federal and provincial politics in Canada.

MacNaughton (2005) has argued that greater attention needs to be paid to the intersection of language, discourse, politics, and research. She claims that Foucault and other postmodernists

> have argued that language is connected intimately with the politics of knowledge and that those politics are evident in the language we use to think of ourselves (our subjectivities) and to describe our actions and our institutions. Poststructuralists have also challenged the idea that individuals can think and act freely outside of the politics of knowledge. . . . Consequently, identifying the stories of (individuals or societies) that are silenced or marginalized and then sharing them is a political act. (p. 4)

Shonkoff (2000) has articulated in some detail how—especially in collaborative research—stakeholders representing different professions/interest groups must recognize the substantive differences between the groups in terms of their respective values, goals, and vocabularies. Shonkoff has pointed out that the *cultures* of research, practice, and policy differ greatly, requiring that successful collaborations address the fundamental differences between these three worlds. Each culture has its own distinct *rules of evidence*, with researchers emphasizing empirical studies, professionals drawing upon organizational or clinical experience, and policy officials relying upon political agendas and financial considerations. The three cultures also have different perspectives on *ideology and values*, with researchers tending to assume an objective or neutral stance, community professionals operating on social advocacy, and policy officials focused on public opinion. All ten studies in the CHILD Project have dealt with these very real differences in the cultures of research, policy, and practice. The challenge and promise of the CHILD Project was that the ten studies represented ten case studies with ten different kinds of community partners and, therefore, ten different kinds of university-community collaborative relationships. For this reason, the CHILD Project provided the opportunity to observe varying forms of interdisciplinary and different manifestations of university-community collaboration in the ten studies under one programmatic umbrella.

The CHILD Project provided unique opportunities and challenges to the study of early child development and, in particular, the dynamics and outcomes of university-community collaborations within and across each of the ten studies. A wide range of very different collaborative relationships developed within CHILD due to the varied community partners involved in the ten studies, including public health nurses; a childcare resource and referral agency; individual childcare centers; early intervention programs; a municipal social planning department; a non-profit family counseling agency; and parents, elders, and professionals in on-reserve First Nations. Despite these important differences, each of the ten partnerships produced successful collaborations that added to the overall strength and credibility of the CHILD Project as a whole. The partnerships—as in any relationship—confronted challenges and were able to negotiate positive working relationships that were of benefit to both the researchers and to the community partners.

Through our continuing meetings, retreats, position papers, and other activities, a number of key examples of the *power of words and words of power* were identified, and we discuss three of these in the following section: the notions of *choice*, *safety*, and *surveillance* in early child development.

Choice

The Child Care Policy Study examined the impact of federal and provincial childcare policies on the provision of childcare services in BC. In addition to the *Child Care Policy Study*, however, other studies were also collecting data on different aspects of the ecology of childcare in BC, and all of them raised issues around the notion of *choice*. Two of the universal programs, *The Outdoor Play Spaces Study* and *The Safe Spaces Study*, were both situated in childcare centers in Vancouver. Three of the targeted studies—*The Income Assistance Study*, *The Parent Counseling Study*, and *The Indigenous CHILD Study*—all received parent reports on the importance of childcare in their lives and the contributions that stable, high-quality childcare services would make to their lives and especially to the lives of their children. In this summary, Mary Russell (2011) explains the importance and the lack of childcare for low-income parents:

> This accords with McKendrick's (1998) observations that lone mothers are highly motivated to improve their quality of life through self-improvement, but feel constrained by lack of opportunities. Economic deprivation and a lack of child care were reported as primary barriers. In describing the means to reach the goal of an improved quality of life, mothers described both furthering educational efforts and acquiring experience through their volunteer labor. (p. 77)

Kamerman and Kahn (1988) reported that childcare services that are near to the home, reasonably priced, and of decent quality were the single most important service for lone parents and the highest priority on their *wish lists*. Thus, while the targeted studies were learning from parents that childcare was both important and hard to find, *The Child Care Policy Study* undertook to find out on a population level why childcare policies were not providing sufficient childcare programs. Official provincial policy seemed to endorse the importance of *choice* in finding childcare for their children:

> The provincial government recognizes the fundamental importance of child care to a prosperous economy. The government of British Columbia partners with child care providers to create and support a sustainable child care system in which families can choose from a range of affordable, safe, quality child care options that meet diverse needs. (Government of British Columbia, 2011, n.p.)

What, then, accounted for the widely reported lack of choice in finding suitable childcare? The initial analyses revealed that over an eight-year period (1997–2005), the overall number of childcare spaces remained relatively constant. A closer analysis, however, revealed that in that same period, there was substantial turnover in the provision of childcare services. That is, during this time frame, 34 percent of the childcare centers and 48 percent of the family childcare homes had closed. New centers and homes appeared, but the overall effect on families was that the supply of childcare spaces was sporadic, inconsistent, and unstable. The federal Conservative government adopted a policy upon their election in 2006 that cut back on funds to existing childcare centers and homes and, in the name of *choice*, decided to offer parents CAD$100 per month, per child under six years of age, for any service or product they may wish to purchase. By using the term *universal* to describe this program, the government was attempting to frame their policy as one that allowed for parental choice:

> The Universal Child Care Benefit (UCCB) provides financial assistance to all Canadian families with young children, regardless of where they live, whatever their family circumstances or preferences. Parents receive $100 a month for each child under six. For some parents, this might mean using the benefit to pay for some of their child care fees. A parent who stays at home may want to use it on a preschool program or to purchase learning material, other parents may even wish to deposit all or part of the benefit in a Registered Education Savings Plan (RESP) or Registered Disability Savings Plan (RDSP). The UCCB, which was introduced in July 2006, provides about $2.6 billion each year to 1.5 million families for 2 million preschoolers in Canada. (Government of Canada, 2011, n.p.)

The political agenda had adopted *universal* and *choice* as key words of power in the discourse on children's programs and services. Under these schemes, parents could *choose* to use their *universal* benefit for hard-to-find childcare programs and, even if they were successful in finding such programs, the CAD$100 per month would do very little in terms of defraying the overall cost of childcare.

Safety

The concept of *safety* also emerged as a focal point in our research and in our language. Just as *choice* took on specific meanings in our different studies and in government policies, *safety* raised different issues in the universal studies and in the targeted studies. The *Outdoor Play Spaces Study* focused on the development of play spaces and play structures that stimulated physical, motor, intellectual, social, and language development in young children. They found that planning regulations and rules influenced how play spaces were developed and thus, child development. In some ways, *safety* was a catch phrase that really meant, "Make sure that no on sues us because of this playground." Fear of litigation, then, became synonymous with safety in designing outdoor play spaces (Pivik et al., 2011).

Safety took on a different meaning altogether in the two Aboriginal studies. Centuries of oppression and cultural damage sensitized these families and communities to their need for *cultural safety* in both programs and in research. During the life of the CHILD Project, the Aboriginal leadership in Canada articulated four key principles that would guide program development and research studies involving indigenous peoples in Canada. Collectively, these principles are known by the acronym *OCAP* (Schnarch, 2004):

> *Ownership* refers to the relationship of First Nations to their cultural knowledge, data and information. This principle states that a community or group owns information collectively in the same way that an individual owns his or her personal information.
>
> *Control.* The principle of control affirms that First Nations, their communities and representative bodies are within their rights in seeking to control over all aspects of research and information management processes that impact them. First Nations control of research can include all stages of a particular research project from start to finish. The principle extends to the control of resources and review processes, the planning process, management of the information and so on.
>
> *Access.* First nations must have access to information and data about themselves and their communities, regardless of where is it currently held. The principle also refers to the right of First Nations communities and organizations to manage and make decisions regarding access to their collective information. This may be achieved, in practice, through standardized, formal protocols.
>
> *Possession.* While ownership identifies the relationship between a people and their information in principle, possession or stewardship is more concrete. It refers to the physical control of data. Possession is a mechanism by which ownership can be asserted and protected. (Schnarch, 2004, p. 1)

Safety also arose as an issue in the various studies that dealt with screening and early intervention. In some studies, the basic operating principle was that population safety could be assured through large-scale, wide-spread, population-based screening measures that could identify individual children who were in need of treatment and remediation. In other studies, the participants felt the need to feel safe from unwanted government intrusion into their personal and family lives. These issues were also raised in regard to the word *surveillance*, which we turn to next.

Surveillance

As noted above, the research process was highly dependent upon communication in general and on language in particular. The articulation of research questions, the development of appropriate methodologies, and the collection of data were all dependent upon mutually understood language conventions and definitions among all of the research partners. Language can serve as a bridge across different disciplines and across the policy-academic-community divides and can also serve as barriers between these key players. In CHILD we experienced both the bridges and the obstacles.

Much of the work in the CHILD Project, especially in the early screening cluster and to some extent in the indigenous cluster, was based on the power of language to conduct, interpret, and communicate the results of developmental assessments on young children. Language was the medium needed to connect children with the professionals assessing them, to connect professionals from different disciplines, and to build meaningful, constructive relationships between professionals and parents. The words that are used in assessment practices have enormous power to affect both positive and negative changes for children and their families. Respectful and sensitive language during child assessments can allow all participants in the assessment process to have meaningful conversations, as well as disagreements and arguments. With the use of words comes great power, which must be used cautiously and carefully. Many of the parents, teachers, childcare workers, and elders in the *Indigenous CHILD Study* and in the *Income Assistance Study* reported very negative experiences with child assessments. Their complaints included not being informed of test results and the tests being used to place children in special education programs without consultation with parents. In short, they felt that the language of assessment—along with the assessment itself—was biased and judgmental against them.

For example, one contentious term was *developmental surveillance*, used by some of the early screening and identification studies. In population health research, the term is used as a neutral description associated with monitoring the overall health and well-being of a population over time. Those projects, however, which dealt with populations that have typically been treated as more marginal and disadvantaged—including families living in poverty and indigenous families—had a particularly negative reaction to the term *surveillance*, which they felt carried connotations of governmental monitoring and control. Many participants in various studies were suspicious of the entire research process, fearing that their participation would result in information being disclosed to various authorities, resulting in unknown consequences for them and their children. The question arose as to whether programs of developmental surveillance represent legitimate and appropriate forms of social support or intrusive and controlling mechanisms. This was an issue that required continued discussion among the university and community researchers in the CHILD Project.

Toward a Conclusion on Collaborative Play

The CHILD Project exemplified and magnified the concept of *cultural competencies* (Reich & Reich, 2006), where different actors, including academics, community service providers, parents, policymakers, and even children had their own values, attitudes, metaphors, jargon, and language. These different cultures influenced how individuals understood language and circumstances, how they conducted the research, and how data were interpreted and, finally, implemented.

Several important lessons emerged from the CHILD Project about facilitating collaboration between different groups, or, as we are calling it, collaborative play (Pivik & Goelman, 2011). First, attention to relational issues is paramount—specifically, nurturing a sense of trust and respect of a person's viewpoint, their language, and the lenses that they use to view the world and their position (parent, service provider, academic, and child). Second, communication needs to be carefully considered. This means understanding that words carry power, ensuring all participants have a voice, and taking the time to understand and share different perspectives. Third, successful collaborations require a shared commitment from all sides and the opportunity for equitable engagement. Finally, collaborators require the time to understand each other and broaden their perspective. These key lessons stand whether the collaboration is between academics, community service providers, policy makers, parents or children, or in the case of the CHILD Project, all of the above.

Acknowledgments

We gratefully acknowledge the support provided to this program of research by the Social Sciences and Humanities Research Council of Canada, first through their Research Development Initiatives Program for the "UBC Child and Family Project" (1999–2003) and then through the Major Collaborative Research Initiatives Program for the "Consortium for Health, Intervention, Learning and Development Project (CHILD)" (2003–2007). We also thank the Human Early Learning Partnership, the Office of the Vice-President, Research, the Office of the Vice-President, Academic, and the Dean of the Faculty of Graduate Studies at the University of British Columbia for their active support for this program of research.

Notes

1. QUAD—Quality, Universal, Accessible and Developmental.
2. While different groups prefer to use different terms to refer to Canada's original inhabitants, in this chapter we use the terms *Aboriginal, First Nations,* and *Indigenous* interchangeably.

References

Anstett, S. & the MCFI Screening Task Group. (2002). *Phase 1: Framework for MCFI Integrated Early Identification Screening program.* (A discussion paper). Chilliwack, BC: Kids First Project.

Anstett, S., & the MCFI Screening Task Group. (2003). *Child development guide.* Chilliwack, BC: Kids First Project.

Ball, J. (2004, February). *Principles and protocols for research about First Nations children and communities in Canada.* Paper presented at the Thirty-third Annual Meeting of the Society for Cross-Cultural Research, San Jose, CA.

Ball, J. (2005). Nothing about us without us: Restorative research partnerships involving Indigenous children and communities in Canada. In A. Farrell (Ed.). *Exploring ethical research with children* (pp. 81–96). Berkshire, UK: Open University Press/McGraw-Hill.

Ball, J., & LeMare, L. (2011). Lessons from community-university partnerships with First Nations. In H. Goelman, J. Pivik, & M. Guhn (Eds.). (2011). *New advances in early child development: Rules, rituals and realities* (pp. 69–94). New York: Palgrave MacMillan.

Barer, M. L., & Evans, R. G. (eds). (2006). *Healthier societies. From analysis to action.* Oxford : Oxford University Press.

Beach, J., Friendly, M., Ferns, C., Prabhu, N., & Forer, B. (Eds.). (2009). *Early childhood education and care in Canada, 2008.* Toronto, ON: University of Toronto, Childcare Resource and Research Unit.

Beatch, M., & Le Mare, L. (2007). Taking ownership: The implementation of a non-Aboriginal early education programme for on-reserve children. *The Australian Journal of Indigenous Education, 36,* 77–87.

Bronfenbrenner, U. (1979). *The ecology of human development.* Cambridge, MA: Harvard University Press.

Canadian Coalition for the Rights of Children. (1999). *The UN Convention on the Rights of the Child: How does Canada measure up?* Ottawa, ON: The Canadian Coalition for the Rights of Children.

Canadian Council on Social Development. (2001). *Children and youth with special needs: Summary Report of Findings.* Ottawa, ON: Canadian Council on Social Development.

Chen, E., Matthews, K. A., & Boyce, W. T. (2002). Socioeconomic differences in children's health: How and why do these relationships change with age? *Psychological Bulletin, 128,* 295–329.

Chen, E., Fisher, E. B., Bacharier, L. B., & Strunk, R. C. (2003). Socioeconomic status, stress, and immune markers in adolescents with asthma. *Psychosomatic Medicine, 65,* 984–992.

Cynader, M. S., & Frost, B. J. (1999). Mechanisms of brain development: Neuronal sculpting by the physical and social environment. In D. P. Keating & C. Hertzman (Eds.). Developmental health and the wealth of nations: Social, biological, and educational dynamics (pp. 153–184). New York: The Guildford Press.

Dahinten, V. S., Ford, L., Canam, C., Lapointe, V., Merkel, C., Van Leeuwen, S.,...Sahraei, V. (2004, July). *The Kids First project: A partnership to promote early school readiness.* Poster session presented at the annual conference of the American Psychological Association, Honolulu, HI.

Dahinten, V. S., Ford, L., & Lapointe, V. (2004, May). *Validation of the Nipissing District Developmental screen for use with infants and toddlers.* Poster session presented at the annual meeting of the Society for Prevention Research, Quebec City, QC.

Dettling, A., Gunnar, M., & Donzella, B. (1999). Cortisol levels of young children in full-day childcare centers: Relations with age and temperament. *Psychoneuroendocrinology, 24*(5), 519–536.

Fiske, J., & Gervais, L. (2006, January). *Recent findings on the Income Assistance North Project.* Paper presented to the CHILD Learning Forum, Vancouver, BC.

Goelman, H. (1992). Day care in Canada. In M. Lamb, K. Sternberg, C.R. Hwang & Broberg, A. Anders (Eds.). *Child care in context: Cross cultural perspectives* (pp. 223–266). Hillsdale, NJ: Lawrence Erlbaum Associates.

Goelman, H., Ford, L, Pighini, M., Dahinten, A., Synnes, A., Tse, L.,...Hayes, V. (2011). What we learned about early identification and screening. In H. Goelman, J. Pivik & M. Guhn (Eds.). *New approaches to research in early child development: Rules, rituals and realities* (pp. 95–116). New York: Palgrave Macmillan.

Goelman, H., Forer, B., Kershaw, P., Doherty, G., Lero, D., & LaGrange, A. (2006). Towards a predictive model of quality in Canadian child care centers. *Early Childhood Research Quarterly, 21*(3), 280–295.

Goelman, H., Pivik J., & Guhn, M. (Eds). (2011). *New advances in early child development: Rules, rituals and realities.* New York: Palgrave Macmillan.

Government of British Columbia, Ministry of Children and Family Development. (2011). *Child Care.* Retrieved from www.mcf.gov.bc.ca/childcare

Government of Canada, Ministry of Human Resources and Social Development. *Universal Child Care Plan.* (2011). Retrieved from www.hrdc.gc.ca

Grunau, R. E., Whitfield, M. F., & Davis, C. (2002). Pattern of learning disabilities in children with extremely low birth weight and broadly average intelligence. *Archives of Pediatric Adolescent Medicine, 156,* 615–620.

Hack, M., Friedman, H., & Faranoff, A. A. (1996). Outcomes of extremely-low-birth weight infants. *American Academy of Pediatrics, 5,* 931–937.

Harris, S. R., & Daniels, L. E. (1996). Content validity of the Harris Infant Neuromotor Test. *Physical Therapy, 76,* 727–737.

Harris, S. R., & Daniels, L. E. (2001). Reliability and validity of the Harris Infant Neuromotor Test. *Journal of Pediatrics, 139,* 249–253.

Hayes, V. E., Harris, S. R., Megens, A. M., & Backman, C. (2004, November). *Early identification of infants' motor delays in nursing practice: Development of the Harris Infant Neuromotor Test (HINT)*. Paper presented at the research symposium of the International Pediatric Nursing Association, Montreal, QC.

Herrington, S., & Lesmeister, C. (2006). The design of landscapes at child care centres: Seven Cs. *Landscape Research, 31,* 63–82.

Hoekstra, R. E., Ferrara, T. B., Couser, R. J., Payne, N. R., & Connett, J. E. (2004). Survival and long-term neurodevelopmental outcome of extremely premature infants born at 23-26 weeks' gestational age at a tertiary centre. *American Academy of Pediatrics, 113,* e1–6.

Houbé, J., Lisonkova, S., Klassen, A., Synnes, A. R., & Lee, S. K. (2005). Canadian neonatal network: Patterns of health care utilization among children four years after discharge from NICU. *Pediatric Research, 55,* 480A.

Kamerman, S. B., & Kahn, A. J. (1988). *Mothers alone: Strategies for a time of change.* Dover, MA: Auburn House.

Keating, D. P., & Hertzman, C. (Eds.). (1999). *Developmental health and wealth of nations: Social, biological, and educational dynamics.* New York, NY: Guilford Press.

Kershaw, P. (2004). "Choice" discourse in BC child care: Distancing policy from research. *Canadian Journal of Political Science, 37*(4), 927–950.

Kershaw, P. (2005). *Carefair: Rethinking the responsibilities and rights of citizenship.* Vancouver, BC: UBC Press.

Kershaw, P., Forer, B., & Goelman, H. (2005). Hidden fragility: Closure among child care services in BC. *Early Childhood Research Quarterly, 20,* 417–432.

La Pine, T. R., Jackson, J. C., & Bennett, F. C. (1995). Outcome of infants weighing less than 800 grams at birth: 15 years' experience. *Pediatrics, 3,* 479–483.

Lipset, S. M. (1990). *Continental divide: The values and institutions of the United States and Canada.* London: Routledge.

Lorenz, J. M. (2001). The outcome of extreme prematurity. *Semin Perinatol, 25,* 348–359.

MacNaughton, G. (2005). *Doing Foucault in early childhood studies: Applying poststructural ideas.* New York, NY: Routledge.

Moster, D., Lie R. T., & Markestad, T. (2008). Long-term medical and social consequences of preterm birth. *New England Journal of Medicine, 359,* 262–273.

Pivik, J., & Goelman, H. (2011). Lessons in university-community collaboration. In H. Goelman, J. Pivik, & M. Guhn (Eds.). *New approaches to research in early child development: Rules, rituals and realities* (pp. 155–173). New York: Palgrave Macmillan.

Pivik, J., Herrington, S., & Gummerum, M. (2011). Nurturant environments for children's social, emotional, and physical well-being. In

H. Goelman, J. Pivik, & M. Guhn (Eds.). *New advances in early child development: Rules, rituals and realities* (pp. 117–140). New York: Palgrave Macmillan.

Ramey, S. L., & Ramey, C. T. (1997). The role of universities in child development. In H. J. Walberg, O. Reyes, & R. P. Weissberg (Eds.). *Children and youth: Interdisciplinary perspectives* (pp. 13–43). Chicago, IL: Sage Publications.

Reich, S., & Reich, J. (2006). Cultural competence in interdisciplinary collaborations: A method for respecting diversity in research partnerships. *American Journal of Community Psychology, 38*, 51–62.

Resnick, M. B., Gomatam, S. V., Carter, R. L., Ariet, M., Roth, J., Kilgore, K., . . . Eitzman, D. V. (1998). Educational disabilities of neonatal intensive care graduates. *Pediatrics, 102*(2), 308–314.

Riley, K., Roth, S., Sellwood, M., Wyatt, J. S. (2008). Survival and neurodevelopmental morbidity at 1 year of age following extremely preterm delivery over a 20-year period: A single centre cohort study. *Acta Paediatrica, 97*, 159–165.

Russell, M. (2011). What we learned about poverty and vulnerability. In H. Goelman, J. Pivik, & M. Guhn (Eds.). *New advances in early child development: Rules, rituals and realities* (pp. 53–68). New York: Palgrave Macmillan.

Russell, M., Harris, B., & Gockel, A. (2008a). Canadian lone mothers describe parenting needs: European solutions explored. *Canadian Social Work Review, 25*, 169–185.

Russell, M., Harris, B., & Gockel, A. (2008b). Parenting in poverty: Perceptions of high-risk parents. *Journal of Children and Poverty, 14*, 83–98.

Sauve, R., Etches, P., Robertson, C. M., Christianson, H. E., & Jain, S. (2004). Are long-term outcomes of fetal infants improving? *Pediatric Research, 55*, 370A.

Schnarch, B. (2004). Ownership, control, access, and possession (OCAP) or self-determination applied to research: A critical analysis of contemporary First Nations research and some options for First Nations communities. *Journal of Aboriginal Health, 1* (1), 80–95.

Schonert-Reichl, K. A., Smith, V., Jaramillo, A. M., & Zaidman-Zait, A. (2004, May). *Translating theories of emotion into prevention and treatment in early childhood: Examples of current programs.* Paper presented at the Second Annual Symposium on Assessment in Early Childhood Education, Vancouver, BC.

Schonert-Reichl, K. A., & Jaramillo, A. M. (2005, May). *"How do I feel about going to school?" The role of emotions in children's school readiness.* Paper presented at the Third Annual Symposium on Assessment in Early Childhood Education, Vancouver, BC.

Shonkoff, J. P. (2000). Science, policy and practice: Three cultures in search of a shared mission. *Child Development 7*(1), 181–187.

Shonkoff, J. P. & Phillips, D. A. (Eds.). (2000). *From neurons to neighborhoods: The science of early child development.* Washington, D.C.: National Academy Press.

Synnes, A. R., Lisonkova, S., Houbé, J. S., Klassen, A., & Lee, S. K. (2004). Canadian neonatal network: Targeting follow-up needs of premature survivors. *Pediatric Research, 55,* 474A.

Watamura, S., Donzella, B., Alwin, J., & Gunnar, M. E. (2003). Morning-to-afternoon increases in cortisol concentrations for infants and toddlers at child care: Age differences and behavioral correlates. *Child Development, 74,* 1006–1020.

Westheimer, M. (Ed) (2003). *Parents making a difference: International research on the Home Instruction for Parents of Preschool Youngsters (HIPPY) Program.* Jerusalem, Israel: Magnes.

Whitfield, M. F., Grunau, R. V., & Holsti, L. E. (1997). Extremely premature (<or= 800 g) schoolchildren: Multiple areas of hidden disability. *Arch Dis Child Fetal Neonatal Ed, 77,* F85-90.

Willms, J. D. (Ed.). (2002). *Vulnerable children: Findings from Canada's National Longitudinal Survey of Children and Youth.* Edmonton, AB: University of Alberta Press.

CHAPTER 11

Conclusion: Reconceptualizing Early Education; Crossing Borders to Build Community

Sarah Te One and Judith Duncan

INTRODUCTION

This book represents our attempt to challenge existing borders to partnering with families and *whānau* (extended family) in Early Childhood Education and Care (ECEC) services. In so doing, we argue for a reconceptualized purpose to these services: one that enhances community wellness through a process of conscientization (Freire, 1993)—a political awareness of how social, cultural, and economic conditions influence perceptions of children, of childhood, of families and of ECEC services—and one that places children and their families at the heart of communities. In this reconceptualization, children, families, *whānau,* and teachers in ECEC services are active partners together working to improve their quality of life and that of their respective communities. While the rhetoric of partnership with families and community appears in the *public sphere* via technologies (Duhn, 2006) such as curriculum documents, regulations and policies, research argues that ECEC services, children, and families are often relegated to the *private domain* (De Visscher & Bouverne-De Bie, 2008) and are therefore rendered invisible and powerless (John, 2003). This book documents the impact of neo-liberal economic policies during a global recession and how, not surprisingly, conservative government responses deal with the most vulnerable most harshly—theirs are the voices silenced by class, a lack of cultural capital, and by linguistic diversity, ethnicity, sexuality, or nonconventional life styles. How then, can ECEC services challenge the dominant discursive regime to promote inclusive, socially just, democratic participation?

Dalhberg, Moss, and Pence (2007) highlight tensions between the socially constructed nature of ECEC services, which reflect the status quo and accordingly aim to reproduce the ideal maternal home, and the economic rationale for service provision as a necessary corollary to increasing mothers' participation in the labor market. These tensions influence how children are perceived as dependent, weak, socially inept, and in need of protection, or as dangerous and potential threats to social stability. In direct contrast to this are views of children as actively asserting agency over their own experiences—in other words, children as (responsible) rights-holders—and a view of ECEC services as locally based sites for democratic engagement with families and communities.

A more recent trend in social policy suggests that families alone cannot provide all that is needed to raise future global citizens, thus positioning ECEC services as an essential complement to parenting (May, 2007). Over a relatively short period of time, an intergenerational bond, based on shared experience and the wisdom of parenting and family, has been usurped by experts. Where once children were considered at risk if they participated in ECEC services, the opposite is now true (Duhn, 2006; May, 2007, Te One, 2003). Despite an intense spotlight on the fundamental importance of the early years and of early education of high quality (e.g., see OECD, 2006; UNICEF, 2008), in many countries, including those represented in this volume, ECEC services have low status, and economic investment in children per se is below OECD averages (OECD, 2006). More needs to be done to achieve a socially just quality of life for all children and their families (Walden, 2011) and, in our view, more needs to be done to recognize the enormous potential of ECEC services embedded in communities, actively engaging with families, *whānau*, and children, to enhance social well-being.

This book brings together a wide range of international exemplars to illustrate the power of relational pedagogy based on tolerance, inclusiveness, and acceptance of diversity at a grass- roots level as well as at a macro policy level. The chapters in this book represent international experiences of how community wellness and active adult participation in ECEC services empower and enhance experiences for all involved. Using diverse methodologies and theoretical paradigms, the chapters in this volume challenge existing discourses and re-present traditional interpretations to illuminate possibilities for reconceptualized partnering within ECEC services. All chapters engage, to some degree, with notions of disruption and disturbance to current discourses of influence in early childhood. All actively engage with social inequities to highlight the silence of the indigenous voice and of marginalized populations. Critical, reflective, and discursive arguments weave throughout the book to present a refreshing take on ECEC services. The scope is global; the discussions are local with an underlying intention to demonstrate that communities, wherever and whatever these constitute, hold a key to social, cultural, and community well-being.

Strength-Based Approaches

The research reported on in this book ranges from meta-analyses of large (and very large) projects (e.g., Duncan; Goelman & Pivik; Joanou et al.) to small, discrete, localized community-based research findings (see Duncan et al.; Jones et al., Lee; Munford et al.; Sumsion et al.; Te One). All, in one way or another, position ECEC services as pivotal in establishing respectful, responsive, reciprocal relationships with people in space and place (Ministry of Education, 1996).

An overarching theme throughout the volume argues for *strength-based* possibilities, which build on existing *funds of knowledge* within communities. Cogent arguments favoring integrated, universally provided ECEC services challenge the current rhetoric, which singles out the vulnerable as targets for intervention, further marginalizing and diminishing the integrity and dignity some families may experience. An alternative to this deficit approach is a *quality of life* discourse that concentrates on what makes life worthwhile (Stainton Rogers, 2004). Stainton Rogers (2004) argues that this approach holds more potential for enhancing quality for the following reasons: first, it is a strengths-based as opposed to a deficit approach; second, it shifts the focus from the individual to the situational and in so doing removes unhelpful perceptions such as blaming a child or a family for their circumstances, a stance that ignores the social, economic, and political contexts that may have created adverse circumstances in the first place. In *the quality of life* discourse, the route to change is political action.

This political action can be seen when natural disasters present new challenges and new opportunities for localized communities.

EARLY CHILDHOOD EDUCATION AND NATURAL DISASTERS: THE ULTIMATE COMMUNITY EXPERIENCE[1]

At the time this book was being written, both Aotearoa New Zealand and Japan had experienced devastating natural disasters in the early months of 2011.

Christchurch had experienced a 7.1 magnitude quake on September 4, 2010, and while property damage had been extensive, no lives were lost. The next months were, however, a constant reminder that the world was still moving, with aftershocks continuing on a daily basis. On February 22, 2011, another aftershock turned into a catastrophic new event—a 6.3 magnitude quake right under the center of the city. While the 6.3 (magnitude) rating made the quake appear to others to be less fearsome than many, the combination of factors involved in this one quake produced devastating consequences for everyone in Canterbury: that is, where the fault lies (under the city), the length of time of the shaking (20 seconds), the trampoline effect it produced (up and down as well as side-to-side), and the impact of gravitation forces twice the normal rate.

No one in the city and surrounding areas has been untouched—from those who lost loved ones in collapsed buildings (final death toll was 182) and the thousands who lost homes and work places, to the many thousands whose lives have changed, who cannot now access community facilities (libraries, swimming pools, halls, places to gather), shopping facilities (including major malls), flush toilets, or travel safely on the roads around the city. Spaces and places where families went for support or wider community connection were lost. With the basics for safe healthy living no longer available, and nerves and personal safety threatened, local communities responded to those around them quickly and effectively. This was seen in the immediate post-earthquake hours and days where those in each geographical community immediately turned to one another for help and support. This type of response effort helped to maintain not only residential homes and properties but the *lived communities*—the links, networks, and sense of *belonging* and *location* that support the social capital of families and maintain resilient and well communities.

The Eastern Japan Great Earthquake of March 11, 2011, of 9.0 magnitude, followed 30 minutes later by a devastating tsunami, completely destroyed communities and lives (more than 15,000 lives were lost, with another 7,305 missing and 206 disaster orphans under 17 years of age). The stories from Japan mirror those of Christchurch, with individuals and communities immediately responding to those around them. Months on, the sense of rebuilding the community is the focus of many of the press releases from Japan. For example:

> First the earthquake, then the devastating wave which rushed in and destroyed a part of the coastal city of Iwaki, then there are the radiation waves that are coming into the area as well. The volunteers rebuilding the city certainly have their work cut out for them, but just like the city itself, the people who live there need to have their spirits rebuilt as well. In an effort to keep the community emotionally strong, organizers have called in an acting troupe from Tokyo. Its members say their goal is to provide something beyond simple entertainment....And with an understanding that there is still much more work that needs to be done, the people are working to keep their community together, rebuilding the city one step at a time. ("Volunteers across Japan unite to rebuild devastated towns and lives," July 6, 2011)

These events are a stark reminder of the pivotal place that geographical community plays in the lives of those who live in them. In Aotearoa New Zealand research has demonstrated the changing understanding of *community* for children and their families, and the different experiences of childhood that children in the twenty-first century have from those who grew up in the nineteenth or twentieth centuries (Freeman, Quigg, Vass, & Broad, 2007). However, the earthquakes and the Japanese tsunami created situations where the geographical community were required to respond and care for each other in ways that emphasized the importance of relationships and cohesion in communities.

Rebecca Solnit (2009), writing about American disasters and the "extraordinary communities that arise in disaster," provides a compelling argument that while disasters themselves should never be welcomed, the opportunities that they create for reconceptualizing social relations and meaningful work, plus the windows they present for change at all levels of the human existence, are not to be ignored. Discussing a range of disasters from the San Francisco earthquake in 1906 to Hurricane Katrina in New Orleans in 2005, Solnit (2009) argues that people do not act as selfish individuals, prone to violence, mayhem, violence, and looting as is supposed, but rather neighbors turn to one another, strangers become rescuers in the streets and buildings, and whole populations turn their gaze to help stricken areas.

This response by others in the community after the Christchurch quakes, while the official local and national government attention was focused elsewhere, was the most significant factor in supporting and restoring families and their lives within the suburbs. Neighbors cranked up barbeques and cooked food for the whole street (using the food from freezers and fridges that would otherwise spoil from lack of power) and boiled water on gas rings for those who had no forms of heating sources. Springs that appeared in the middle of lawns and living rooms were plumbed out to the street with signs advertising the free availability of water (in communities where the water mains had burst and no water was available). The "Student Army," as they have come to be known, provided hundreds of youthful volunteers who, with shovels in hand, swept through the suburbs, clearing paths and digging residents out of their homes and properties. All of these responses occurred in the following hours and days of the quakes, prior to any national or governmental response. Such actions were the key to personal survival, reconnection of social relationships, and positive hope.

The New Zealand Prime Minister John Key, speaking at the Memorial Day for February 22, summed up this situation well:

> Whether it's been an Urban Search and Rescue team, or whether it's been someone taking their neighbour's water containers to be filled, the assistance which has been given to the people of Christchurch has been of enormous practical benefit, and has lifted our spirits when we most needed it.... We have learned the power not only of individuals who have done more than they ever dreamed they could have, but also the power of a community, whether it's a neighborhood, a school, a nation or the international community. We have witnessed in these past three weeks the very best of the human spirit. We have seen the coming together of a city, and of a nation. We have learned a lot about our capacity to do good. There is much talk that ours is a selfish generation, focused only on money and individual gain. What I have seen in our country, and especially here in this city since February 22 puts the lie to that. I have seen people who are resilient, capable, practical and compassionate. New Zealanders have been generous and brave. (Key, March 18, 2011, Speech to National Memorial Service)

MacFie (2011, pp. 26–27), in discussing the government's response to the earthquakes in Christchurch, compared the national action to those of the organized localized community groups who had been working door-to-door with citizens in the suburbs. She quoted community leaders as they worried that the government was focused on "fixing potholes and pipes," while the community leaders emphasized that the rebuilding of community should take into account the "soft infrastructure" that goes beyond the pipes. That is, a community is much more than its bricks and mortar (or steel and concrete).

Solnit (2009) argues that civil society survives after disasters because of its ability to muster creativity and resources to meet challenges; that the power, usually held by the elite, is devolved to the people on the ground; and that the localized responses demonstrate how as a people we "desire connection, participation, altruism, and purposefulness" (p. 306). Elsewhere, Duncan, Bowden, and Smith (2005) have argued that early childhood education services are the ideal places for supporting families, developing family resilience, enhancing social capital and overall community well-being (for further discussion see Citizens Preschool and Nursery, 2008; Duncan, 2009; Duncan et al., 2005, 2006a, 2006b), and in times of crisis, big or small, the importance of the early childhood center, within the community, becomes even more obvious.

Reported examples from Japan describe similar community responses, with a key to the success and survival of many of the children being attributed to the teachers' close ties to the community:

> Most of the teachers/caregivers lived in the community, having sense of the locals, information on human and other local resources, and knowledge of traditions and legends of the area. Therefore, they could make rational and effective judgment at the time of emergency. There were many day nurseries without any casualties even though they were completely damaged by the Tsunami. (Suzuki et al., 2011)

This deep connection to the community, both geographically and relationally, was a lifesaver in both countries where teachers were required to respond to natural disasters. The social and educational responses, which came next, in both the Japanese and Aotearoa New Zealand early childhood communities, provide examples of how and why individual early childhood services are the *heart of our communities*. Jan Dobson, supervisor at New Beginnings Preschool in Christchurch, wrote an account of the day and weeks following the February 22 quake:

> One of the most valuable resources we have at *New Beginnings* is the inner resource within my team members of well being which supports an ability to remain calm and to create this around them, and this is what our families walked into when they came to pick up their children. I have heard enormous praise from our parents for our team at *New Beginnings*, for the *manaakitanga*[2] care and respect that they as parents received when they walked in the door, as they were

comforted and calmed by staff before going to their children, and for the warmth, care and calmness, *aroha*, that was wrapped around their children while they waited....There are also stories from our team where teachers have momentarily lost their homes, or are in areas where there is still no sewerage. On the day of the earthquake it took one of my teachers seven hours to get home where it would usually take 20 minutes, and with no cell phone coverage, we became increasingly concerned about her wellbeing and whereabouts. Throughout all of this we have helped each other, supported each other and have continued to be resourceful, resilient and committed to maintaining the well being of our community. (Duncan et al., 2011, p. 13)

Flexible postearthquake and tsunami responses to children, families, and provisions of ECEC in these areas have presented new possibilities, new ways of organizing enrollments, programs, patterns of attendances, places to play, and places to come together. New ways to reconceptualize ECEC as democratic sites, as places to build family resilience, community wellness, and create positive learning outcomes for all children and their *whānau.*

Solnit (2009) concluded in her description of American disasters and the community responses they provoked:

Disaster sometimes knocks down institutions and structures and suspends private life, leaving a broader view of what lies beyond. The task before us is to recognize the possibilities visible through that gateway and endeavor to bring them into the realm of everyday. (p. 313)

These possibilities, and the everyday life of ECEC, are the content of this book.

THE POSSIBILITIES OF RECONCEPTUALIZING ECEC

In addition to an affirmation of a *strength-based approach,* several subthemes emerge throughout the book, but three stand out. First, there is the notion of *belonging* and *connectedness* in communities; second is the role of *collaborations* and *networks* within, among, and between communities; and third is *resilience* and *identity* within communities.

Belonging and Connectedness

Notions of belonging are central to community. Without a sense of belonging, there can be no meaningful participation. How to gain entry, how to find common ground, how to build trust, and how to reveal powerful messages that exclude and prevent families and *whānau* from engaging with ECEC services are complex in part because feeling a sense of belonging is often assumed and *taken-for-granted*. Lee, for example, explores how *hospitality as curriculum* facilitated entry into the day-to-day life of an ECEC service for lesbian mothers. A combination of skilled facilitation (leadership), established a climate of openness and curiosity within a culture of care, based on trusting relationship, afforded first-time parents' permission to be novices in their role but also experts with their baby (Te One). ECEC services afforded opportunities for families to develop a sense of belonging to a group, of having a sense of place, and this enhanced community connectedness. However, there are key barriers that obstruct participation at a community level and in communities—transience, different philosophical values, life styles, languages, poverty, and locality counter inclusiveness. Living in a community does not equate to belonging (Joanou et al.; Goelman & Pivik).

Collaborations and Networks

Finding workable collaborations and developing effective networks, formal and informal, as well as local, regional, and national, are foregrounded throughout the book. Large-scale research projects (Goelman & Pivik) explored exciting relationships across disciplines, methodologies, and regions to successfully build collaborative networks with multiple benefits for all concerned, not the least of which were enhanced understandings of one another's roles. Economic rationalizing necessitated creative solutions at a provider level when funding and services folded. New collaborative networks between providers of ECEC services emerged out of necessity, and preexisting conditions (such as lack of transport) were overcome (Joanou et al.). Integrated services models, such as *Te Aroha Noa* (Munford et al.), Ngala, and Gowrie SA (Sumsion et al.) exemplify the notion of collaborative action as a result of mutual demand for responsive ECEC services. To remain effective, networks must evolve—this ongoing dynamic stems from respectfulness from within ECEC services (as in Lee; Te One) and from opportunities to expand in new, unconventional, and unexpected ways that challenge the norm of power and control being located within institutions (as in Duncan; Jones et al.; and Sumsion et al.). Collaborative action potentially revolutionizes existing perceptions of ECEC services as bounded by their location and constrained by technologies such as curriculum, policies, regulations, and funding and philosophies, usually heavily *child-centered*. Descriptions of effective, dynamic networks in this volume illustrate how, if afforded the opportunity, a wider family and community discourse can exert influence within services via for example, curriculum (Lee; Duncan et al.) and, in mutually beneficial ways, at a community level where local knowledge is respected (Munford et al.). When there is a strong sense of trust, based on belonging to a community, there is a sense of flow between ECEC services, families, *whānau,* and communities.

Resilience and Identity

A particularly salient theme is one of building resilient families. For whatever reason, and there are many cited within, unless dominant discourses about who can and does belong to *a community* are disturbed, the chances to thrive in sustainable ways are diminished. The affordances and opportunities are not complicated even though the contexts out of which they emerge are extremely complex. Linguistic barriers, prison timetables, cultural suppression, marginalized, *below-the-radar* immigration situations, single-sex families, and a societal fear of difference compound to isolate families from communities. However, personal relationship-building, over time, and in culturally safe environments, proves to be effective in developing resilience and in establishing identity (Munford et al.; Jones et al.; Sumsion et al.). Committed, critically reflective teachers assuming a critical and reflective stance to their pedagogical practices are key determinants to promoting resilience (Sumsion et al.) The process is not one-sided: as teachers or other professionals working with families note, moving into new space or rearranging the familiar environment (Duncan et al.) potentially creates new options for relationships to develop on different terms, creating new possibilities for challenging inequities (Jones et al.). Strengthening local, community-based relationships through *korerorero* (dialogue) epitomizes democracy in action (Sumison et al.). Opening up to new possibilities is not comfortable, but to move the agenda of ECEC services toward enhancing community wellness, this book suggests it is necessary.

Notes

1. Sections of this chapter have previously been published in Duncan, J., Wegner, A., Dobson, J., & Foote, L. with Teachers from Otago and Southland. (2011). Early childhood education: Community when and where it counts. *Early Education, 49* (Winter), 12–20.
2. *Manaakitanga* is the Māori word for hospitality or kindness.

References

Citizens Preschool and Nursery Centre of Innovation. (2008). *Collaborations: Teachers and a family whānau support worker in an early childhood setting. Final report for Centre of Innovation Research (2005–2007).* Wellington, NZ: Ministry of Education.

Dahlberg, G., Moss, P., & Pence, A. (2007). *Beyond quality in early childhood education and care. Languages of evaluation.* (2nd ed.). London and New York: Routledge. Taylor & Francis.

De Visscher, S., & Bouverne-De Bie, M. (2008). Children's presence in the neighbourhood: A social-pedagogical perspective. *Children and Society, 22* (6), 470–481.

Duhn, I. (2006). The making of global citizens: Traces of cosmopolitanism in the New Zealand early childhood curriculum, *Te Whāriki. Contemporary Issues in Early Childhood, 7*(3), 191–201.

Duncan, J. (2009, November). *Building communities: Begins in the early years.* Keynote presentation to the Anglican Social Services Conference: "Strengthening Our Communities." Napier, NZ.

Duncan, J., Bowden, C., & Smith, A. B. (2005). *Early childhood centres and family resilience.* Report prepared for the Ministry of Social Development, Wellington, NZ.

Duncan, J., Bowden, C., & Smith, A. B. (2006a). A gossip or a good yack? Reconceptualizing parent support in New Zealand early childhood centre based programmes. *International Journal of Early Years Education, 14*(1), 1–13.

Duncan, J., Bowden, C., & Smith, A. B. (2006b). Aotearoa New Zealand early childhood centres and family resilience: Reconceptualising relationships. *International Journal of Equity and Innovation in Early Childhood, 4*(2), 79–90.

Duncan, J., Wegner, A., Dobson, J., & Foote, L. with Teachers from Otago and Southland. (2011). Early childhood education: Community when and where it counts. *Early Education, 49* (Winter), 12–20.

Freeman, C., Quigg, R., Vass, E., & Broad, M. (2007). *The changing geographies of children's lives: A study of how children in Dunedin use their environment.* Dunedin, NZ: Department of Geography, University of Otago.

Freire, P. (1993). *Pedagogy of the oppressed* (20th Anniversary ed.). New York: Continuum.

John, M. (2003). *Children's rights and power: Charging up for a new century.* London and New York: Jessica Kingsely Publishers.

Key, J. (2011, March). *Speech to National Memorial Service. Hagley Park, Christchurch.* Retrieved from http://www.beehive.govt.nz/speech/speech-national-memorial-service

Macfie, R. (2011). Frustration grows: Letter from Christchurch. *Listener, April 16–22,* 26–27.

May, H. (2007). *Politics in the Playground. The world of early childhood in postwar New Zealand.* (2nd ed.). Dunedin, NZ: Otago University Press.

Ministry of Education. (1996). *Te Whāriki. He whāriki mātauranga mō ngā mokopuna o Aotearoa: Early childhood curriculum.* Wellington, NZ: Learning Media.

OECD. (2006). *Starting strong II: Early childhood education and care.* Paris: OECD Publishing.

Solnit, R. (2009). *A paradise built in hell: The extraordinary communities that arise in disaster.* London: Viking Penguin.

Stainton Rogers, W. (2004). Promoting better childhoods: Constructions of child concern. In M. J. Kelhily (Ed.). *An introduction to childhood studies* (pp. 125–144). Maidenhead, UK: Open University Press.

Suzuki, M., Naito, T., Kamigaichi, N., & The Japanese National Committee of OMEP. (2011). *A brief report on conditions of Kindergartens and Day Nurseries affected by the Eastern Japan Great Earthquake on March 11, 2011* Tokyo, Japan: The Japanese National Committee of OMEP.

Te One, S. (2003). *Te Whāriki*: Contemporary issues of influence. In J. Nuttall (Ed.). *Weaving Te Whāriki. Aotearoa New Zealand's early childhood curriculum document in theory and in practice* (pp. 17–49). Wellington, NZ: New Zealand Council for Educational Research Press.

UNICEF. (2008). The child care transition. A league table of early childhood education and care in economically advanced countries. *Innocenti Report Card 8.* Florence, Italy: UNICEF Innocenti Research Centre.

Walden, C. (2011). *Monopoly games in the nursery. Community, inequalities and early childhood education.* Retrieved from www.salvationarmy.org .nz/socialpolicy

Volunteers across Japan unite to rebuild devastated towns and lives. (2011, July 16). Retrieved from http://rt.com/news/japan-volunteers -earthquake/

Index